Shoot-Out with a Wild-Eyed Moderate:

Riding Herd on the Bible, Rust, Sun Belts, and the Beltway

Featuring an Introduction by Brewster Barlow, the Original Wild-Eyed Moderate

Howard Denson

Dedicated to

My many outstanding teachers and professors, ranging from Iris Taylor Johnson (Central Elementary, Jasper), Ms. Watson (C.A. Weis, Pensacola), Ms. Wilson (Blount Junior High, Pensacola), Arch Manning (Norview High, Norfolk), George Goodwin (Pensacola JC), James Cox (Florida State), Hubert Harper (U of Alabama at Birmingham), Howard Bahr (U of Southern Miss), and others.

Disclaimer

This is a collection of humor, whimsy, and even serious opinion, but a sharp reader will detect instances when pieces are partly (or fully) fictional. The persona of the belovéd Edgar Bergen makes an appearance. He shouldn't be confused with the historical Edgar of the family. It will be sheer coincidence to find individuals actually named Brewster Barlow, Franklin T. Foxwhistle, Bob Such, Francis Xavier Pert, Marty Skagmore, Millard Fillmore, and so on. If they exist, I'm sure they are fine fellows all.

http://howarddenson.webs.com

Title ID: 3981453
ISBN-13: 978-0615692739

Printed in the United States of America

CONTENTS

INTRODUCTION BY THE ORIGINAL WILD-EYED MODERATE

By BREWSTER BARLOW

Imagine my surprise when some kid shows up at the retirement home wanting me to write an introduction for his book. He also wanted my okay for him to use my old handle, the "wild-eyed moderate." That's what they called me back in the 1930s when I starred in a couple of Westerns. My big claim to fame was *Shoot-Out with a Wild-Eyed Moderate*, not that anybody cares or remembers. I did have a tape of the movie that my family located, but it went up in smoke when I accidentally set fire to the retirement home again.

You don't find my movie listed in Leonard Maltin's book on films, but, heck, he hardly mentions any black-and-white Westerns unless they were directed by Pappy Ford or Howard Hawks. Don't bother googling it or looking it up on Wikipedia because you'll strike out.

I can remember a little about the picture, though. It was supposedly taking place in Wyoming, but, of course, it was all done on the studio and on a farm out in the sticks. I forget the name of the town, Dry Fork, Wet Spoon, or something, but the town in the movie was being torn apart because the cowmen hated farmers and sheepherders, and the sheep men hated the ranchers, and the farmers hated everybody. A preacher cried out, "We've got to cut out the killing and just learn how to live together!" So both sides shot him. The factions had also gunned down the past five sheriffs, two druggists, and a Singer

Sewing Machine salesman. It was about that time that I rode into town to wet my whistle at Taggart's Tumbleweed Saloon. All of the bad guys in cowboy movies were called Taggart.

The movie crew didn't spend much time making us up, but somebody must have gotten a flake of dried makeup in my eyes because I was blinking like crazy, and one of the cowboy actors ad-libbed something close to "Damn, he's a wild-eyed mother." The director called "cut" and got him to say the line again but change it to "Darn, he's the wild-eyed moderate." I think that was the only scene that had more than one take in the entire movie.

So they shot the film and made me blink in all the other scenes, and I thought I had a full-time job for the rest of my life. All I had to do was blink and say, "Yup, nope, yessum, nome," and then toss down a whiskey glass of apple juice. The guys thought it was funny to pour in Jack Daniels, but, hell, I was all right with that, too.

The studio did one other "wild-eyed moderate" Western. Nobody said they didn't like *Gunfight with the Wild-Eyed Moderate*, but, after that, I found myself working just as a member of a gang or a posse in other pictures. For a while, I got to say a few lines, like "What's that, Boss?" whenever Charles King or Roy Barcroft said he had a sure-fire plan to take over the water rights and the town.

Was I bitter? Oh, sure. I saw myself as another Buck Jones, Tom Mix, Hoot Gibson, or Tim McCoy, with their big houses and fine automobiles. That was before they brought in the singing sissies who looked like fruitcakes.

You could say that I had a drinking problem back then, but I mainly had trouble sipping whiskey AND smoking. I'd get sloppy drunk and then the booze would put out my cigar or cigarette, except when the whole thing caught on fire. They claimed I was difficult to work with on the sets, so they put me back caring for the horses, which I was good at. A horse is happy if you just leave him alone, and I was an expert at that. Same thing for women, but my ex-wives would disagree.

To be honest, I had sort of hit bottom in the Forties, but managed to get a job wrangling horses on tours. When I traveled with Gene Autry to a rodeo in Birmingham in 1946 or so, I met the very kid who wanted me to write this introduction. This goofy kid was a real little feller then, about five or so, and wore a monocle, but he came right up and said, "Howdy, Mr. Wild-Eyed Moderate."

Gene Autry overheard that and said, "How about that, you've got a fan!" He seemed surprised that anyone would pay attention to this broken-down drunk.

"Do you know me, kid?" I asked in the kindly way that I had heard Gene talk to young-uns.

"Yes, sir. You're Ambrose Barlow." I was impressed that he knew my real first name. "Brewster Barlow himself, the wild-eyed moderate."

"And you are?"

He gave me his name, which I promptly forgot. I never remember a person's name until he has bought me three or four drinks. If he buys me five or six drinks, I forget my own name.

I did ask him about the monocle, and he said his other big hero was Charlie McCarthy. I figured he was going to have a hard time going through life admiring a wooden puppet and a drunk known as a wild-eyed moderate, but I didn't say anything.

Gene fired me when he caught me with one too many bottles and blondes. On screen and the radio, he was real friendly, but his theme song should have been "I'm a Sour-Puss who's Back in the Cash Register Again."

I found a kindred spirit, however, working with Lash Larue. Everyone called him "Lush" Larue, and on some days nobody would work with him when it came time for him to do one of his bullwhip tricks. But me and him were a perfect match. He was too blind drunk to hit anything, and I was so smashed that it didn't hurt when he popped my hand instead of the six-shooter I was holding.

When he quit starring in Westerns, I was hired by Whip Wilson's company at Monogram. Whip was a nice guy, sober and respectful, but I had to quit when he pestered me to death about joining Alcoholics Anonymous.

After that, I was traveling all about. When we played the Pal Theatre in Vidalia, Georgia, this monocle kid pops up again, this time also sporting what looked like a top hat. It was made out of cardboard and had been painted black. He was there to see Tommy Cook, the little boy who played the first Little Beaver in the "Red Ryder" films.

The monocle kid almost ruined the gig when he stood up in the theater and hollered, "We want to see Brewster Barlow, the Wild-Eyed Moderate!" That shout came right when Little Beaver was trying to yell, "Gitty-up, Papoose!"

The other kids got to chanting it, though I could tell none of them knew who Brewster Barlow was.

To hush them up, I stepped out from behind the curtain and waved at them. "Hey, kids. Ain't Little Beaver great?"

It broke my heart when they groaned at the sight of me.

In the early 1950s, I once again saw the kid with a monocle when I was in the crew that traveled with Smiley Burnette.

I was drunk and thought we were appearing in Brownsville, Texas, but it turned out to be the Brownsville community of Pensacola, Florida. Smiley could play practically every instrument there was and some that he just outright invented, so I didn't have a whole lot of horse wrangling to do.

After the show, while Smiley was signing autographs, this kid with the monocle pulled on my sleeve backstage and grinned that he was now calling himself "the Wild-Eyed, Cock-Eyed, and Cross-Eyed Centrist." He had found a black hat like

Lash Larue's but stretched it up a little like a top hat. He also said his sidekick was Mortimer Kabibble, but I could see that he was only dragging around a two-by-four that he had painted up to look like a puppet, sort of.

A few years later, I was waiting for Roy to finish up a number on a radio show and saw that Edgar Bergen himself had slipped in and settled into a chair in the last row just to watch and listen. When I eased into a seat next to him, he whispered, "Hello, Brewster. Haven't seen you since the charity rodeo."

When they were doing a commercial, I told Bergen about the goofy kid who idolized Charlie and wore a monocle and at times a home-made top hat.

"Is he touched upstairs or just enthusiastic?" Bergen asked.

"I dunno," I said and went on to tell about his sidekick Mortimer Kabibble.

"Not Snerd?"

"No, sir, Kabibble. He's calling himself 'the Wild-Eyed Moderate,'" I added. "I think he views himself as some kind of centrist, politically and socially."

"Interesting," Bergen said. "Candice practically hates Charlie and won't go into his room. It didn't bother Kris so much. Of course, he's just a babe. For her, worst case of sibling rivalry I've come across." He sighed. "Too bad Charlie didn't have an older brother that he could pal around with."

"Well, he's got Mortimer."

Bergen shook his head sadly. "Not really. They're friendly, but they really don't have anything in common. Charlie's smart and sophisticated, and Mortimer's a hayseed. He's sweet but not very bright." He sighed. "But they're both my boys."

We were getting close to the end when Bergen sat up straight. "Just remembered: Are you still wrangling horses?"

"Yes, sir. You got any?"

"Oh, no, no. Thought of having a horse figure once.

Couldn't decide between the names 'Parking Citation' or 'The Postman Always Whinnies Twice,' but I dropped the idea. Have to stay away from words that have 'p' in them, too hard to say without moving my lips. You've heard how Charlie fusses at me about it."

"Yes, sir. He's hard to please sometime."

"Definitely. I wanted to tell you that my wife Frances is going to be on TV in Desilu's new show *Yancy Derringer*, about sort of a Rhett Butler adventurer. She'll be playing Madame Francine."

"A madam of a —" I searched for a polite word. "—a 'sporting house?'"

"Oh, no, no. A gambling emporium in New Orleans."

"Are they going to need any stagehands or wranglers?"

"I don't know that, but Frances says they are going to need actors who can take a fall. Jock Mahoney's the star."

"The stuntman?"

"Right, his sidekick in the series is X. Brands. He plays a silent Indian who only uses hand gestures."

"That couldn't be hard. I could even play that part."

"Yancy saved his life, so he's always saving Yancy's. He uses a sawed-off shotgun that blows the bad guy away."

"Damn, they can't show what a shotgun does on television."

"You're right, Brewster. They have a rig and harness on the bad guy, and, when the gun goes off, they jerk him way back into a wall. You don't get a chance to see any gore."

"Oh, I could certainly do that, no lines to learn, not even sign language."

"But sometimes the bad guy will be shot off a balcony, through the banisters, and down to the floor."

I made the mistake of letting Bergen recommend me to Frances, Jock, and the Desilu people. During that season, they busted my tailbone about seven times. It still acts up when the weather changes or there's a political ad on TV.

Years later, I was set to work with Jock and "real Indians." Since I got along well with X. Brands, or Mr. Jay X. Brands, I figured I could handle a real-life Arapaho or Navajo. I was wrong on two things: X. Brands was a German American who'd talk your head off, except when he was doing his Indian bit, and Mahoney was going to India and Thailand to do Tarzan movies with real Indians. He came back as skinny as Fred Astaire because dysentery and dengue fever almost killed him. I guess Dr. Jack Daniels destroyed all the germs I was taking in.

Years later, I got a call from Edgar Bergen's secretary. The whole family was going to Birmingham, Frances' hometown, where Edgar, Charlie, Mortimer Snerd, and Effie Klinker were to perform on a street corner on one of the closed-off streets during an arts festival. I was to wrangle their luggage this time because Bergen was getting too old to do much more than his act.

So, after the performance in downtown Birmingham, I was putting Charlie away, and Bergen was talking to Mortimer, the goofy country bumpkin puppet:

"Well, Mortimer, would you like to elucidate what the artistic endeavors in Birmingham should signify to us?"

Mortimer gave the audience a look to see if any of them figured out what Bergen was asking and then drawled, "No, I don't think I would…nope…I sure wouldn't."

I got uncomfortable when Bergen called up that horny old maid Effie Klinker. She was about as ugly as Mortimer, but I can tell you that, after I had knocked off a bottle or two of the Jack, she got to looking awfully good. Later Bergen would have to give me The Talk: "I'm really ashamed for you, Brewster. This is disgusting. I forbid you to see her again."

Once I protested, "But she's a grown woman," but he glared at me. "She's a figure, Brewster, a puppet."

Since I wasn't inebriated enough yet for Effie to interest

me, I scanned the crowd and saw what had to be the monocle kid. He had to be in his twenties but looked like he was fifteen, and he had on a green top hat.

After Effie's routine, Bergen was answering questions from his street-corner audience, and the kid drifted over to me.

"Howdy, Mr. Brewster."

"You've grown up, kid."

"Well, I'm taller than Charlie."

"Still being the 'Wild-Eyed Moderate'?"

"Yes, sir, and I've been working on a code to go along with it."

"A Code of the West-type thing?"

He frowned and leaned forward confidentially. "Actually, I based it on the 'categorical imperative' of Immanuel Kant."

"You don't say."

"I do."

"I'll bite: What *is* a categorical imperative?"

"It's a saying, sort of a grand universal principle."

"And what would that be, kid?"

"Kant says, 'Act only according to that maxim whereby you can, at the same time, will that it should become a universal law.'"

I didn't know what the hell that meant, so I said, "So that's your code, eh?"

"Only briefly. Whenever I said that, people looked about like Mortimer does when Bergen uses a big word."

"So what's the code now, kid? 'Kiss your mom and your horse, stay away from whiskey and wild women, and smile, podner, whenever you say something sarcastic?'"

He cocked his head and repeated what I said and began scribbling them down. "—whenever you say something snarky. I can add those."

I checked to see if the Bergens were ready to go, but Mrs. Bergen was having a great time talking to one of her high school friends. It was safe to talk to the kid a little longer. "So what do you have so far?"

"Let's see: 'A man has to keep his word.' He can't just trim what he says for whoever he's talking to."

"Does that apply to politicians, too?"

"Especially them."

"Well, good luck with that. What else?"

"I like this one: 'Do unto ranchers, sheepherders, and farmers as you would have them do unto you.'"

"Does that apply to, say, used car salesmen?"

He shook his head. "No, sir. It doesn't apply to bank robbers, car salesmen, bank presidents…or members of Congress."

"What does the code say about women who work in saloons and cathouses?"

"You treat a lady like a lady."

"Even when she's not a lady?"

"If she's fallen, that doesn't mean you have to fall, too."

"What if she's a member of Congress who robs banks and sells cars?"

"Even then."

"Is that all of the code?" I asked.

He shook his head. "'If you are in favor of something only because it will make you a buck, then you are lying to yourself and to the public.' I know that's harsh."

"When you go from town to town, do you give out silver bullets?"

"Lord no. Too expensive. When Clayton Moore appeared as the Lone Ranger in the parking lot of the Piggly Wiggly in Vidalia, he gave me a silver bullet, but it was just plastic that had been spray-painted silver."

"So what do you give out?"

"I was going to give out ball bearings spray-painted copper, but I didn't realize what 'brass balls' meant."

Mrs. Bergen was raising her voice for me to hear and telling one of her friends how won-der-ful it was to see her again and to keep in touch.

The kid looked panicked and blurted out. "Lead weights. I ride away—actually drive away—and shout out, "Good people, remember: Get the lead out!"

So that was that until he tracked me down in the retirement home.

Big complication, dang it. I found out that I had made a colossal mistake in cooperating with the kid when he told me that he wanted me to do an introduction to a book. He said I could talk it into a tape recorder, which I did. He listened to the tape, but then said he wanted me to say something about the stuff in the book.

The kid's so darned serious that I thought the reading would be rough going. I decided to give myself a reward for each chapter I got through: I'd open a new bottle of Jack Daniels. The retirement home staff put a stop to that, so I trudged on till the end.

Frankly, it was all I could do to keep from busting out laughing during some of the pieces. I kept a straight face because I didn't want to hurt his feelings.

I have to admit that half of the time I didn't know what he was talking about. That could be partly because I don't read much. He mentions Harry Potter in several pieces. I do know about him, of course, because I have to sit through those movies when folks' grandkids visit them at the retirement home. I have a hard time figuring out what the English actors are saying.

The kid also has interviews with George Washington, Thomas Jefferson, and Millard Fillmore, sort of. I believe they were all presidents, and I think I met Millard Fillmore when he visited the set of *Gunfight with the Wild-Eyed Moderate.*

There's a quiz in there on writers in movies. I didn't get a single one right. If it had been about riders, like horse riders in movies, I would have done much better. He has a piece on Igor from the Frankenstein movies. Tom Tyler, one cowboy actor, said those scary pictures paid his rent after he finished Westerns and the Captain Marvel serial. When he began to suffer from rheumatoid arthritis, he said he was lucky to play the Mummy because it didn't matter if his movements were jerky.

The kid calls himself a moderate, but I guess the pieces won't hurt you if you are an extreme right-winger or extreme lefty. So go ahead and dive right in, even if you don't have a bottle of whiskey to help out.

PAST LIVES, LOVES, AND LOSSES

"You'll be wanting to publish a case history about me," I told my eminent therapist. "Everyone will be speaking of you as the famous Dr. —"

"No, absolutely not," he interrupted. "I'll write nothing, and, if you ever speak or write about our treatment, you will refer to me as—let's see—ah, yes, Franklin T. Foxwhistle. Is that clear?"

"And not —?"

"No, it'll be 'Dr. Franklin T. Foxwhistle,'" he insisted. "Not what you've been erroneously calling me."

"But all your diplomas say your name is —"

"That's when I was in a witness protection program," my therapist maintained. "The feds made me go into hiding when I figured out that George W. Bush was born outside of the U.S. on the islets of Langerhans."

I realized that Dr. Foxwhistle resembled John Gotti, or perhaps J. Edgar Hoover, if you pressed a finger to the side of each eyeball and squinted at him just so.

But I don't recommend that you thumb your eyes around him, because that will panic this, ah, Dr. Foxwhistle, who will then interrogate you for an hour that will cost you $150 and leave you no wiser than before. Besides that, your eyes will hurt.

"Your problems are hidden," Dr. Foxwhistle had announced at our tenth session.

"No, they're not. I'm an adult grandchild of an alcoholic. I voted for Richard Nixon three times, almost, and would do it again if somebody dug him up and put him on the ballot."

He held up his hand to silence me and shook his head. "Hypnotism may help."

"Oh?" I asked, since I have often wanted to stand on a kitchen chair and *cock-a-doodle-do* at family members. The action would rid them of their complacency and make them wonder if I had started getting into the bottle, too.

"Yes, I'm running a special on hypnotism. Only $150 extra." He leaned forward confidentially. "That's cheaper than a getting a crown."

That puzzled me. "I'm quite certain that Queen Elizabeth II is not me mum."

Dr. Foxwhistle gave me a long look, which I knew meant he would be asking me to schedule three more sessions. "I was talking about a *dental* crown."

That set off an anxiety attack. As I huddled on the floor and sucked on my clip-on tie, Dr. Foxwhistle settled my nerves by twirling a pocket watch in front of me. "Look at the watch," he droned. "You are relaxing."

I relaxed and then felt a sharp poke in the ribs.

"You are relaxing, but you are NOT snoring. Do you understand?"

"Well, I do have sleep apnea."

"No matter," he said as he gritted his teeth and stared at his walls. "Your snoring has peeled off the wall paper." In a few seconds, he droned, "We are going back to when you were a baby. Going back, back, back." Eventually he asked, "Are you a baby now?"

A voice not quite my own *goo-goo*ed that I was.

"Do you hear music? Your mother singing?"

I *goo-goo*ed, "Mummy sings 'God Save the Queen.'"

Another poke in the ribs brought me back to the present, and he regressed me again. This time, Dr. Foxwhistle emphasized that I was not heir to the throne of the United Kingdom. "There's never been an English king or prince who talks like Goober Pyle," Dr. Foxwhistle maintained. "Kings like kippers and bangers, not black-eyed peas and grits."

Again the ritual went on, and Dr. Foxwhistle asked, "As a baby, what music are you hearing?"

Goo-goo: "Take it off, take it off, cried the boys from the rear!"

"Good Lord, that's 'Strip Polka,' isn't it?"

Goo-goo: "My favorite song: 'and she stops, and always just in time.'"

Dr. Foxwhistle sighed, "That explains one compulsive fixation."

A week later, Dr. Foxwhistle announced, "It must be earlier, this great problem of yours."

"How can it be earlier?" I asked. "You've got me back to six months old."

Dr. Foxwhistle drummed on the table and declared, "This is revolutionary, but we're going to have to take you back, back, back."

Shocked, I asked, "Even backer than before?"

"Definitely, much backer."

"Not *before* I was born?"

"Even before you were *conceived*," he announced and twisted the pocket watch again.

Later, Foxwhistle asked, "What year is it now?"

"It's April 1912, guv."

"Ah, where are you?"

"On 'oliday, guv."

Excited, Foxwhistle leaned forward and adjusted the volume on his tape-recorder. "What's your name? Do you know that?"

"Right-o, guv. 'Erman Doodle, Bookseller. On me first 'oliday in twenty years. My wife Bertha insisted that I get away, so we're sailing to the States to visit our daughter in Perth Amboy."

"And what's your ship?"

"Top 'ole vessel, guv: the *Titanic*."

Dr. Foxwhistle poked me in the ribs and ended the session. "That accounts for your cynicism and your doom-and-gloom that unnerves the Suicide Survivors Encounters Group. But it's not the whole story."

The next week, he twirled his watch and droned until he asked, "Where are you now?"

"In the Mermaid Tavern."

"Do you know the year?"

"No, sir, I wouldn't be knowing that, no, sir."

"Then do you know what city you're in."

"No, sir. Just in the City, where I've always been."

Dr. Foxwhistle snapped, "Well, tell me *who* are your customers?"

"Well, there's Dr. Johnson, and —"

"What's his first name?"

"Oh, I wouldn't be knowing that, sir, no sir, but he's the bloke what knows all them big words."

"Would one of his friends be a Mr. Boswell?"

"Right, sir, a Scottish gent."

"How do you know that, if you didn't know Johnson's name?"

"Easy, sir, because every time he came in, the doctor always said, 'My God, here comes Bosley, that idiot from Scotland.'"

"That's 'Boswell,' but no matter. Now look about the room and tell me what Dr. Johnson is doing now."

"Oh, yes, sir, he's shouting them big words at me again."

"Such as?"

"I don't know if I can say them, sir. But I think he said something like *contemptible*, *despicable*, *atrocious*, *deleterious*, *obnoxious*, *calamitous*, and —"

"What have you done to make him angry?"

"Nothing much, sir. Today's his 'clean shirt day,' and all I did was spill a tankard of ale on him again."

"Again?"

"Yes, sir, it's them big words sets me off, and people who drink a lot sort of unsettle me, sir."

A poke in the ribs brought me to the present again, and Dr. Foxwhistle glared at me. "You spill ale on Dr. Samuel Johnson every time he comes in, and you can't remember a single witty thing he ever said. It's disgusting!"

"And *odious*, *repugnant*, and *loathsome*, the Doctor always said."

At the next session, Dr. Foxwhistle snapped at me, "Get on the couch, for God's sake! Hurry!" A few minutes later, he asked, "Now where are you?"

"Oh, the Globe!"

"The what? A regular globe or —?"

"The acting place, on the south bank of the River Thames."

"You sound happy." He cocked his head and looked at me suspiciously. "*That*'s different."

"It should be. I'm one of Master William's key actors: I'm the sixth clown, and I get to perform when the understudy of Will Kempe's understudy is sick."

"Master William—now exactly who is he?"

"*Who*? *Who* in the bloody hell is Master William? You're asking that?"

"Those are my words."

"Master William, sirrah, is our director, our paymaster, and the play-writer, you know: the great scribbler."

"Shakespeare?"

"Right, that's him, always going on with that quill, *scratch-scratch* here and *scratch-scratch* there."

"What is Shakespeare doing now?"

"Oh, that's easy, sir. He's not speaking to me. He's sitting over there glaring at me. No gratitude in him, sir, for all his greatness. I suspect he'd fire me if he could get any of the other clowns to clean up after the horses out front."

"Why should he be grateful to you?"

"*Why*? Why? You're bloody hell asking me *that*?"

"I think those are my words, if you'll answer."

"Well, I cleaned up after the horses, as I always do, because I put myself into my work, if you understand what I mean. Then they asked for me to fetch some victuals, which I did, even though I'd already et, you see."

"Then what happened?"

"Oh, sir, it was summat in the food, and they all got sick: Master William and the whole cast."

"That something in the food, could it have been fingers with horse manure on them?"

"No, sir, wouldn't think so. At least, it had never bothered them before."

"So they were all sick?"

"Right and lined up to the privy and everyone asking for any extra copy of Marlowe's *Doctor Faustus*."

"To read?"

"No, sir, for the paper, you see. Anyway, Master William is deciding to cancel and tells me, 'Will, we'll have to call off this evening's production of *Hamlet, Prince of Denmark*. Go out front and tell them to come another afternoon."

"Your name is Will?"

"We was all Will: Will Shakespeare, Will Kempe, and me: Will, son of Will the Hog Slopper."

"So you cancelled the play?"

"No, sir, not by a long shot, sir, not Will son of Will, no sir. I did the play all by meself because I'd heard all the lines and liked the play. I enjoyed parts like 'Two bees or not two bees, the question, honey, is where is the hive?' I knew that I had the whole play down pat."

"So you, all by yourself, did the whole play of *Hamlet*? How did you manage to pull off that feat?"

"With sock puppets, you see. I'd have Hamlet on my left hand, and then I'd give Ofeelme, my right-hand puppet, a good tongue lashing and tell it to 'get thee to a gunnery.' Right fierce, I was too."

"I'm afraid to ask, but what do you think was your best scene?"

"Oh, the graveyard scene, sir, with the skull of Yogurt. I pretended to talk to the gravedigger down in the hole and then I'd pick up the skull. I was about to say, 'Alas, poor Yogurt, I knew him, Horatio,' when I thought of a line that Master William would love, you know, if he had been cleverer and had just the tiniest bit of imagination."

"Go on," Dr. Foxwhistle said. "I've taken a couple of Valiums."

"There was this wench amongst the groundlings in the theater, so, just as Master William stumbled into the theater, I was saying, 'A *lass*, poor Yogurt,' and then I moved the jaw of the skull and threw my voice so that Yogurt's skull was saying, 'Swounds, that *is* a fetching lass. What're you doing tonight, Poopsie?'"

"I suspect the Bard was ecstatic."

"No, sir, not at all. He didn't have much of a sense of humor. I don't care how many comedies he wrote."

"What did the Bard do?"

"At the next rehearsal, he stuck in this scene of Hamlet with the players. Burbage—that big tub of conceited lard—had to memorize the lines overnight, not that his Hamlet was half as good as mine, you understand. So there he's saying, 'And let those that play your clowns speak no more than is set down for them, for there be of them that will themselves laugh, to set on some quantity of barren spectators to laugh, too, though in the meantime some necessary question of the play be then to be considered.'"

"But those lines weren't necessarily directed at you."

"Oh, they were, too. Let me tell you: Richard Bloody Burbage and the Barb were looking daggers at me. You know, *la de dah*, like I can't figure out who the Barb is talking to, when Hamlet says, 'That's villainous, and shows a pitiful ambition in the fool that uses it.'"

"The Barb?"

"Right, I always called him the 'Barb of Stratford on Avon.'"

"It was *Bard*, a word for a poet."

"And *not* for that nasty disposition, with him always telling me, 'Will, you say the words that I put on paper,' like I can read writing and all that?"

At the next session, Dr. Foxwhistle seemed mellow and hummed, "Oh, lithium, my lithium, oh, how I love you, lithium." He patted me on the head and grinned. "You've upset Dr. Samuel Johnson, you've horrified William Shakespeare, so who am I to complain if you've thrown my life and practice into disarray?"

I wasn't quite sure what kind of answer he wanted and didn't get a chance to pursue his line of thought when that pocket watch started spinning again.

A voice asked by and by, "How far back are you?"

"I don't know."

"What year is it?"

"It's now."

"Okay, *where* are you?"

"Here."

"Where is *here*?"

"It's an apple orchard."

"Very good, and what's your name?"

"Will, Son of Will the Hog Slopper."

"What was your *grand*father's name?"

"Oh, he was a Will, too, also Son of Will the Hog Slopper. We all be Hog Sloppers, to the beginning of time, and we all be Wills."

"Very well. What are you doing, Will?"

"Oh, I'm holding up a pig so he can nibble apples from the tree. He's et fourteen of them already."

"You're holding a pig while he eats fourteen apples? Doesn't that take a lot of time?"

"You're joshing me, sir. After all, what's time to a pig?"

A week later, Foxwhistle glared at me and got me under so fast I couldn't even talk about the weather. "Where are you?"

"In a pig pen, sir."

"You're slopping hogs, right?"

"No, sir. I'm in charge."

"Of what?"

"Of eating this end of the slopping trough."

Dr. Foxwhistle poked me in the ribs again and hastened me out the door. While I drove home, I wiped off the dirt from the potted plant container in which I had been rooting.

The whole year of therapy had been a waste of time. I was no closer to figuring out the big mysteries of my life: why I hate ocean voyages, why I refused to work as a waiter in college, why *Hamlet* fascinates me so much, why the sight of an apple orchard simply makes my arms hurt, and why I have this pug nose.

I also wonder what sent Dr. Foxwhistle off the deep end.

THE HOLY CODE TO GETTING RICH QUICK

The lawsuit in London against Dan Brown for his *The Da Vinci Code* started my little gray cells to cogitating like mad about copyright and plagiarism. Of course, I'm wrong about half the time concerning the way that courts decide their verdicts, but the Court of Denson came down on the side of Dan Brown. (The British court agreed with my brief and my briefs, but not my boxer shorts nor my night-shirt.)

His novel, of course, is a bunch of silly nonsense. I don't mind his claiming that Jesus was married to Mary Magdalene and had a child. That wouldn't shake the beliefs of this defrocked Baptist.

Quick digression: Actually "defrogged" Baptist is more accurate due to an unfortunate encounter with nature during my full-immersion baptism in Lugswater Creek. We'll skip over the turmoil of that service.

Jesus was a rabbi, and a rabbi is generally married and all that by his thirties.

I also don't mind that Robert Graves in *King Jesus* had Mary as a "temple virgin" and that he wrote a novel about Jesus actually having royal blood and a claim to the throne. That was an interesting approach.

It doesn't bother me that Jewish-writer Sholem Asch had

a center section of *The Nazarene* entitled "The Gospel According to Judas Iscariot." That was fascinating because it explored more motivations for the betrayal other than "the devil made me do it." I found Asch's gospel to be more grounded in the New Testament than the actual, putative *Gospel of Judas*, which was written about 180 A.D., discovered in the 1970s, and first translated in 2000.

However, I do object to assertions that Mary Magdalene was depicted in Leonardo's "Last Supper" as being one of the apostles and sitting to Jesus' right. My chief art advisor, former Governator Schwarzenegger, states that the figure is sort of a girly man, but Leonardo painted other effeminate males.

Even with that flaw, Brown is entitled to create a narrative that entertains. Since various sources say Brown's novel has sold more than 40 million copies worldwide, we recognize that it is satisfying some readers. That represents a potful of money that went into the coffers of Random House.

And that alluring cash, that folding stuff, and that money-money-money was enough to entice two other Random House authors, Michael Baigent and Richard Leigh, to beseech some court to shovel a good portion of the loot their way. They claim that the central premise of *The Da Vinci Code* was taken from their nonfiction book, *Holy Blood and the Holy Grail* (which was published in 1982).

The Court of Denson agreed with Random House's British attorney, John Baldwin, QC (Queen's Counsel), who said Baigent and Leigh's allegations were "spurious and bogus."

Baldwin said, "Many of the ideas complained of are not even in both books, some are not even in either, so they cannot have been copied from one to the other."

He adds, "In the main, the ideas complained of were not

original to HBHG anyway." It is argued by Denson, RCC, MP (Royal Crown Cola and Moon Pie) that Frederick Jackson Turner's work has long been in the public domain, but let's pretend Turner published his concept of the expanding frontier only back in 1983 instead of in 1893. He would not have a legal complaint if someone was writing about Dan'l Boone, perhaps in this manner:

> DAN'L: It's an expanding frontier that's driving us all, Buddy.
>
> SIDEKICK: Mebbe.
>
> DAN'L: Mebbe, nothin'. There's a driving force at work in us settlers. We have a rendezvous with destiny, with the Pacific and a Hard Rock Café.
>
> SIDEKICK: The only expanding frontier, I'm interested in is the backside of that new gal at the tavern.

And so on.

One's a non-fiction book, and the other is a novel or screenplay.

By the same token, if you have a best-selling non-fiction book, you and I do have some limitations. For example, *A Beautiful Mind* by Columbia's Sylvia Nazar caught the attention of Hollywood. Frank McCourt's *Angela's Ashes* is non-fiction, but it took McCourt's permission for it to be made into a film. Neither you nor I may produce a novel or a screenplay about his family's poverty-stricken story.

A quick rule of thumb is this: Does my adaptation take money out of anyone's pocket? If I write a novel or screenplay about Dr. Samuel Johnson and rely on Boswell's biography, I'm not depriving the Scotsman of any payment since he has been as dead as Monty Python's parrot for a couple of centuries. But, if someone has a new biography of

Dr. Johnson and if Oprah, Jon Stewart, and others praise it to high heaven, you and I can get into trouble if we adapt that particular bio.

It's comforting to know that, if you only end up selling 500 to 5,000 copies of your book, you probably won't have to worry about any "spurious and bogus" lawsuits.

But if you sell one or two million copies, then you'll begin to hear the greedy hum of "money, money, money" from clients and their attorneys.

THE GRANDMA MOSES CODE

Dr. Franklin T. Foxwhistle discourages me from writing about my weekly therapy sessions, but he says for me to go ahead since it may cut down on my complaints about his office motto: "If you want to whine, I've got the time—$150 per 60 minutes."

I keep telling him that *whine* and *time* don't really rhyme.

However, he won't listen to a word I say and claims that they could be half-rhymes.

Okay, I argue, if he's going to use half-rhymes, he should only charge $75 for the hour.

During the last session, I guess I was going on a bit about Dan Brown's obscene success with *The Da Vinci Code.*

Let me be honest:

First, I was complaining about his selling 40 gadzillion copies of his silly book, which didn't hold together.

Second, Brown refuses to respond to my letters demanding $20 million "for the hell of it since you have so much extra change."

Dr. Foxwhistle said, "Zilch—that's about the same response that you received from J.K. Rowling?"

I agreed and asked, "What's wrong with these people?"

"How did you open your last letter to Ms. Rowling?" Foxwhistle asked. "Was that the tenth or fifteenth letter?"

"Actually, the sixteenth," I said. "This time, I opened it with 'Dear Fat Limey Cow, I'm guessing you don't know how to write letters either. To prove that you do, send me 20 million."

"Dollars or pounds or euros?"

"Doesn't matter. I'm flexible."

"I hate to quibble, but I've seen the PBS specials on Ms. Rowling. She's really quite slim, not a 'fat, limey cow' at all."

"Go ahead, Foxwhistle. Take her side."

"I saw on the internet that she's now worth $1 billion." Foxwhistle licked his lips and had a faraway look. "That's a wonderful weight for any woman."

"She's married," I reminded him.

He frowned and looked down at his legal pad. "Was 'dear fat limey cow' the most diplomatic salutation you could have used?"

"Are you saying I should have sucked up to her for such a trifling sum?"

"Why 20 million pounds or whatever?"

"Oh, it's the code I discovered when studying the paintings of Grandma Moses."

"A code? Does it prove God or Santa doesn't exist, or something?"

"It proves many different things, according to the Level of Understanding. That's what I call it."

"A Level of Understanding? I'm afraid to ask."

Then I explained to him that I was scrutinizing some paintings by Grandma Moses, when I read some biographical information. Then, using a Chaldic system of numerology, I immediately saw great significance in her actual name: Anna Mary Robertson Moses. "I went through the number value of each word and used a Chaldean scale to convert them to English, so 'Anna Mary Robertson Moses' actually means 'Send $20M to Denson ASAPDQ.'"

"That won't work. Her name has several 'a' letters, and you've given them different values."

"Of course, due to the linguistic shift of the obliquity in the dialectic."

Dr. Foxwhistle seemed to get one of his migraines and popped a couple more of his pills. Then he sighed and asked, "And ASAPDQ?"

"As soon as pretty damn quick."

"Wow! Look out the window."

I looked but didn't see anything.

Then he said, "Darn, you missed it. Oh, I see our time is up."

"No, it isn't. You changed the time while I was looking out your window."

"Not so. Next time, should we talk about your paranoia?"

"Paranoia, my eye. See?" I grabbed his wrist and pulled up his sleeve until we could see his Rolex. "You didn't have time to change your watch. We've still got forty-five minutes."

He stared at the watch, slouched in surrender, and sniveled, "All right, get on with it."

"I will ASAPDQ."

"Stick a sock in it."

"I beg your pardon?"

He said, "I meant, 'Freud would say stick sex in it.'"

I tried to look him in the eye to see if he was telling the truth, but he had a coughing fit and was spinning in his swivel chair until it cleared up. As he spun, he also twirled a finger for me to continue.

"So 'send $20 million,'" I said, "that was the message at the first Level of Understanding. Let me explain in detail. You see each cow was crudely depicted with the right side legs 20 percent off from the left side, so 20 percent, then $20 million, and —"

"I'm sorry to interrupt, but it may be more beneficial for you to explain the next Level of Understanding."

"Oh? Well, all right. Then I noticed she was born in 1860 and then died in 1961, and there it was!"

"Okay, there was what?"

"She was calling for a second War Between the States."

"Numbers told you that?"

"Not at all, the colors of the letters did."

He raised a dubious eyebrow.

"Oh, not the colors in the book," I said. "All of the printing was black, but each letter cast a different color psychologically."

"For example?"

"All of the 'a' letters are gray, and gray is the color of the Confederacy. When you have 'n' and 'm' letters, you have the diagonal crosses of the battle flag, where the stars are. And get this: The 'o' letters give you red, and the 'r' and 't' combine to give you blue."

Dr. Foxwhistle looked at his pad. "How do you account for the 'b,' 's,' and 'y' letters and their colors? Do they mean 'the South is going to rise again'?"

"Not at all. Grandma Moses was from New York state. At one time, some businessmen wanted it to secede from Manhattan, Staten Island, and so on, but they were waiting for a charismatic leader to emerge. In the movie, I think he should be played by Tom Hanks."

"I believe we really are out of time."

"I've sent a letter to him —"

"And it says, 'Dear Mr. Hanks, send me $20 million by return mail."

"Actually, it says send it 'ASAPDQ.'"

HARRY POTTER E-MAILS

[AUTHOR'S NOTE: I cannot vouch for the authenticity of what is purported to be an e-mail exchange between J.K. Rowling and two of her editors. I discount the suggestion that the exchange is purely imaginary since all of my friends claim that I lack inventiveness and got all of my jokes from the old Jack Benny radio show. In addition, I am very much aware that Rowling's publisher is Scholastic.]

Jo: Thanks for letting us know the title for the last (can we talk about this?) Harry Potter book. *Harry Potter and the Deathly Hallows* is all right, I suppose. As a title, it's better than *HP and the Half-Breed Prince.*—BG

BG: The title will be fine. I wish you and the other publishing minions trusted my judgement more.—JKR

Jo: Good Lord, we trust you implicitly and without reservation. You have made everyone filthy rich: yourself, Publishing Minions Inc., and the movie companies. I suppose it's just human nature—or business nature—not to want to see the gravy-train get derailed. The youngsters in the books have become young adults, and the young readers have become young adults, too. It's just that there are lots more HP stories out there. In the attachment, I'll include some titles of possible new works. They don't have to be 700 pages long. A mere 200 or 300 pages would do fine.—BG

BG: I'm sorry, but I can only assume that the entire office must have been smoking something when you came up with your list. *Harry Potter and the Testicles of Steel?* What were you people thinking of? It's a wonder you didn't include *HP Rides Again*, *Son of HP*, or *The Ghost of HP.*—JKR

Jo: Okay, when we sobered up, some of us spotted some potential problems with *HP & TOS*, so I'll concede that. But the series does beg to have other story lines included. For example, switched identity: HP changes into Hermione or Ron (or vice versa). Or an evil entity makes himself look like HP. Or they step into an alternate universe where HP's parents are still alive, but he's a regular bloke, a muggle, and HP the muggle steps into regular HP's universe. Hagrid is a midget in that universe. Scenes filled with potential danger or laughs.—BG

BG: I don't mind a Guinness or two myself, but please don't put on your thinking cap when you're hanging out in a pub with TV writers. Just drink, unwind, and take a taxi home. Don't try to come up with story lines. I must insist.—JKR

Jo: Sorry for the disconnect for several weeks, but I just got out of rehab. Everyone in there suggested that HP should be doing their jobs: nurse, nurse's aide, physician, social worker, chef, maintenance, etc. They suggested that HP could sort of do like the American cable show, *Dirty Jobs*, with HP running a cafeteria in one book or driving a milk-truck in another (*HP and the Rutabagas of Provencal* and *HP and the Sour Disposition* were suggested as titles).—BG

BG: I'm glad you're feeling better. It's not necessary to relay every suggestion to me. You really need to check out my website, www.jkrowling.com, where I have all sorts of rumors and suggestions from faithful readers.—JKR

Jo: I enjoyed the website. I chased the butterfly all over the page, but the spider scared me out of my wits.—BG

BG: That explains things (ha ha).—JKR

Jo: I'm sorry to be a nuisance, but my supervisors here at BG Inc. are insisting that I bring up the issue of what comes after book No. 7. If you don't want to continue with HP himself, they also like a series about someone like Hermione and, for any films, there are thousands of actresses who'd kill for the role. Pamela Anderson has been practicing an English accent, though the character might need to be Canadian for her to handle it. The honchos tell me some test footage shows she is a very convincing in the opening as a fifteen-year-old whose only goal is to work at Hooter's.—BG

BG: No.—JKR

Jo: I don't mean to be a bother, but I'll be history if I don't do a decent enough pitch for some sequels. Ron or someone very much like him has graduated and becomes a private eye and magician for hire. He's doing kids' birthday parties until a villain frames him for some felony. In the big house, thugs try to molest him, but he changes them into chimpanzees. When he's released, he tries to escape his past and to redeem himself. Suggested title: *I the Judge, Jury, and Conjurer.* (One of the chimps becomes his partner. Other possible title: *Ron Weasley and Bonzo.*) As he gets older, he could drive a Maxwell and always claim to be only thirty-nine years old.—BG

My Dearest Ms. Rowling: As per your suggestion on the phone yesterday, BG has moved on to greener pastures, and I've taken over his responsibilities. I can't tell you how much I'm looking forward to working with you. I've seen almost all of the Harry Potter movies and am up to page 119 of the first book. (Wow, you really write long. I'm impressed!!!)

The guys in the office were really enthusiastic about your agreeing to do a book No. 8, 9, etc.; they said all I had to do was close the deal. A round number of 10 or 12 would be fine, but a baker's dozen (that's 13, I found out) might even be better.

The guys were pointing out that HP is a good-looking stud and that he would really appeal to the chicks. One of the suggested titles (see attachment) is ideal for a magical bedroom romp. They don't have to be steel. Iron, brass, or bronze might do as well.—Philip

GONE WITH THE MUGGLES

It's almost impossible to pick up a newspaper or magazine today without finding an article about someone whining about being ripped off by Harry Potter or kept from publishing a great work by the heirs of, say, *Gone with the Wind.*

Lest you sit around moping that, dammit, it's an unjust world with J.K. Rowling fleecing some poor lady, let me give you as much as peace of mind as my therapist, Dr. Foxwhistle, does when he drops a couple of Valiums in my decaffeinated diet Buffalo Rock ginger-ale.

I had my serious misgivings when a lady named Nancy Stouffer first claimed that *Harry Potter and the Sorcerer's Stone* was stolen from her *The Legend of Rah and the Muggles*. I had seen enough people stand up at writers' conferences, waving manuscripts and claiming that they had sent the ideas for scripts to *Golden Girls*, *Designing Women*, or *Friends*: "They returned my manuscript, but my exact ideas appeared within a month or so." As I searched at length for the book, I saw that Stouffer's book wasn't mentioned in the databases of the Jacksonville Public Libraries, the twenty-eight state colleges' libraries, or the University of North Florida's library.

No copy had found its way into the maze of Northeast Florida's Chamblin's Book Mine, which holds more old books than any building since Caesar's troops burned the great library of Alexandria, Virginia, during the Sibyl War (trust me on that since I'm excellent in history and give helpful pointers to Ken Burns all the time).

Mind you, this lack of mention portends no good for someone claiming that her work was so captivating that Rowling stole it. She even claimed that her company had received orders worth $6.5 million and that her books were on the way to earning $1 billion. Unfortunately, a snow storm, she claimed, had, ah, collapsed the roof of her home studio (yes, that was it), and, ah, destroyed the records that would prove her point, darn it.

Of course, it did, dearie, and, as I keep telling Dr. Foxwhistle, I'm Stinko, the flatulent Marx brother.

She complained that she had trademarked the term "muggles" and that Rowling appropriated her invention. However, we see that Stouffer used "muggles" to refer to mutant humanoids on earth after a nuclear conflagration (hey, Phillip Boule heirs, pay attention to this possible ripoff of your *Planet of the Apes* franchise). By contrast, Rowling used "muggles" to refer to normal folk like you and, well, me at times.

The M-volume of *The Oxford English Dictionary* has a couple of entries on "muggles," a bad sign if you're claiming to have made it up. The first recorded use of the word goes back to 1205. It has an obscure origin, perhaps from Kent, and it referred to "a tailed man." The *OED* also contains quoted uses of the word from 1450, 1607, 1617, and then refers to "Muggletonian," a member of the sect founded about 1631 by Lodowicke Muggleton and John Reeve.

So, sorry, Ms. Stouffer, you can't trademark "muggle" any more than Disney can copyright the word "dwarf," a word that goes back to the 800s, according to the *OED*. On the other hand, Disney can copyright "Doc," "Sneezy," "Dubya," "Blitzen," "Barfy," and all the other dwarfs.

Ms. Stouffer noted that her book had "Larry Potter,"

which shows, she said, just how blatant Rowling's theft was.

Except...

Almost any British novel will have a character with the last name of "Potter" or "Trotter." Such names have a solid middle-class ring and the character's forebears were from good yeoman stock, either working with pots or horses. Moreover, you often encounter "Harry," which, by God, is a solid, even heroic, name that will take you once more into the breach, dear friends.

Ms. Stouffer noted other similarities between the two books. For example, she had "worry stones" (mood rocks?) and Rowling had a "sorcerer's stone."

Except...

Rowling originally had a "philosopher's stone," which the American publisher changed to "sorcerer's stone" because we Yanks and Rebels are too bone-head ignorant to know that alchemists claimed philosopher's stones transformed base metals into gold.

Next, Ms. Stouffer noted that Harry Potter had glasses, just like Larry Potter did in her book. They were even drawn alike, she claimed. I won't ask you to go through illustrated books, movies, and TV for images of kids having adventures. The regular kid probably looked a lot like Opie Taylor; the smart kid had glasses and either dark hair or red hair; and the fat kid could have any color hair.

I have yet to see a copy of Stouffer's opus, but, by and by, I saw it discussed in an article by Linton Weeks in *The Washington Post.* He pointed out this distressing fact: Ms. Stouffer's book had (get this now) only twenty-four pages, whereas each Harry Potter book ranges from 600 to 700 pages. Moreover, Stouffer's opus was an activity book with games, puzzles, and pages to color. In other words, the Harry Potter book is to Stouffer's pamphlet as *Gone with the Wind* is to the label on a box of Uncle Ben's rice.

But coincidences do occur, and, when they do, we have the option of filing suits or recognizing coincidence. Back in the 1970s, for example, I wrote a post-holocaust novel set almost fifty years in the future. I entitled the manuscript *2020 Vision*. After a couple publishing houses rejected it, I set it aside, but was startled one day when I saw a paperback version of *2020 Vision* on a bookrack in K-Mart. That caused me to bite through nails until I thumbed through that book and saw that it had nothing in common with my effort. Another writer and I had simply hit upon the same idea for a title. (It's what I call Grade C Level of Creativity.)

Similarly, mystery writer Kevin Robinson wrote a mystery called *Mall Rats*. He told me that, when a movie of the same name appeared, he and his attorney licked their chops with anticipation until they saw that the film was about kids hanging at the mall but not about a murder investigation by someone like his wheelchair-bound private eye, Stick Foster.

That brings us to the wicked heirs of Margaret Mitchell, who filed suit against Alice Randall's *The Wind Done Gone*, a novel that told the *GWTW* story from the African-American perspective. The news stories all seemed to hint that the "heirs" were simply being selfish troublemakers.

Let me blow a whistle and throw a penalty flag.

GWTW is a money-making franchise. Not only is the novel itself still selling, but the Mitchell heirs approved the publication of *Scarlett*, a 1991 sequel by Alexandra Ripley. Even if not a critical success, it still made a profit, both as a novel and a mini-series. Pat Conroy was approached to do another sequel, but declined the honor. However, Mitchell's estate authorized Donald McCaig to write a second sequel titled *Rhett Butler's People*. The novel covers the same territory as *GWTW* does, except from Rhett Butler's perspective.

Some critics thought it just fine that a book-sized parody of *GWTW* would be penned. These included Harper Lee (*To*

Kill a Mockingbird), Civil War historian Shelby Foote, John Berendt (*Midnight in the Garden of Good and Evil*), and some others. They said, "The discussion of the painful legacy of slavery is ongoing among American citizens across the nation. Now is the time for the American public to hear another perspective."

Let's have another penalty flag here, for unnecessary roughness of common sense. You cannot take over someone's intellectual property, another's franchise, and open up your alternate version. Politicians gas on about keeping inheritance laws and taxes from forcing heirs to sell family farms or businesses. Well, like it or not, *GWTW* is a family farm, and, if you don't extend and defend your copyright, you can lose it. That's the reason the Disney people slap lawsuits on two-bit day-care outfits that paint Mickey, Donald, and Goofy on their signs.

It's one thing for Carol Burnett to brilliantly satirize *GWTW* in the sketch in which Scarlett sashays down the stairs with the curtain rod across her shoulders from a dress made out of drapes. It would have been another thing if Carol had planned to have Rhett, Ashley, Melanie, and Mammy exchanging quips in a weekly comedy series, *Scarlett Fever*. That would have gone from protected parody to franchise infringement. In fact, *Scarlett Fever* was the name of a stage musical shut down in 1979 in Atlanta because of copyright infringement.

A lower federal court eventually sided with Alice Randall's legal argument. The *GWTW* publishers probably waited to see if the satire made any substantial money before deciding to appeal the case to a higher court. The book only had modest sales.

Generally, if you use a copyrighted character, you have to get permission from the writer or that writer's heirs. By now, Sherlock Holmes (who may be in the public domain) has probably appeared in more books, films, or TV shows than he appeared in original pages by Sir Arthur Conan Doyle. The Doyle estate kept the copyright alive for ages in part because Adrian Conan Doyle (1910-1970) wrote some stories in the 1950s. Each new Holmes film, story, or novel (whether authorized or not) helped the estate by increasing readership in the original stories. You will find Holmes appearing in *The Seven Percent Solution* by Nicholas Meyer, in at least two books entitled *The Private Life of Sherlock Holmes* (a collection of stories by Vincent Starrett and then a novelization of the Billy Wilder film. Each work said "based on the characters created by Sir Arthur Conan Doyle." In an introduction to Starrett's collection, Michael Murphy said "one is grateful to his amanuensis, the late Sir Arthur Conan Doyle, and the estate of Sir Arthur, with whose gracious permission this volume was made possible."

Of course, "gracious permission" is often code for "the writer graciously pays a percentage of any sales to the estate." For example, the late Vladimir Nabokov's publisher was dead set against Pia Pera publishing *Lo's Diary* (Lolita's perspective) until Pera and Foxrock Publishers forked over some of the profits to Nabokov's son.

In fact, let's see what happens if you write to Harper Lee and Ken Kesey's estate that you're working on *One Flew over the Mockingbird's Nest,* telling her novel from the perspective of Boo Radley. Tell John Berendt that you're working on *Morning, Noon, and Night in the Garden of Good and Evil.* You'd be hit with infringement suits so fast your head would spin like Linda Blair's in the *Exorcist.*

The perspective of the historical equivalents of African Americans can still be told. Although the name Tara is staked out so definitely, you can write about such historical sites as Monticello, Mount Vernon, Twelve Oaks, and hundreds of other sites. Or you can write about Mount Muggles, comparing the folks in the big house to the folks in the field. Besides African Americans, publishers also overlook the stories about the yeomen white farmers. The material is begging to be used.

Moreover, Scarlett wasn't the only spoiled and beautiful girl on a plantation or estate. If William Makepeace Thackeray were around and in a litigious mood, he might want to argue that Scarlett is a mite too similar to Becky Sharp of *Vanity Fair* for his liking.

If a writer wants to scribble a novel about a mythical breeding plantation, he runs the risk of infringing on Frank Yerby's heirs, if the characters are too much like those in *Mandingo.* Ashley Carter (penname for a kindly man, the late Harry Whittington) stepped in at one writer's death to continue penning "slave gothics" for the *Falconhurst* series. If you wanted to write regional soft pornography, you could create your own breeding plantation, filled with whips, sex, and cruelty. You just can't use Mandingo or Falconhurst.

Other writers' characters and situations can also be used because the copyrights have lapsed. In this case, we have Lenore Hart's *Becky: The Life and Loves of Becky Thatcher* (Tom Sawyer's girlfriend), Greg Matthews' *The Further Adventures of Huckleberry Finn* (after Twain's *HF*, of course), George McDonald Fraser's Flashman series (Thomas Hughes' *Tom Brown's School Days*), Tom Stoppard's *Rosencrantz and Guildenstern are Dead* and John Updike's *Gertrude and Claudius* (both playing off Shakespeare's *Hamlet*), Sena Jeter Naslund's *Ahab's Wife* (Melville's *Moby-Dick*), Jean Rhys' *Wide Sargasso Sea* (Charlotte Brontë's *Jane Eyre*), Peter Carey's *Jack Maggs* (Charles Dickens' *Great Expectations*), and others.

Parodies or pastiches don't have to infringe on a copyright, as we can see by Matt Helm, Derek Flint, James West, and Austin Powers following in the steps of James Bond. August Derleth's Solar Pons series quite seriously duplicated the spirit of Sherlock Holmes, but the names were changed to keep Derleth and publisher out of hot water. Now the Sherlock copyright has lapsed, and you can have at it.

A good example of a parody NOT infringing on a copyright is what *Galaxy Quest* did with *Star Trek*. While the fictional *Galaxy Quest* series had its equivalents of Kirk, Spock, and company, the film focused more on the present, as bickering actors picked up spending money at SF cons and yearned for something more or at least for their former glory when *Galaxy Quest* was on the air. The names and costumes of the fictional characters differed from those that Gene Roddenberry and Gene Coon developed at Desilu and Paramount for the Trekisodes, but they certainly were in the same spirit.

The film also parodied the fans and their infatuation with a series. Although these fans are often perceived as hopeless geeks and nerds who need to get a life, in *Galaxy Quest* they become a cavalry that rides to the rescue at the end.

Oops.

Time to get back to work on *The Case of the Jungle Man*. I'm writing about Perry Mason defending Tarzan on a charge of murdering Sheena of the Jungle (he says she was aping him), and James Bond is called in to take on Dr. Rhino, the evil genius behind the misdeeds.

It's going to be great, and mine, all mine.

THE DREADED CHICKEN PSYCHOSIS OF SCOTLAND

Exhilaration overwhelms me whenever I admire the essays and books by the great Shakespearean scholars. Each has chiseled a unique niche for himself in the marble halls of criticism: John Dryden, Samuel Johnson, Samuel Taylor Coleridge, William Hazlitt, William Peol, A.C. Bradley, Sir E.K. Chambers, and A.L. Rowse. Their names sparkle with brilliance as scholars or interpreters of the Bard.

However, despite their erudition, these scholars have failed to answer a startling puzzle in Shakespeare's shortest play: What went wrong in Macbeth's Scotland? I feel smug because I, the wild-eyed moderate, know the answer to the riddle. The evidence has long been there all the time. For the puzzle to be solved, the text only required a fresh perspective and a mosaic mind unhampered by stodginess.

With humility, I offer myself as being worthy of a niche alongside Chambers, Rowse, and Coleridge, thanks to Denson's Theory of the Dreaded Chicken Psychosis in *The Tragedy of Macbeth*. In these opening years of the 21st Century, we have been acutely aware of the danger of illnesses transmitted by birds. Avian flu or "bird fever" may yet transmute into a more communicable form and kill millions.

So it was, I argue, with the Dreaded Chicken Psychosis of several centuries ago, and Shakespeare's play provides evidence to prove this.

My thesis depends upon an intuitive leap, and, although I must wait patiently for historians to locate the documents that will entirely validate my conclusion, I trust its soundness enough to permit it to be appraised by fair and impartial critics.

Let us begin by emphasizing that historians know there was an Ur-*Hamlet.* A popular revenge play was probably performed by the Chamberlain's men for Henslowe at Newington Butts on June 9, 1594. Shakespeare apparently saw this effort (possibly by Thomas Kyd) and then transformed it into his own *Tragedy of Hamlet, Prince of Denmark.* Although the actual script of the Ur-*Hamlet* has not survived, we have enough references to it in others' writings to realize that Shakespeare reworked a potboiler about murders and revenge.

Since the Ur-*Hamlet* did exist, my intuition suggests that some lesser playwright must have adapted an Ur-*Macbeth* from Raphael Holinshed's *Chronicles of England, Scotland, and Ireland* and that Shakespeare, seeing another popular subject being butchered by the efforts of a second- or third-rate playwright, dashed off his own melodrama about the villainous Scot who had killed his own king. Unfortunately, we also do not have a copy of the Ur-*Macbeth.* That manuscript may have perished in the fire that destroyed the Globe on June 29, 1613, or, if it survived that, it may have been lost in the Great Fire of London in September 1666. Lest critics dismiss my thesis because of the absence of an Ur-*Macbeth* manuscript, we should also remember that we lack actual copies of the Ur-*Hamlet* or any of Shakespeare's plays in his own handwriting. Unquestionably, the absence of the Ur-*Macbeth* manuscript should not impede the acceptance of Denson's Theory of the Dreaded Chicken Psychosis.

A close reading of Shakespeare's play will permit us to deduce what had to be in the Ur-*Macbeth.* Once we examine a list of the characters' actions, we will realize that the actual villain in Scotland was a psychosis, not just the damage caused by an ambitious couple. To be specific, all but one of the thanes of Scotland suffered from a mental delusion, the Dreaded Chicken Psychosis: This is to say that they thought that they and their families were chickens.

Macbeth was the notable exception to this pattern of mental illness. However, in having to live in the unstable environment, Macbeth suffered from *folie à deux* or "shared madness." This Shared Psychotic Disorder may be called *folie à trois*, *folie à quatre*, *folie en famille* or even *folie à plusieurs* ("madness of many"). Since Macbeth was forced to interact with the psychotic Banquo and Macduff, he unconsciously focused on the psychosis and often reacted to what the psychotics thought that they were seeing.

Examples to prove this point abound in Shakespeare's play, and we can only assume that the Ur-*Macbeth* would have been more explicit about DSM-IV, as it is listed in the *Diagnostic and Statistical Manual of Mental Disorders*. As it is, many casual readers of the existing text of Shakespeare will claim that the brain of Macbeth was scrambled by wicked ambition.

To keep his sanity, the hen-pecked Macbeth struck out against the world. Imagine Macbeth's horror when he found himself infected with this psychosis, as when he addressed his wife before they murdered King Duncan: "Be innocent of the knowledge, dearest chuck, till thou applaud the deed." *Chuck* was slang, not for "woodchuck," but for "chick" or "chicken."

Macbeth did not have to scratch very far to discover that the infection originated with Macduff, the thane of Fife.

Even the doomed Banquo, having also come into contact with Macduff, had trouble keeping his sanity, especially as he was being carved up by the three murderers sent by Macbeth. As he died, he crowed to his son: "Fly, good Fleance, fly, fly, fly!" Clearly, if Banquo had not been suffering from the dreaded chicken psychosis, he would have shouted, "Run, good Fleance, run, run, run!"

We deduce that the Ur-*Macbeth* would reveal more of Macduff's Humpty-Dumpty fall and of his infection of everyone. But what was the cause of his illness? To understand the origin of the ailment, we need only consult the witches' remarks to Macbeth to "beware Macduff" and anyone "not of woman born." Macduff's unusual birth made him susceptible to the dreaded chicken psychosis brought to Scotland, as we will see, by the Danes.

As every student should know, Macduff was "untimely ripped from [his] mother's womb." Hence, that caesarean birth meant that the thane of Fife did not go through the normal birth process. Psychologically, that C-section turned Macduff into a basket case. Macduff was the odd man out because he was not born as most humans and mammals were. He was sort of hatched, as it were, like a chicken.

Lady Macduff humored him by calling their son "poor bird," and, sad to say, when Macbeth got in a foul mood and decided to sack Macduff's castle, he sent henchmen to wring the necks of everyone there. As the murderers killed little Macduff, they showed scant sensitivity to the household psychosis by taunting the child: "What, you egg! Young fry of treachery!"

Reports eventually reached Macduff, who was perched in England with Malcolm. Ross told him, "Your castle is surprised; your wife and babes savagely slaughtered…."

Macduff asked, "All my pretty ones… What, all my pretty chickens and their dam at one fell swoop?"

The news really ruffled Macduff's feathers, although Malcolm was more hard-boiled about it and tried to egg on his desire for revenge. Malcolm says, "Dispute it like a man," which we understand also meant, "Quit acting like a chicken."

Few dramatic productions, whether by the Royal Shakespeare Company or the Alabama Shakespeare Festival in my home state, have properly staged the death of Macbeth.

Instead of hopeless defiance, the actor portraying Macbeth should say his lines with heavy sarcasm, since Macbeth is facing a battle with a man who thinks he is a chicken. After Macbeth draws his sword and raises his shield, he taunts Macduff with "*Lay* on, Macduff! And damned be him that first cries, 'Hold, enough!'"

Shortly thereafter, Macduff finds himself the victor of the cock fight and, reminded of his psychosis, turns demure and henlike. An Ur-*Macbeth* would have positively shown him strutting and fretting around the body of Macbeth, *puck-puck-puck*ing, and trying to lay the egg that Macbeth had challenged him to produce.

No doubt, such an image had already been considered by Shakespeare in *Hamlet.* The Bard had seen the line in François de Belleforest's *Histoires Tragiques*, in a section that inspired the scene in which Polonious was killed: "Hamlet came into [his mother's] chamber, pretending in his madness to be a cock, and beating his arms (which struck the curtain); then he fell upon the eavesdropper. He slew him with his sword, cut the body into pieces, boiled them, and fed them to the hogs." Clearly, we see that the historical Hamlet fixated on being a chicken. Very probably, the Danes brought the psychosis to the British Isles when they conquered and settled the area known as the "Danelaw," which ranged from Essex up to Yorkshire, near (where else?) Scotland.

In Macduff's delirium, he has his soldiers offstage whack off the head of Macbeth and deposit it at the feet of a grateful, but perceptive Malcolm, the new king of Scotland. Malcolm recognizes that the head is merely a surrogate egg, and, although he probably feels despondent over the psychosis in his kingdom, he appreciates the accuracy of two maxims: Chickens do come home to roost, and you shouldn't count your chickens before they hatch.

The above thesis, although inspired by my intuition, has

also benefited from my self-awareness that too often intuitive minds have made grand leaps into the abyss of error. I trust that a sensible precaution and a dedication to Shakespeare's text have enabled me to avoid such an academic pratfall.

THE X. PERT INTERVIEWS

Professor Francis Xavier Pert is a pompous windbag who fancies himself as an expert on Everything That Matters. Agnes Bromide, now thankfully in recovery, has shared several of her interviews with Professor X. Pert.

PROFESSOR FRANCIS X. PERT ON PROPER ENGLISH

Q. What is the best way to improve English language usage?

A. As sure as my name is Professor Francis Xavier Pert, I know that the bestest way is to get rid of the rules. Let people talk and write any way they wants to, Ms. Bromide, irregardless of so-called proper English.

Q. My word, may I ask what institution has named you a professor, just out of curiosity?

A. Ah, yes, the University of Hard Knocks, if it's irrelevant to the matter at hand.

Q. I assume at the University of Hard Knocks that it's all right to say "irregardless"?

A. Oh, it are, it are!

Q. Then I also assume that rules about subject-verb agreement are passé.

A. You imply what I infer exactly.

Q. I did well?

A. You done good, like you should.

Q. What do you say to people who complain about *good* being used as an adverb?

A. I say it don't make no never mind, no how and no way.

Q. That does seem to accentuate the negative.

A. Between you and I, I'm enthused about the negatives.

Q. I don't mean to be rude, Professor Pert, but—

A. X. Pert. Let's not disremember the initial.

Q. Very well, Professor *X.* Pert, I've noticed several letters and articles from English teachers opposing your position that anything goes.

A. They has taken that position because they refuses to read my book, *Fiting the Gramer and Hanbook Cabal.* I love its wonderful cover, by the way.

Q. These critics have self interests, you're saying?

A. Imprecisely so. All the high school teachers, college teachers, editors, handbook writers, handbook publishers, all of them has a interest in getting us to buy they books and hire them.

Q. I see. I couldn't help noticing—

A. You "couldn't hardly help but noticing."

Q. Whatever, Professor X. Pert. At any rate, as I look at your "wonderful cover," I see you do have misspellings in *grammar* and *handbook* in the title of your book. And in *fighting.*

A. I disagree.

Q. Somehow I thought you would.

A. Despite the spelling, you got the idear that I meant *grammar* and *handbook*, so, if you figgered out what I was saying, then it's spelled all right. Here's my motto on my business card: "Only litle mimes spel wurds one weigh."

Q. "Mimes"? Like in Marcel Marceau. Don't you mean *minds*, Professor X. Pert?

A. You ain't nothing but a trouble-maker, are you, Miss Bromide?

Q. Oh, don't throw yourself into a chair and sulk so, Professor X. Pert. If there's nothing for me to do, I might be tempted to read the papers on your desk.

A. Whom cares if you does?

Q. Okay, Professor X. Pert, I apologize if I've hurt your feelings, and I'll quit skimming your papers.

A. I are much too big for hurt feelings, but your apologies is excepted.

Q. I also apologize for glancing through your correspondence lying on the desk.

A. Laying on the desk.

Q. If you say so. I noticed you use perfect grammar and spelling in this letter about a speaking engagement, and in the letter to your publisher about a $5,000 advance on your next book, your writing is flawless.

A. Of course, Ms. Bromide. You don't think I'm going to confuse them with bad grammar and mixed constructions, and actually give them an excuse for *not* paying me my money. Good Lord, woman!

Q. Thank you, Professor X. Pert. Everything is quite clear now.

X. PERT DECONSTRUCTS WORDS AND MEANINGS

Q. Goodness gracious, Mr. Pert, you look a mess today, lying there in your hospital bed, part of you in a body cast, your legs and arms raised, your eyes blackened, your nose—

A. That's enough, Miss Bromide. Sticks and stones are bad enough, but even your words are hurting my bones.

Q. Sorry, Mr. Pert.

A. Excuse me, Miss Bromide, but my name is Professor Francis Xavier Pert, or Professor X. Pert, if you must shorten it.

Q. Yes, Professor, and mine is *Ms.* Bromide, not *Miss*?

A. All right, if you're that picky about what people call you. It's a sign of insecurity, you know.

Q. Professor, how in the world did you wind up in such a fix?

A. It was my research into the English language. I was busy breaking new ground.

Q. Do you have an example, Professor X. Pert?

A. Indeed! I heard this big, hulking worker plop his large derriere onto a stool next to me in a drugstore. He ordered one of their "great" banana splits. "Ah ha," I said to myself, for I like talking to someone of great intelligence and discernment; consequently, I converse with myself frequently.

Q. Yes, I understand, but what about the banana split?

A. It's the word *great.* Can a banana split actually be great? It may be delicious or delectable, but hardly great. You don't have banana splits carved into any Mount Rushmores, do you?

Q. I'll concede that point, Professor.

A. To confirm my hypothesis, I sneaked a spoonful of the ice cream when I thought this big gorilla went to the restroom. *Tsk-tsk*, it was merely tasty.

Q. You *thought* he went to the men's room?

A. Alas, he caught me in the act of sampling his dessert. That accounts for the black eye.

Q. You poor man.

A. That's another word, you see? Truly, I'm not *poor*, else I wouldn't be able to afford all the specialists from the Humpty-Dumpty Medical Center, as they try to put me back together again.

Q. That accounts for the eye, but what about the other injuries?

A. When I was going through the park, I noticed the signs saying, "Wet Paint." It's my theory, Ms. Bromide, that each city has entire departments of workers who do absolutely nothing except go around to city benches and put out signs saying "Wet Paint." I discovered that, out of twenty-five benches, only one of them was wet, so that means that ninety-six percent of the time we don't mean *wet* when we put out a "Wet Paint" sign.

Q. So, if someone wanted to mention fast-drying paint on hot summer days and concluded you were "all wet" in this area—

A. That misguided person would be wrong ninety-six percent of the time.

Q. I assume you informed the city workers about their laxity regarding their signs.

A. Indeed, Ms. Bromide! I gave them a proper tongue-lashing. It was so proper that some city worker named Bubba gave me this broken nose in exchange.

Q. How about the missing tooth?

A. That occurred when I then called him a "Neanderthal." He kept saying, "No, I'm not! I root for them 'Jag-Wires!,'" thinking, no doubt, I was accusing him of being an enthusiast of some obscure team in the National Hockey-Stick Football Conference.

Q. That deluded man.

A. Exactly. Anyway, my further research revealed that, since words don't mean what they are supposed to mean, healthy people park in handicapped spots, usually without penalty. In addition, I discovered that it's all right to fold, staple, or mutilate most things that tell you *not* to fold, staple, or mutilate them.

Q. But—

A. But me no buts, Ms. Bromide. Moreover, I, Professor Francis Xavier Pert, discovered that entire schools of literary criticism say that you can take a book, such as—

Q. *Moby-Dick*?

A. Splendid, that'll do! It's the story of a boy and his whale, plus a captain with an attitude. You can throw out Melville's words, put in other words about the boy, the whale, and the captain, and you'd still have *Moby-Dick*. You can make anyone of them the albino! "Captain Ahab the Albino"—how's that?

Q. Frightening.

A. It's a liberating epiphany…but that insight also got me here.

Q. How so?

A. My research into street signs revealed that many dangerous curves weren't hazardous at all. When a sign said "maximum speed thirty-five mph," you could take the curves at forty-five or fifty-five miles per hour. When it said "yield," you rarely had to. And when the lights are blinking and the railroad crossing is down—

Q. Oh, no, you didn't.

A. Unfortunately, Ms. Bromide, I did, though I made it through twenty-four out of twenty-five crossings.

Q. That's ninety-six percent.

A. I know, but I hadn't factored in the disastrous consequences inherent in the four-percent exception to the rule.

Q. You could have been killed.

A. And would have, too, Ms. Bromide, if I hadn't had serious doubts about the meaning of the words, *Always fasten your seatbelt.* I didn't, and the train knocked me clear into the lobby of the Humpty-Dumpty Medical Center here. All in all, though, my research proves that words mean little and are steadily losing whatever power the oral and written traditions conferred on them.

Q. No power? Hmm, I wonder. Professor X. Pert, in that body cast, have you been detecting any areas that needed scratched?

A. No, not really. I am immobile, but quite comfortable otherwise.

Q. Oh, how about around your left shoulder blade? Is there a little spot that is beginning to tingle now? And now a bit more, and begs you to reach in there with—

A. Stop it, Ms. Bromide, this isn't funny!

Q. To reach in with anything, perhaps a clothes hanger, a long stick, anything, to scratch that spot that's really, really itching you now, that's TINGLING all over, even down the backbone, and now in the front, and

all over. My God, your whole body's itching, and it's almost KILLING you, it's so bad.

A. Hey, come back here! Come on, it's driving me crazy, Ms. Bromide! You've got to help me, or call a nurse at least, you sadistic creature!

X. Pert Finds His Roots

Q. I'm talking to Professor Francis Xavier Pert, who I suspect represents the academic WASPs.

A. Please, Miss Bromide.

Q. *Ms.*, if you don't mind, Mr. Pert.

A. That's *Professor* X. Pert, just to be accurate.

Q. Whatever. Look, yes or no: *Are* you representing academic WASPs?

A. Not really, Ms. Bromide. Besides, I object to the label, WASP.

Q. "White Anglo Saxon Protestant"? What's wrong with it?

A. Well, it's redundant: If one is "Anglo" and "Saxon," it's sort of difficult to be anything other than "white."

Q. Or red-nosed and liver-spotted?

A. Yes, quite clever, Ms. Bromide. After all these years of your interviews, I'm surprised to finally hear you say something intelligent *and* witty.

Q. Maybe we'll both be lucky today, Professor X. Pert. I suppose it's too much to ask you to learn something relevant instead of being so WASPish.

A. What's more relevant?

Q. Computers, data processing, IBMs, clones, Macintoshes.

A. Macintosh is a good Celtic name.

Q. I don't know basketball, Professor. To move things along, what would you prefer to be called?

A. Simple: My roots are of a "Celtic Appalachian American" background, or a "C.A.A.," for short, and it has nothing to do with bouncyball.

Q. Isn't that term the same thing—no offense intended, Professor X. Pert—as a "hillbilly"?

A. No offense taken, my dear lady, though I do prefer the more formal "mountain-william."

Q. When did you decide you were, ah, a Celtic Appalachian American?

A. Or, "when did I find my roots?" Is that what you're trying to ask, Ms. Bromide? Let me write it on the board here: "You're asking with baited breath about my roots?" as my father used to say.

Q. That's b-a-t-e-d, Professor X. Pert.

A. Normally, it would be *bated*, but my pater used to fall into the lake while inebriated.

Q. Why was the lake inebriated?

A. Quite droll, Ms. Bromide. It was my *father* who was tanked to the gills, and he often fancied he was a catfish and nibbled the bait off his neighbors' hooks. Hence—

Q. *Baited* breath, yes, I see.

A. Quite correct, Ms. Bromide.

Q. What specifically caused you to become aware of your roots?

A. Hollywood, of course. I went to a Celtic Film Festival and saw *The Prince of Donegal*, *Kidnapped*, *Rob Roy*, and *Braveheart*, plus a History Channel re-enactment of the Battle of Culloden. Then I went to our local Highland Games. All of those bagpipes, tossing the tapirs, wearing the kelp—they transformed me.

Q. You mean "tossing a caber," don't you? A tapir is a South American animal that looks a bit like a pig.

A. And hits the ground a bit like one, too! No, none of us could lift the taber.

Q. *Caber*, Professor. A tabor is a small drum.

A. Ah, I misspoke myself. Usually I would say *caber*, Ms. Bromide, but McDoodle works at the zoo near the tapirs, and—

Q. And weren't you misspeaking when referring to wearing kelp instead of a *kilt*?

A. A good kilt costs $400, Ms. Bromide. I'm afraid we made do with kelp, since—

Q. Professor X. Pert, let me interrupt. You aren't setting me up with some long, tedious, and politically incorrect story about you and a bunch of guys in kiltish kelp or whatever going into a gay bar?

A. Your cynicism does you no credit, Ms. Bromide. Besides, that was last year.

Q. And this year?

A. I was transformed, you see. Then I saw the grocery store and went charging into the Piggly Wiggly in my kilt-substitute and swinging my claymore and Dirk. A claymore is a sword.

Q. I know, and a dirk is a knife.

A. Actually, he's someone I met last year.

Q. Could you move it along, Professor X. Pert?

A. Ah yes, so I was swinging my claymore and wiped out every can of English Peas in the Piggly Wiggly.

Q. Gracious!

A. I was fighting down the aisles to the English muffins, when the assistant manager stopped me in my tracks.

Q. With a gun?

A. Hardly, Ms. Bromide: with Scott tissues. They restrained me with a case of Scotch Tape.

Q. Could we get back to your designated ethnic group, "Celtic Appalachian American"? That's eleven syllables, a

real mouthful, and certainly not likely to unseat "WASP," with its one syllable.

A. I don't care. "WASP" is still redundant.

Q. How about "ASP"? Would that make you feel better in some serpentine way?

A. Well, Ms. Bromide, I'll admit that it's not wordy, but what about Anglo-Saxon Jews or Druids? They exist, you know.

Q. And Catholics?

A. Certainly, we Celtic-Appalachian-Americans have some Catholic old-timers who want Latin in the liturgy, not to mention the Second Vatican Ecumenical Council Catholics who prefer Bubbonics.

Q. And what is that?

A. English as spoken by Bubbas, whether Baptist, Catholic, Jewish.

Q. Do you have an example?

A. Of course, here's an old one: *Jeet yet*, meaning "Did you eat yet?" It's listed in all the reputable tomes at Stuckeys about *How to Speak Redneck* or *Talkin' Southern the Rat Way.*

Q. *Rat*?

A. Right. *Oy vay, jeet yet?*—that's for those liking collards and gefilte fish.

Q. Look, Professor, aren't you stealing lines from Jeff Foxworthy about *jeet yet* and so on?

A. No, I'm not.

Q. Yes, you are. I've seen his special on the comedy channel about fourteen times. Those lines are from Foxworthy.

A. Well, he stole it first.

Q. Oh, really? From whom?

A. Those books from Stuckey's: *How to Talk Southern* and things like that, you know.

Q. Okay, I do remember seeing those.

A. Can you believe it? He got rich from a ninety-eight-cent pamphlet from Stuckey's.

Q. If so, you should try the same thing, Professor.

A. Exactly, Ms. Bromide. I've just gotten the galley proofs for *You Can Tell If You're a Celtic-Appalachian- American by the Number of Pralines Wrappers in Your Pickup*. You might want to proofread it.

Q. I, ah, just noticed that I have another interview in fifteen minutes, Professor.

A. It has a chapter on "The C-A-A and Beef Jerky," not to mention a chapter on—

Q. I'll wait for the movie, Professor. Ta ta.

X. PERT TACKLES ILLITERACY

Q. Professor *X.* Pert...notice I got it right this time.

A. Very good, *Ms.* Bromley, and notice that I returned the courtesy.

Q. Actually, it's *Bromide*, but never mind. My sources tell me that you have been doing research into illiteracy and cultural literacy.

A. Indeed, I have a three-hour presentation: fifteen action- and fact-packed minutes per grade. Now, in the first grade—

Q. Professor X. Pert, could we focus on just a sampling of the grades? How about the last four?

A. Oh…today's my birthday, and I thought you could indulge me. This could sort of be my present, you understand.

Q. Yes, but it's also my editor's birthday, and she wants me back in the office in an hour or so. So what's noteworthy about the ninth grade?

A. Very well. To begin with, I found three groups. Check out the video. We haven't added the sound yet, but I'll narrate the action for you. See, in Group 1, the subject is shown a book. He examines it with curiosity, smells it, *tastes* it. Now notice what happens when the pages are flipped.

Q. Goodness, he's screeching and grabbing for the light fixtures.

A. Typical reaction, Ms. Bromide. Now here's a typical member of Group 2. He sees the book in the lab assistant's hands. Then he recoils and screams.

Q. What's he screaming?

A. "Get that thang away from me. Get it away! You know I hate them thangs!" It's clear that some sadist in the past has tried to make him read one.

Q. On the screen, I'm guessing we're coming to someone from Group 3. I see that he takes the book, turns to the title page, and flips through, reading pages at random.

A. Yes, I'd encourage those in Group 3 to get a good education and attend a Real College.

Q. What would you do with the other two?

A. Oh, the Taster-Smellers and Recoiling Screamers would go to some institution that's looking for warm bodies.

Q. Let's move onto the tenth grade. Is there any change here?

A. Absolutely. Some of the Taster-Smellers can be trained to see that books don't have to be opened at all, and those nasty pages don't have to go flap-a-flappa. Electronic books may be helpful. We do have luck with some of the Recoilers in enticing some of them at least to touch a book. We hope to teach them that books are not slimy or slippery, contrary to many people's ideas.

Q. So they will learn there is a place in the world for books?

A. Indeed, now the members of Group 3 may have transferred to real schools here and there. They may also learn how to use computers and word processing programs, not to mention understand how to print out their work. Many of them will use the small type.

Q. Oh?

A. They'd be called elitists.

Q. I suppose. Moving on, what happens in their junior year?

A. Regression has occurred in the learning experience of the typical Smeller-Taster.

Q. That's awful.

A. Not necessarily. In learning math or playing the piano, the student will sometimes feel as if he or she is back-sliding and forgetting everything…and then there's a jump forward.

Q. What causes the regression for the Sniffer-Tasters?

A. Most often, they drop a book on their foot, perhaps on bare toes if they are wearing sandals. They may return to their status in the tenth grade, but, if you use large type books so they can see them from a distance, you may be able to regain some confidence and let them know there's something on each page.

Q. I assume that pictures help.

A. Indeed, Ms. Bromide, but I counsel teachers to keep a straight face if the student asks, "You mean you're going to try to tell me those marks mean something?"

Q. Are there any changes in the Recoilers at this level?

A. Some of them will have become aware of idioms in English involving the word *book*: "I make book on the horse race," "Book him, Dano," "Throw the book at him," "The embezzler cooked the books." They try out each idiom literally, generally to the detriment of the book itself, which ends up being sticky or charred.

Q. Regarding "throw the book," would that—?

A. The record distance at our school is three hundred feet, but technically he missed his target, Maynard Tagwell III. We had several juniors who could pop Maynard in the ear at a hundred and twenty feet, though. Maynard's parents have since transferred him to another school.

Q. I would hope so. Now, let's go to the twelfth grade, the year of graduation.

A. Ah yes, since graduates will have to face new challenges, the Taster-Smellers have been encouraged to open books and to turn the pages. They may have been able to recognize some of the words, even some of foreign origin.

Q. What's an example?

A. An Old Frisian word: *the.*

Q. As in "give me *the* ball"?

A. Absolutely, although our students are apt to say "put *the* money in *the* bag and don't hit *the* alarm button."

Q. My word. At any rate, I infer that they are not actually reading entire books.

A. True, Ms. Bromide, but let's put that in its proper perspective. Proportionally how many books are read, or left unread, by those who *can* read? When a reader encounters Kant or Joyce, is that person's comprehension necessarily superior to the person who has difficulty with another book?

Q. For the sake of time, I won't argue the point, Professor X. Pert, but tell me more about the Recoilers from Group 2.

A. The Recoilers should be able to master several competencies.

Q. *Competencies*?

A. Yes, that's a scientific word meaning "things."

Q. Often pronounced "thangs," right?

A. True. Now, to graduate, the Recoilers will have to learn how to carry the book, how to open it, and how to recognize the book again.

Q. By reading the title?

A. Not necessarily. They just memorize the design and color on the cover.

Q. One possible problem, Professor. Your study seems to focus only on books and not on the electronic forms, e-readers and all that. Are you updating the data to factor in those?

A. We were signing up student volunteers downtown in the registration building, but, alas, alas.

Q. Why so glum, Professor chum?

A. They wind up in accidents because they were texting and reading while driving.

Q. One final question, Professor X. Pert: Have you read any good books lately?

A. No, but *The Joy of Collards and Hog Jowls* is my favorite. It *smells* and *tastes* grand, Ms. Bromide.

X. Pert and Student-Hegemony Applied Management (SHAM)

Q. My editor said you have an innovation that will revolutionize education, Professor X. Pert.

A. Exactly, Ms. Bromide. It came to me that our colleges are far too timid to adopt the Total Quality Management—that's TQM. It uses the principles that Lemming brought to Japan.

Q. I believe that's *Deming*, Professor.

A. In Japan, this American innovator had the goof-offs jumping into the Pacific, and—

Q. No, sir. It's still *Deming*. It has nothing to do with lemmings or anyone committing suicide by jumping off a cliff into a lake or river. Besides, lemmings are only trying to swim across bodies of water.

A. I'll have you know that I saw it in a cartoon.

Q. And you also saw the coyote running in air in a cartoon, right?

A. I knew that. Anyway, as Leming said—

Q. Excuse me, it's still Deming when talking about management.

A. Are you sure?

Q. Absolutely, Professor.

A. Hmm, then I suppose it'd be a wise move if I revise the paper I'm presenting tomorrow.

Q. If you are only speaking to professors like yourself, maybe they won't notice.

A. Good point, Ms. Bromide. Anyway, I will urge that colleges move beyond TQM.

Q. How so?

A. My TQM argues that students who learn well generally know *why* they learn well and know the classroom procedures that work best for them.

Q. Could that be reworded to say that "Students know more about learning than teachers"? Or "students know about how and what should be taught"?

A. You're being negative again, Ms. Bromide, disagreeing with high-paid educational consultants.

Q. Oh, you're high-paid?

A. No, but that's my goal as I present my new innovation, Student-Hegemony Applied Management.

Q. Hmm, the acronym would be *SHAM.* Are you sure you want that?

A. Well, I was considering calling it Student-Hegemony Applied Management Excellence, but in two syllables that would be pronounced *SHA-may*, whatever that means in Latin or French.

Q. Or something in one syllable in English.

A. What's that again?

Q. Nothing, Professor, but tell me: What are the, ah, shameful principles of SHAM?

A. "If one student in a class has failed, the faculty member has failed as a teacher."

Q. So, if a doctor loses one patient, she has failed as a doctor? If one house burns down, the fire fighter has failed?

A. Exactly. Principle No. 2 is "Since students know what works best for them and what should be taught, they also know the grades they should receive."

Q. Just as a batter in baseball knows best whether or not a pitch was a ball or strike?

A. Ms. Bromide, I like the way your mind works. Figuring grades is always such a bother, so it also makes sense to have each student encode his or her own grade.

Q. What principles does SHAM have for attendance and calling roll?

A. Good point, Ms. Bromide. Required attendance is inappropriate in global villages and electronic "classrooms," which may even be in terminals in students' own homes.

Q. What if a student doesn't log on?

A. An effective teacher will inspire his or her students to log on regularly or to attend classes. SHAM believes that, if the students aren't attending classes, then the classes simply aren't interesting, compelling, or significant.

Q. But wouldn't that simply produce students who didn't *know* anything?

A. Ms. Bromide, I'm surprised at you. So-called facts are always changing in a high-tech world. What's the point of knowing something that's going to change tomorrow?

Q. So what would a course do?

A. It would emphasize *process*.

Q. Then you are saying that *process* would enable them to do well on tests?

A. Ah, tests, tests, tests—such archaic instruments. A test only measures what a student does not know.

Q. But if you aren't teaching *anything*, then—

A. Ms. Bromide, the student may not do well on a test, but may be an excellent product of SHAM-style education.

Q. Very well. What about assignments?

A. SHAM argues that assignments should only focus on what is significant.

Q. That is reasonable, Professor X. Pert.

A. And since what most students do on assignments won't matter in ten, twenty or a hundred years, the assignments themselves are *not* meaningful.

Q. Assuming that SHAM doesn't quite catch on, Professor X. Pert, do you have any other goals?

A. Certainly, Ms. Bromide. I mainly want to escape a full class load, since that seems to be what educational consultants, high or low paid, enjoy the most.

Pert Makes Sense of the Calendar

Q. Okay, Professor Francis Xavier Pert, my editor said you called about some major breakthrough in communication, something about the calendar.

A. Yes, Ms. Bromide, I've simplified the English language. It's a major triumph, one that will rank with—

Q. The invention of the whoopee cushion?

A. Please, Ms. Bromide. Vulgarity isn't necessary.

Q. I apologize, but I've driven fifteen miles in bumper-to-bumper traffic in a driving rain, just to get here on a Monday night.

A. Stop right there: *Monday night*—see the problem? *Day* and *night* in the two words? If it's night, it's obviously not day, so step one of my simplification is to shorten our time references.

Q. How so?

A. We will have *Sunnight*, *Monnight*, *Tuesnight*, *Wednesnight*, *Thursnight*, *Frinight*, and *Saturnight*, and I'm working on simplifying the spelling to just *Sunight* or *Monight*, and *Wenight.*

Q. And I guess you'd have *Monnoon* and *Thursnoon* for things that happen at high noon?

A. Brilliant, Ms. Bromide! My thoughts exactly! You're beginning to think like me, old girl!

Q. Dear God in heaven.

A. I thank Him, too, my dear, for helping me come up with *Friaft*!

Q. Not for "the back of a frying pan," I bet, but for "Friday afternoon?"

A. Exactly, and *Monmid* for "Monday midnight."

Q. Why couldn't it stand for "Monday midday?"

A. What? Yes, I see: a bit ambiguous there. That'll give me something to work out tonight. Maybe I can get a grant to study the puzzle for an entire year.

Q. At least you won't have any time on your hands.

A. No, indeed, because I've also addressed the problem of a month, a year, and the names of the months.

Q. I don't see any problem with a month, Professor.

A. Ah, I misspoke. *Month* is pretty acceptable. It derives its name from the time it takes the moon to circle the earth. *Moon* and *month*, you see?

Q. Okay, and twelve of them to make up a year.

A. But *year* is troublesome. That's the time it takes the sun to circle the earth, so logically the annual name should be *sunth*. *Month* and *Sunth*, got it?

Q. There is a small problem as I might expect, Professor. The sun doesn't circle the earth. It stands still, basically, and the earth circles it.

A. You're joshing me, of course.

Q. No, sir. You can read about it on the internet.

A. One of those unreliable sites, no doubt. At any rate, we still have the problem of the names of the months, which can be divided into these categories: the *ary*-ones—

Q. *January*, *February*, and what else?

A. None else, old girl. Consistency says we should have *January*, *February*, *Marchuary*, *Apruary*, *Mayuary*, and so on.

Q. Which would sound silly.

A. True. Next, we have the *ber*-months.

Q. *September*, *October*, *November*, *December*.

A. Very good. Now these are "counting months" for seven, eight, nine, and ten.

Q. Except—

A. Right, they're the ninth, tenth, eleventh, and twelfth months, thanks to the system being thrown off by the "people's names" months.

Q. I beg your pardon?

A. *July* for "Julius Caesar" and *August* for "Augustus Caesar."

Q. I see, I suppose.

A. Now how about some consistency here? *January* is named after a mythological figure, Janus, the god who looked both ways.

September and so on are counting months. *July* and *August* are political figure months, and then we have the one-syllable months.

Q. *March, May, June.*

A. Absolutely no pattern, you see. Then it dawned on me that they could all be one-syllabled: *Jan, Feb, March, Apr, May, June, Lie*—

Q. Not *Jool*?

A. Please, Ms. Bromide. Does *Jool* sound like a month? My goodness.

Q. I apologize.

A. Very well. Then we have *Aug, Sept, Oct, Nov,* and *Hol.*

Q. *Hol* and not *Dec*?

A. No, Ms. Bromide, *Hol* for the *Holiday* month.

Q. So that's what you're recommending, all of those one-syllable months? You got me to drive through traffic on a Monight just for this nonsense?

A. No, Ms. Bromide, I slept on it and decided the one-syllable names wouldn't work. I then tried the *ber*-system: *Janober, Febober, Marchober,* and—

Q. I get the picture, so you're going with that, or have you decided to go strictly with great men and women: *July, August, Einstein, Babe Ruth*—

A. Enough, Ms. Bromide. Besides, I had *Michael Jordan* instead of the *Babe*. No, I want your esteemed publication to announce to the world that I've simply renamed the months: *Month 1*, *2*, *3*, *4*, and so on, the way the Japanese do it.

Q. That's it?

A. Of course, Ms. Bromide. My brilliance let me understand that we don't name each story of a building.

We give numbers to each floor, except *13*. In football, we don't say, "The Rug Rats have the ball on their opponents' February." We simply say the ball's on the Rug Rat 20 or the Wildcats' 34.

Q. As I check through my notes here, I see one question hasn't been asked. Why not simply spell *night* as *n-i-t-e*?

A. *Nite*, as in all the ads and notes from silly girls who dot the *nite* with a heart or circle?

Q. Oh, come on, I was only fifteen when—

A. When what, Ms. Bromide?

Q. Nothing, nothing. Okay, I guess I better go now.

A. So when will the story appear, Ms. Bromide?

Q. Probably during a very cold day in Month 8 when the Mississippi River freezes over.

A. Thank you, old girl. Delighted!

PROFESSOR X. PERT GOES ONLINE

Q. Professor, what are you doing in the news room?

A. Looking for you, Miss Bromide. Our dean at Sitting Bull College has delivered one of those computer contraptions in my office, so I have to learn lines.

Q. "Learning lines"—like for a play?

A. I don't think so. Oh, silly me. He probably was ordering me to learn line dancing.

Q. As with country and western music?

A. I think so. How about it...Big Momma? That's the way they talk, I believe.

Q. Professor, if you call me "Big Momma" again, you'll be talking through jaws that are wired shut.

A. Well, about "Little Lady"? You could call me "Francis" or "Xavier."

Q. I can call you something in a harassment affidavit, Professor, if that's what you want.

A. Very well. I'll get back to that computer.

Q. Just a moment, Professor. Don't you think the dean really just wanted you to learn how to go online, onto the internet—using email, exploring websites, and perhaps learning how to use the internet in your classes?

A. Good Lord, probably so. But I've already been doing that, just to keep my mind off wearing cowboy boots in the online dancing. I've had quite a few insights, you know.

Q. Such as?

A. Well, I've written a trifling monograph on *The Grammar of the Internet.*

Q. And what are your conclusions?

A. The parenthesis is their indispensable key. For making winks, smiles, frowns, and guffaws, as in *;) :) :(:P*

Q. Yes, everyone knows that.

A. They *do*? Well, how about the fact that they use the abbreviations for "bug-eyed monster" and "bacon lettuce and tomato" all the time.

Q. No, they don't. You're thinking of *BTW*, not *BEM* or *BLT*. *BTW* is short for "by the way."

A. I sort of missed that one.

Q. Of course, you could write, "BTW, look out for the BEM who is terrorizing the city until it gets a decent BLT."

A. Which will never happen, of course.

Q. Anything else in your grammar?

A. Ah yes, the apostrophe is used in any word that has an *S* in it, or it's not used when you expect it to be there. Look at this: "Its time for fan's of Garth Brook's to as's'emble and sing his' great praise's. Dont miss' the rally's."

Q. Aren't you exaggerating here, Professor X. Pert?

A. Maybe, but I've been busy researching textiles and engines.

Q. As in what?

A. The dean wanted me to report on serge engines, but serge may make a decent suit, but hardly—

Q. Excuse my interruption, Professor, but couldn't the dean have meant "search engines"?

A. "Search"? Oh, well, silly me. One thing: What's a search engine? Don't you just lift the hood, and there it is?

Q. No, it's a computer program to help you find things. It comes from companies like Yahoo—

A. Ha, what an insult. I punched out a guy in the computer lab for calling me a Yahoo: "I know what you want, Yahoo," he was saying, so—*pow!*—I let him have it. He didn't expect Francis Xavier Pert to be such a pugilist.

Q. You're not the petty, paranoid individual who picked on the thirteen-year-old internet genius in the lab, are you?

A. I'm hardly petty and paranoid. I don't care what all those people say. Besides, he was big for his age.

Q. Once again, I end an interview feeling thoroughly ashamed of having known Francis Xavier Pert.

A. Make that "*Professor* Francis Xavier Pert," Ms. Bromide.

THE REVOLUTION COULD BE REVOLTING

One of the great stand-up comedians of American history was Thomas Jefferson. Few people know that he, George Washington of the Sainted Presidents of Greatness, Millard Fillmore of the Obscure Presidents of the Middle Years, and others helped make American comedy what it is today.

“Punch It Up, Tom! Nobody Likes to Read Anymore”

“It’s too long, Tom. People won’t read this in 200 years.”

“How do *you* know?” Thomas Jefferson snapped without looking up from his writing table.

Marty Skagmore grinned knowingly, pulled his coat-tail over his time-belt, and distracted Jefferson by strumming his business card over his fingernails. When the noise infuriated Jefferson enough for him to stop writing and tighten his jaws, Skagmore popped the card onto the writing table and announced, “Marty Skagmore at your service: the Marvelous Marvel of Marketing.”

Jefferson glowered at the card and dipped his quill into the ink again. “If it’s important,” he said through thin lips, “people *will* read it.”

Skagmore slapped his forehead with the flat of his hand. “Tom, baby. Tom, Tom.”

“Now what, Skagmore?”

“You gotta punch it up before we can get a United States of America, and a Congress, and all that. Let me go through each point one more time. All right, sweetheart?”

“I am *not* your sweetheart.”

“Hey, big guy, calm down. I’m not here to diss you, but, come to think of it, your love life is naughty-naughty…or is it your *lust*-life?”

Jefferson spat out each word. "Dispense with the gossip. What, is, your, point?"

"Just this: You rattle on forever in this piece. But nobody likes to read anymore."

"It's important, Skagmore. It's about the future of a new country. Ours."

"Yes, Tom. I understand what you *think* you're doing, but trust me: Who's going to read the thing?"

Jefferson stiffened. "What do you mean, Skagmore? I'm noted for my style."

Skagmore shook his head sadly and patted Jefferson's head. "Thomas, they were talking about your natural 'do, not this insipid prose. Listen to it, Tom-baby: 'When in the course of human events.' Now what's that supposed to mean, other than the obvious?"

"Well, you know, Skagmore, 'during our history,' 'the history of people,' you see?"

"Thomas, look at your first sentence: 'When *blah blah blah*, it becomes necessary *blah blah blah*, a decent respect *blah blah blah* and *blah blah*.' Count them, Tom-baby: *seventy-one* generally multi-syllabic words in one sentence! And you've used 'Nature' twice, and you're referring to a 'people' and 'mankind.' You see what you're doing, kid?" Skagmore saw that the criticism had struck home and rubbed it in by smirking condescendingly.

Jefferson began nervously looking around and chewing on the feather end of his quill. "Well, I, ah —"

"Look, everything that happens *is* part of our history, you see? We don't have 'declarations' written by, or about, chickens, or clouds, or daffodils. Do we?"

"Well, I guess not."

"Of course, we don't." Skagmore snatched Jefferson's quill and drew a rectangle on the parchment. Inside the rectangle, he wrote: "—— happens".

"What happens, Skagmore?"

Skagmore exhaled in disgust. "I can't believe it, and you a college man and all that. Four spaces: Can you think of any four-letter words?"

Jefferson brightened and counted them off on his fingers: "*Love*, *laws*, *free*, *king*, *jury*, *life*, *hang*, *ring*, and —"

"Tom-baby, look at the horse out there, on the ground, near the back. See what I mean?"

Jefferson made a big *O* with his mouth. "*That* happens?"

"Now you got it, Tom-baby." As Skagmore tried to hide the felt-tip marker with his hand, he sketched madly. "Look at my storyboard: We have this sticker on the back of a mule, on the tailgate of a wagon, on a cart, everywhere, you see? '*It* happens,' you got it?"

Jefferson frowned and pulled at his upper lip. "It sounds fatalistic, like there's nothing we can do about our problems."

"So? Don't fret it: *KISS*, Tom-baby."

"I beg your pardon." Jefferson pulled back noticeably.

"'Keep It Short, Simple'—great advice for writing."

"But I was hoping to work in something about 'certain unalienable Rights…Life, Liberty, and the Pursuit of Happiness'—that sort of stuff."

"You're kidding me, Tom-baby. Does that meet the *KISS* test, hmm?"

"But, Skagmore, it's what we're about. The *ideas* are important."

"You start talking about 'pursuit of *happiness*,' and you're going to have your 'lust life' on the cover of *The Colonial Enquirer*."

"They wouldn't do that to me."

"Tom-baby, let me explain why they would in four words: Cir-cu-la-tion. Got it?"

A melancholy Jefferson pulled some notes from his pocket and sighed. "And I was hoping to put in some grievances against the King: 'He has excited domestic insurrections amongst us, and has endeavoured to bring on the inhabitants of our frontiers, the merciless Indian Savages, whose known rule of warfare is—'"

"*KISS*, Thomas, *KISS*." Skagmore put his hand confidently on his heart. "I, Marty Skagmore, the Marvelous Marvel of Marketing, know whereof I speak."

Jefferson took out a fresh parchment and carefully made the letters within the rectangle.

"Cheer up," Skagmore said. "It can still be a petition. Who do you think will sign it?"

"John Hancock," Jefferson said with a sigh, "Roger Sherman, and Ben Franklin, and lots of fellows with high ideals."

Skagmore blanched. "Fellows with high *heels*? No, no!"

Jefferson ground his teeth and imagined he had his hands around Skagmore's neck. "*Ideals*, Skagmore, not heels."

"Thank goodness," Skagmore exclaimed.

"A document expressing our high *ideals*," Jefferson enunciated, "may help us start a new country and perhaps 200 years from now enable us to celebrate the Fourth of July."

Pleased with the vision, Skagmore beamed. "But write it real short, Tom-baby, because—let me repeat—nobody likes to read anymore." The vibrating beeper in Skagmore's pocket went off and warned him about the time-phase point. He scooted out of the hotel in Philadelphia and zapped back to the early 21th Century.

Thirty seconds after materializing, he was already forgetting the details of his latest marketing triumph…or even the broad outlines of that great accomplishment. No matter, he told himself as he whistled confidently while driving by Traitors' Hill. When he was in school, he could name almost all (well, a couple anyway) of the trouble-makers that were all hanged a couple of centuries ago.

As he approached the Parliament building of the Commonwealth of North America, he admired the campaign that he had done for the Queen, though, come to think of it, she was a bit of a stick in the mud about the slogan he had suggested.

"YOUR IMAGE NEEDS CHANGING, GEORGE"

Marty Skagmore pulled back the flap of General George Washington's tent and asked, "Do you have a minute?"

The haggard and tired Washington lowered his quill. "What can I do for you?"

"I'm Marty Skagmore, the Marvelous Marvel of Marketing and head of East Coast operations for Fenwick Arnold Associates, the public relations experts."

"I'm working on some battle plans," General Washington said. "So I —"

Skagmore interrupted, "I've been sent over to see if we can improve your public image."

"Look," Washington sighed, "I need supplies from the Continental Congress, plus troops who —"

"I'm aware of that, George."

"*Huurrrmph*!" Washington stiffened at the use of his first name.

"*Er*, General," Skagmore corrected, "you've got to have public opinion behind you." He pulled a roll of papers from his laced gray-flannel waist-coat. "Now a survey by John Adams shows that a third of the colonists back the revolution, a third are Tories sticking with King George, and the rest don't care."

Washington's fingers went *rat-a-tat* on the table top.

"That means," Skagmore explained, "you can't afford to offend many people or you'll turn the public against you."

"If you'll leave forthwith, sir," Washington said with penetrating blue-gray eyes boring into his visitor, "I'll plan a battle that might win us the war."

"Please, please," Skagmore said, "you're only the general. *We* have to mold the public." He thumbed through his papers. "Now you remember crossing the Delaware?"

Washington smiled. "A masterful bit of strategy. Caught them completely off guard."

"Strategy, my eye!" Skagmore snapped. "That was one of the stupidest blunders in the revolution."

Washington jerked to his feet and towered his six-foot-two frame over Skagmore. "Whattayamean? We captured over a thousand Hessians and only had four men slightly wounded."

"My dear sir," Skagmore explained, "you crossed the river on Christmas night. Now what sort of press does that get you? 'Blood-thirsty Americans massacre unarmed men singing Christmas carols.'"

Washington sputtered, "Massacre? We only captured mercenaries, and we didn't even attack until December 26."

"Mercenary smercenary," Skagmore declared. "An attack around Christmas is strictly bad press." He tapped his papers. "We did public opinion polls after your folly."

The quill fell from Washington's limp hands. He said hopelessly, "There was…the element…of surprise..."

"Another thing, General," Skagmore continued. "You realize you're a model for the rest of the country."

"I've never been a model in my life," Washington said. With a sigh, he added, "Of course, there were the Christmas frolics when we dressed up as—" Frowning, he remembered Skagmore's presence. "*Huurrrmph*!"

"I mean *role* model," Skagmore said with a disapproving shake of his head.

"Yes, yes, of course. I knew that."

"Well, then, you're not going to improve your image by standing up in a boat, for God's sake, while crossing the Delaware."

"But, but," Washington protested, "I wanted to keep an eye on the troops as they landed and to be sure that the Hessians didn't spot us."

"Any way you slice it, General, people don't have confidence in some doofus who stands up in a boat. On top of that, their kids will be saying, 'If George Washington can stand up in a boat, why can't I?'"

"I…I…"

"Another blunder," Skagmore resumed. "Did you say this? 'I have heard the bullets whistle, and, believe me, there is something charming in the sound.'"

"Well, yes, I—"

"What *are* you, man? A psychotic warmonger?" Skagmore arched an eyebrow and looked with pity upon the poor excuse of a human. "What do you think the wives of the country are going to say about that over the breakfast table?"

"But what I meant was—"

Skagmore cut him off. "And finally, the people are saying that, if this is the *American* Revolution, what are all those French soldiers doing over here?"

"*Huurrrmph*!" Washington cleared his throat and nervously straightened his wig. "They are—ah, *hrrummph*—only advisers."

"Advisers? French ships brought in 4,000 men the other day at Delaware Bay. You mean we need 4,000 advisers?"

Washington squirmed in his seat and giggled uneasily. "*Heh, heh, heh*, well, 4,000 heads are better than one."

Skagmore wasn't amused. "Listen, fella, the country won't buy that." He glanced at his papers. "There's also been talk of making you the president or something if we happen to win this conflict."

"I'd rather be right at home than president," Washington growled, making a gnashing noise.

"Don't grind your wooden teeth," Skagmore chided. "You'll get splinters in your tongue."

Washington pouted and discreetly spit out a splinter.

Skagmore laid the papers on the table. "Now, our studies show that the country does not need a militarist and a war-hawk for its leader. On top of that, you've got too many extremist friends, General."

"What do you mean?" Washington asked.

"Well, nuts like that Patrick Henry fellow. His 'liberty or death' slogan nearly petrified the colonists. Besides, this better-grave-than-knave prattle is bad for the economy. It'd be a great peace move, General, if you'd refuse to head the government. That way, you'd be first in war; second, behind whoever was president, in peace; and third (can't forget Ben Franklin) in the hearts of your countrymen."

The general mused, "First in war, second in peace, and third in the—"

Marty Skagmore folded his statistics and walked to the front of the tent. "Oh, yes, before I forget, Fenwick Arnold, my boss, wants you to say hello to his Uncle Benedict."

"GIVE ME LIVERWURST ON RYE!"

Thanks to Patrick Henry, CIA members had dreaded the opening of the July 1776 meeting in Philadelphia.

Years before, all of the leaders of the colonies made sure to attend all breakfast and luncheon meetings of the Colonial Improvement Association (CIA). Then such hot-heads as Henry had spread dissension through the meals.

Some CIA members had even been asking Tories to leave the meetings so "we can eat in peace."

Henry skipped the Philadelphia meeting, however, because of THE incident, which had occurred a few years before at a CIA meeting in Virginia. CIA members had been struggling to decide on a menu.

"Virginia ham," cried the anti-royalists.

"No!" crown partisans shouted, "Fried chicken and English Peas!"

Henry had thrown aside his menu and declared: "I know not what course others may take, but, as for myself, give me liverwurst on rye."

The phrase, traveling from CIA member to member, changed like a politician's ethics as it went around the room:

"What'd he say?"

"'Liverwurst and die,' I'm sure."

"You mean 'liberty and die'?"

"No, no, I've had the liverwurst here, so he must have said, 'Give me liverwurst *and* give me death.'"

His distorted cry reached a rowdy colonial element, and Virginia was soon rocking from riots, flag burnings, and wig-flipping.

CIA members sadly noted that sales declined during the disturbances. They issued reassuring statements to each other, and then they put up signs saying "buy British," whereupon tranquility returned, somewhat.

An unfortunate incident in Boston not long after sent the economy spiraling downward again. A miscreant CIA member spiked the tea at a dockside tea party, and proper Boston shuddered as reputable, red-nosed businessmen scampered from ship to ship, playing sailors and Indians, whooping, shouting, and then pushing boxes overboard.

Skeptical crown authorities, troubled by each anti-British incident, never bought the "spiked tea" story. George III was told, "The CIA is trying to undermine the British government."

To this, King George nodded wisely and patted a Clydesdale horse, "My daughter here will soon marry a poopdeck," whereupon they carried him off for his vacation at the Royal Funny Farm.

With these tensions around, the Philadelphia luncheon opened cautiously, as the mayor tossed off another pot of ale, hiccoughed, and greeted the group: "It's peachy-dandy to have you in Fillydelphia, the city of 'brotherly love.'"

Virginia's Thomas Jefferson was day-dreaming about the name *Phillip* meaning "horse lover" and muttered, "Or city of horses' brothers."

"Them, too," the mayor agreed.

New England's Samuel Adams grumbled, "What kind of mayor can't even pronounce the name of his town?"

That question went unanswered since the waitresses passed around the menus. The most popular course at the Philly luncheon was the Gotta Go Special: prune pizza, prune jelly, and prune juice. The special was regularly devoured by a restless colonial segment that was often fidgety and fast-stepping.

July 2 passed with CIA members posing for a painting by Gilbert Stuart, who specialized then in still-lifes of knives, forks, and Mulligan stew.

July 3 featured speeches. Sam and John Adams attacked King George III, while the royalists ranted against "brunchmanship."

Eventually, the CIA decided to press for independence using this time-table:

1776: Set up a Life, Liberty, and Pursuit of Pork and Beans Committee to examine the feasibility of independence and to determine the best restaurants in which to hold future CIA meetings.

1780: Hear the report of the Life subcommittee of the LLPPBC.

1785: Hire a special counsel to examine the Life subcommittee for fraud and incontinence. Examine the Liberty subcommittee report.

1790: Hire a special counsel to investigate the previous special counsel. Hear from the Pursuit of Pork & Beans workers, preferably in an outdoor session.

1800: Combine the recommendations and draft a white paper. Hire a not-so-special counsel to see if he can do a better job than the special counsels.

1800-25: Conduct saturation studies on possible adverse effects of independence on textile industry; appoint residents of all even-numbered houses as special counsels.

1825-50: Study effects on shipping; appoint odd- numbered residents as special counsels.

1850-65: Explore the effects on agriculture.

And the time-table went on through the 19th and 20th Centuries and into the beginning of the 21th Century, but they settled on "I-Day" or "Independence Day" as July 4, 2076, and the cry of "the spirit of '76" went through the hall.

Then the unfortunate July 4 came, after which CIA members in Philadelphia discovered that Thomas Jefferson was both sneaky and radical.

Jefferson had waved a large piece of parchment and shouted: "Gentlemen, I have the bill here. They put it all on one ticket. Let's all sign it so we can all go home."

The weak-eyed Franklin, fishing in his waistcoat for his glasses that he had left in his house, squinted at the paper. "'When in the course' ...my, my Tom, we certainly tied on the old feedbag."

John Hancock grabbed the quill after Franklin scribbled his name. With a laugh, he said, "I'll sign it BIG, since I'm on an expense account!" He elbowed Jefferson in the ribs and laughed. "Tom, you know what would be a good joke and really shake up His Royal Basketcase? You ought to send the bill to King George!"

"I will," Jefferson said knowingly, "oh, yes, I will indeed."

POLITICAL JUNKY AND MILLARD FILLMORE

As I walked across the park, I was glad of the many hours I had spent reading Sherlock Holmes stories. The tales sharpen your observation skills and enable you to protect yourself by knowing what's around you. For example, I spotted this guy and concluded immediately he was a political junky. One subtle clue enabled me to make that shrewd deduction. His tee-shirt, you see, proclaimed, "I am a political junky." Sherlock would have been proud of the mental gymnastics.

The guy in the park was carrying a laptop, along with yard-signs and bumper-stickers. Moreover, he clicked and yelped when he walked because of the pins on the campaign buttons in his pockets.

"Who's your candidate?" I asked, a little puzzled. "The election has already passed, and—"

"There's always another one—*ouch!*—for the true believer," he said, wincing when a pin bit into his leg.

"Of course," I agreed, "and *whom* do you believe in truly?"

He opened the laptop and pointed to a slogan on his homepage: "Bring back Millard Fillmore."

"Millard Fillmore? But he's—"

"No, no, my friend, *don't* say it! He lives, I know, somewhere, in Argentina." His eyes twitched, and he rose onto his tip-toes with a giggle. "Would you like a bumper-sticker?

'Fill the Bill with Mill' or 'An Encore for Millard Fillmore' or perhaps just plain 'Vote Whig.'"

"Why Millard Fillmore as a candidate?" I asked. "Why not Jeb Bush, Hillary, Paul Ryan, or Newt Gingrich?"

He leaned forward and looked me in the eye. "We don't need a president named 'Newt' or 'Salamander' or any other lizard."

"So you're saying that 'Millard' is okay?" I asked.

He cast a wily eye on me. "Millard certainly *is* okay. Why? Name one thing that Millard Fillmore did wrong. Just one."

"Well," I stammered, "but then what did he do *right*?"

"Hah!" he scoffed and shook his head. "No one gets praise for successes. It's mistakes that count. As the Bard says, 'The Evil that men do lives after them; the good is oft interréd with their bones.' What evil of Millard Fillmore has lived on?"

As I tried to think of some major gaffe, the Whig clapped his hands in triumph and clicked on a page of sheet music. Before I could stop him, he was singing new lyrics to "My Bonnie Lies Over the Ocean":

A Whig is hiding in Blanco,
Way down in old Argentine;
The U.S.A. needs him now, so
Bring back my Millard to me.
Bring back, bring back,
O bring back my Millard to me!

Since I suffer from what psychologists call the MGM Movie Musical Syndrome (or MG3MS), I go through life fearful that, at any given minute, people will start madly singing and tap-dancing and some male dancers will think I'm the catcher and throw at me all three hundred pounds of Helen Traubel, Kate Smith, or Roseanne. I was about to start running for safety when he choked up and wiped away a tear.

"Why Millard Fillmore?" he sobbed. "He has no vested interest, other than an interesting vest. He's a dark horse, for, if you try to name the five most obscure presidents, you'll list James K. Polk, James Buchanan, Rutherford B. Hayes, Zachary Taylor and Franklin Pierce and never even think of Millard Fillmore."

"True, he's—"

"He's the Forgotten Man of American Presidents, just the man: the Forgotten Millard for the New Millennium."

"Well, what kind of platform do you Neo-Whigs have?"

"Platform? We used to win elections *without* platforms. We were the 'party of organized incompatibility.'" He pulled out a yard-sign: "Millard Fillmore for Vice President."

"Why just vice president?" I asked.

"It's the routine. We only elected two presidents: General Harrison and General Taylor. Both were war heroes, and both died in office. Also, both had unknowns for vice presidents."

"Which did Fillmore go with?" I asked, a little embarrassed at my lapse in knowledge about American History I.

"Remember 'Tippecanoe and Tyler, too,'" the Neo-Whig asked.

"Ah, yes," I said, casually tossing off the information since I did not want to brag about my accomplishments in history, "Harrison fell out of his canoe and drowned, and Tyler took over."

For some reason, the Whig glared at me as if he knew about my *C-* at Pensacola High but finally said, "When John Tyler served out Harrison's term, the party said to him, 'Why don't you run for president…of Mexico?' Then the Whigs picked another candidate and lost."

"Too bad," I agreed.

"Later on, Millard took over after Taylor died. It was a wild time, with a lot of little parties and sectional fighting. As a matter of fact, their actions so weakened the decade that the

1850s lasted a mere ten years, succumbing eventually to the 1860s."

Since I detected a wild look in his eye, I stepped back a couple feet.

"So today," the Whig said, "we pick somebody famous for president. Heck, who knows, maybe General Schwarzkopf, or General Eisenhower!"

"But Eisenhower's dead," I protested.

He brightened, "Even better! We won't have to wait around for It to happen. So, we have Millard for veep; and then we see if the Lord had called home the General, and Millard takes over." A black cloud seemed to settle over his face, though, as he added, "But, back then, Millard never had a chance: the *thirteenth* president, so what do you expect? The party wouldn't even re-nominate him, and the Whigs lost again." He sighed. "Abe Lincoln used to be a Whig, but he too left the party and even said, 'Whiggery is against us.'"

"What kind of man was Millard Fillmore?" I asked.

"*Is* Millard Fillmore," he corrected. "They say he has a pleasing personality and a suavity of manner that disarms political opponents."

"Oh?"

"For example, a guy would come up to him and say, 'Milton, what have you been doing with yourself lately?' And Fillmore'd say, 'Oh, I'm the President.' Then the guy would say, 'Imagine that: Milton Gilmore as president. President of what?'"

By now, the Whig was pulling out his campaign buttons and throwing them to passersby, impaling one formidable woman about the size of the blue-eye-lidded lady on the re-runs of *The Drew Carey Show*. "And the stories they tell about him. Of course, they usually changed his name to Lincoln, Roosevelt, Reagan, or Clinton, so people would know the story was about a president."

The blue-eye-lidded woman was barging through the park with a policeman in tow, and I heard the distant strains of a brass band breaking into a nice little ditty from an MGM movie.

As I broke into a run, I heard the Whig shouting, "Have you ever heard the story about Millard Fillmore and his father's kumquat tree? Well, Millard had gotten an ax and—"

SHAPING UP HONEST ABE

President Abraham Lincoln squinted at the business card and fished in his pocket for his glasses.

"It says 'Marty Skagmore, the Marvelous Marvel of Marketing,'" announced the visitor. "That's me."

Lincoln frowned at the time-belt that Skagmore was trying to cover up. "I've not seen one of those," he said.

"What? This?" Skagmore patted the belt. "Well, it keeps my britches up."

"It looks to me like a time-belt," Lincoln said. "Some of my predecessors left messages warning me about you, Mr. Scummore."

"*Skag*more," the visitor corrected, "and I'm afraid that the prime directive forbids —"

"You're obviously from the future," Lincoln said, "so tell me what you want and get on with your business."

Skagmore sighed. "All I'm doing is coming back to tell a minor president how to improve one of his speeches."

"Minor? Are you sure?"

"Certainly. I was home-schooled, which I can't describe to you because it would reveal too much of what occurs in the future."

Lincoln took a deep breath. "Let me take a stab at it. *Home-schooled* means you took classes at home."

"From books."

"I think I know what *books* are, Mr. Skagmore." Lincoln took a deep breath since that helped him to deal with fools. "Now, which speech are you talking about?"

"Oh, that one in Pennsylvania."

Lincoln smiled and pulled out an envelope. "I've been polishing this for days now."

Skagmore shook his head. "Look, you serve eight years as president, give one almost-decent speech, and then you retire to Illinois, where, ironically, you get hit by a train and become the laughing stock of the country: ex-railroad attorney gets done in by a steam-engine."

"I thought you weren't supposed to tell me the future."

"Right," Skagmore admitted, suddenly rattled and nervously checking the temporal monitor to see if any official had overheard his remarks. "Forget the train remark. You live to be a hundred and six, and they, ah, put up a big memorial to you in Washington. Is that better?"

"Even rail splitters are familiar with sarcasm, Mr. Skagmore."

"Yeah, I guess I was laying it on a bit thick with a memorial for Abe Lincoln, of all things." Skagmore laughed suddenly, but quickly cleared his throat.

"What's amusing?"

"Nothing," Skagmore said, only to strain himself trying to stop a giggle.

"You might as well tell me," Lincoln said.

"It's just a tasteless joke in my mind. When we're in a bar, we try to think of grandiose monuments for the most insignificant presidents, so, of course, your name gets bandied about a lot."

"All right," Lincoln said a little impatiently, "so what outlandish memorial do I get, in these jokes?"

"A thirty-foot-long screw, but upside down, going up into this big chunk of California Redwood. The joke says you're the big *screw*-up, get it? That's especially if you give that horrible speech in Pennsylvania."

Lincoln tapped the envelope. "All right, Skagmore. What's wrong with the speech?"

"Well, the opening for one: 'four score and seven years ago.' Isn't that a bit much? Wouldn't 'eighty-seven years ago' do just as well?"

Lincoln shook his head. "I'm echoing a line from the Bible: 'three score and ten'—the time allotted to a man's life."

"I'm well aware of the source." Skagmore frowned and glanced down at the time-belt. "As soon as I figure out the coordinates, I'll be giving Moses a piece of my mind."

"Okay, what else is wrong with the speech?"

"For one, it's too negative, and it's loaded with passives. Look here: 'all men *are created* equal…Now we *are engaged* in a great civil war…We *are met* on a great battlefield of that war.' And so on till the cows come home."

"What else?"

"All the negatives: 'In a larger sense, we *cannot* dedicate—we *cannot* consecrate—we *cannot* hallow—this ground.' State your message in a positive way, man. Can't you see the need for that?"

"But we *can't*—"

"Don't quibble, Mr. President. It's unbecoming." Skagmore grabbed the envelope and shook his head. "How can you say, 'The world will little note nor long remember what we say here, but it can never forget'? More negatives."

Lincoln sighed and settled into the chair. "I guess it needs more work, but I've been working so *hard* on it already."

The time-belt's transport alert vibrated, and Skagmore hurried out the door. "Gotta go, Mr. President. Got an appointment with an actor, John Wilkes Booth. Got a great idea for a project for him."

Months later, Skagmore reappeared in the room.

"Ah, it's you, Skagmore," Lincoln said with some irritation. "I thought you were out of my hair altogether."

"How did the revised talk go at Gettysburg?"

Lincoln cocked his head as he remembered the scene. "Well enough. I did use *my* speech instead of what you were suggesting."

"Why?"

"Partly because I forgot and left the new one here at the White House."

Marty Skagmore grinned. "That helps to prove that it's all right for me to gad about in time. We can travel, but we can't really change anything."

"Mary says I would have remembered the new draft if I hadn't been so worn out from over-work." Lincoln noticed Skagmore's time-belt vibrating. "I presume it's your time to zip out of here."

"Somewhat." Skagmore felt in his pocket and extracted a couple of tickets. "Look, Mr. President, I *was* thinking about sticking around another day and taking in a play, but why don't you and Mrs. Lincoln go in my place."

Lincoln took the tickets and squinted at the title, *Our American Cousin*—the play that was being performed at the Ford Theater.

"Oh," Lincoln said, "did John Wilkes Booth like your great idea?"

"Ah," Skagmore said, "did I talk to him or have I come back and ruined the sequence?"

"What sequence?"

"Don't know. Time anomaly or something. Whatever happened didn't happen or something." Skagmore tapped his belt again. "Gotta go."

"Thanks, Mr. Skagmore." Lincoln waved the tickets to *Our American Cousin*. "I'm sure I'll get a bang out of the play."

FORWARD TO THE PAST

Marty Skagmore popped his card on the restaurant table in front of Sidney Q. Mock. "The Marvelous Marvel of Marketing meets the Wunderkind of Hollywood, Sid. It's about time. I came out here to make a killing with *Forward to the Past.*"

"You said you have a film project set on a college campus." Mock lit his cigar and gestured. "Pitch it fast. I have to take a meeting with Ted Bimbeau in ten minutes." He cut his head toward a crew from *Tinseltown Tonight.* "Oh, and watch your language. *TT* is taping us."

"Right, it isn't exactly a done deal, Sid, but I tell you, baby, that Michael is interested."

"Michael Keaton?"

"No, that'd look stupid, you schmuck. An old Batman as president of a college?"

"Okay, but you can't mean Michael Jackson, not with all of his complications."

"Right, rigor mortis is a real complication."

"Exactly. Rule #1: Don't reach for a cookie if you don't know how it's going to crumble."

"All right, how about Michael Douglas?"

"No way, Sid."

"I hear he's played Liberace."

"Okay, Douglas *could* do, but I'm after Michael J. Fox, you understand?"

"What?" Mock frowned and shook his head. "Michael's been fighting his illness and doing some TV work, and, besides, he's too old to play the McFly kid in another *Back to the Future*."

"Come on, Sid. Check this out: Can't call him 'McFly,' but we can call him 'McBug' or 'McCrawley' to avoid a law suit. Same basic Michael J. Fox character, but he's grown up, slight physical problem, and plays the president of a college: Acme CC."

"*Si si*—that'd go well south of the border."

Skagmore gave a quick, polite smile. "Sidney, listen to me: It's the letters, *C* and *C*, for community college, a junior college, you see?"

"I see. So who's going to put up $150 million for a junior college flick?"

"Here's the story, Sid. Some clown has set up an organization with heads of campuses, first called 'provosts.'"

"What does *provost* mean?"

"Hell, I don't know, Sid, but it don't matter, you see, because they change the names to 'campus presidents.' So Acme has four of these campus prexies."

"Watch your language, Marty." Mock cut his eyes toward the videocam of *Tinseltown Tonight*. "You don't want to wind up on the '*TT*ing on Hollywood' segment."

"Not that, Sid. *Prexies* is plural for *prexy*, another word for *president*."

Leaning forward, Mock whispered, "Then I can safely say the president of Paramount is a prexy."

"That's funny, Sid." Skagmore laid an organizational chart on the table. "So Acme has these prexies, then lots of vice presidents, associate vice presidents, and stuff. Then each area has an assistant dean."

Mock ran his finger down the page. "Who are the deans?"

"Deans?" Skagmore leaned over and searched each line carefully. "No, Sid. No deans, just assistants."

"That's a pile of actors, Marty, but I don't see a story here. What's the spine? Pitch me a story, kid."

Skagmore rubbed his hands together and leaned forward. "President McBug says he wants to reorganize, and he talks to the Professor and they hop in his machine and go back to the 1970s and study the structure of the bigger community colleges in Florida. The Professor says, 'Marty, stay away from this turkey of a set-up. This system's for dinosaurs, but Marty don't listen, you see?"

Mock took a puff on his cigar. "A lot of Martys seem to have that problem, Skagmore." With a grimace, he tapped the table. "Why is it set in Florida?"

"We can make it in the Orlando studio, Sid, and save money."

"So what happens, Skagmore?"

"Well, President McBug does whistles and bells at the schmucks on the board of trustees, and they swallow it hook, line, and stinker. The plan is implemented, but then it hits the fan."

"How so?"

"East Campus starts believing that the sun rises over it, and the campus president becomes a king or a god, like in the old days."

"Make it a king. I'm not ready to be a Cecil B. DeMille and mess with God, Marty."

"'Ready when you are, C.B.,' so it stays a king. Meanwhile, the prexy of West Campus starts having the guys in maintenance carry him around in a what-cha-ma-call-it, one of those things the guys in wigs rode in."

"Is McBug in a Delorean?"

"Nope, we're using a Ford Escort for promotional purposes, and the bad guys are in the what-cha-ma-call-its."

"Is there a what-cha-ma-call-it chase?"

"Great idea, Sid. There is one now. Now, at River Campus, the campus president just wants to play golf, so he doesn't pay attention to the wicked Academic Dean, who turns into a Prince John. Dean John is smart, cunning, devious, a real back-stabber, you see?"

"Like you, Skagmore?"

"You got a smart mouth, Sidney. I wonder if it's as smart as some of your anterior body parts."

"What else, Skagmore?"

"Piney Woods Campus ends up with a wicked Academic Dean, too, only this one is your basic hillbilly, big belly, but not a brain in his head."

Mock mused, "Meryl Streep could do a redneck accent, and use just a little padding."

"My thoughts exactly, Sidney. So everything turns sour on President McBug. Bureaucracies really get entrenched, academics get trampled, inventories get screwed up because one kingdom don't like another kingdom interfering. In despair, Marty runs to a bridge on a snowy night and is about to throw himself into the water, but just in time the Professor shows up with his Ford Escort and says, 'Marty, snap your heels together three times.' So President McBug runs back to campus and gets all the heels in a meeting. He says, 'If you bums aren't chalking and talking, then start walking.' And those who can teach start getting on with the real business, teaching and then administrating some, and those who can't do anything except sit on their butts get jobs as bench-testers for the transit authority."

Sidney Q. Mock closed his eyes for a second as he tried to imagine the opening credits. Suddenly he shook his head and stood up to leave. "No deal, Skagmore." He leaned close and whispered so the *Tinseltown Tonight* microphone couldn't record him. "Audiences don't care about education. They want T&A, car chases, and blood and gore."

Marty Skagmore slumped in his chair and stared at his business card. He drummed his fingers on the table for two minutes and then screamed, "Eureka."

Tinseltown Tonight caught that moment on tape and showed him that evening announcing the next mega-hit, *Horace Mann Park*: "A dinosaur becomes president of Acme College. There's T&A, tyrannosauruses and allosauruses, car chases as the students try to escape from them, and blood and gore at board meetings, and everything!"

WRITING ON POLITICS OR FINE CUISINE

An adage for scribblers is "write what you know," but many of us want to stretch ourselves to explore areas in which we *think* we would be experts…often with disastrous consequences.

THE COMMON TOUCH FOR COLUMNS

"I'm fixing this elevator on the way to the 30th floor," the man says, "so maybe you should take a different one."

No, thanks. I was hoping to talk to someone like a repairman anyway.

"You ain't one of them writer guys, are you?"

I've written some.

"Then I know what you want: You're like Mike Royko with his Slats Slobbowhatnik, or William Raspberry with his cabdriver. You're trying to get me to be the voice of the Common Man in a column, aren't you? And you're expecting me to say *ain't*, aren't you?"

Lots of people don't say *ain't.* But, for me, all you have to do is shoot the bull with me. It won't hurt.

"Nothing doing. You get to throw lines at me like you're some kind of Brian Peter Brinkley or Diane Chung and hope I'll spout off some instinctive remark from the primal perspective of our species."

Primal, instinctive, perspective? That's some vocabulary.

"Yeah, I listen to radio psychologists."

You don't tune in Rush Limbaugh?

"Naw, I don't listen to fat guys. I don't like *one* fat guy or *lots* of fat guys."

Should I get off? I'm a little chubby.

"Hmmph, you passed *chubby* sixty pounds ago." He pointed to a sign on the elevator. "Fat guys cause us to max out on the weight, so that's why I like people like Cassius, because of his 'lean and hongry look.'"

Ah, the Common Man quoting Shakespeare.

"Watch that 'Common Man' stuff, tubbo. I'm quoting Andy Griffith: 'What It Was, Was Shakespeare.' Big difference."

Sorry, but I really want to make a big impact as a political columnist, so, if you'll bear with me, I'll hurry up. Now, many people were complaining about President Clinton putting American soldiers in Haiti or Kosovo, or Bush putting our young men in Afghanistan and whatever, or Obama going after terrorists. Do you feel, as some critics have said, that Haiti, Kosovo, or Tora Bora Boom Baghdad isn't worth one drop of American blood?

"That's a dumb question. You look at a Sunday paper and it'll tell you about four or five paratroopers getting killed during an exercise in Oklahoma, then three Marines drown when they get dropped into water over their head in full gear in maneuvers in Carolina, two sailors wipe out just going to the base in morning traffic in California, and a B-47 on a pizza-run crashes with ninety-seven G.I.s on board."

What's your point?

"If you got 14 million-zillion guys and gals in uniform, they're going to shed blood just getting their chow in the morning. You don't see members of Congress saying the exercises and maneuvers aren't worth turning two or three Rangers into flapjacks."

So you think we ought to stay in the trouble spots?

"Naw, let's invade the French Riviera and call up some more of the Reserves."

You're angry with the French?

"No way, but we might as well fight some place that we'd actually like to go to. *Oo la la*, and I'm in the Reserves, you see."

Hmm, I guess this is enough working-class wisdom for a political column, but I really need to get your name, Mr. —?"

"Bubba Ali Jones, but my co-workers call me 'Ali Oops.' Mama named me after my Uncle Bubba and, of course, after her favorite boxer."

Interesting. But why have your co-workers nicknamed you "Oops"?

"Hold it, we're about there: floor 28, 29, 30. All the way to the top."

Ah, the door's not opening.

"Yeah, I see. Hand me that wrench there and let me get this ceiling panel off."

Be careful with the brake up there.

"As I was saying, the guys gave me that nickname because—*oops*!"

Holy cow, this thing's dropping faster than Dick Cheney's social conscience!

"As a political columnist, tubbo, you're about to make a hell of a big impact."

Thanks, Common Man. I guess.

"HAUTE, TWO, THREE, FOUR —PASS THE SNAILS PLEASE"

I keep running across individuals who spout such aphorisms as, "You are what you read...or wear...or eat."

In my case, that means I am a wrinkled black-eyed pea with a craving for James Thurber.

I had developed a strong desire to write a cookbook and perhaps a regular food column, so I borrowed a book on haute cuisine and was returning it to a friend, whom I'll call Bob Such, for Such was his name.

My courtesy shocked Bob, who had not had a book returned since Spiro Agnew was copping a plea, and the poor man collapsed until we dragged him to his recliner and roused him with the foul stench of an old athletic sock.

He cradled the book and gasped, "You must stay for dinner."

I regretted my rudeness in dropping by at dinner time and attempted to leave, but Bob's wife Babs grabbed me by the elbow and ushered me into the living room. "You dear thing," she said, "returning a book."

"This one's a thing of beauty and a joy forever," I said, "and it may just help me to become a great food writer."

Bob called, "Bet you can't guess what our little culinary club is having."

"Oh, I don't know. Probably—"

"Escargot!" he exclaimed. "You know: Snails!"

I called upon my military training to hide the panic that was consuming me. Sergeant Ruffbutt used to warn us that gourmands can smell fear of snails from two hundred clicks away. "No, Bob, really, I can't stay. No kidding. I'm late already to go wherever I'm going."

"You told me this morning you didn't have anything planned tonight."

"Hey, so I'm planning already."

Bob and Babs Such cornered me and let me know that it was time for my Southern manners to yield to their gesture of hospitality. "It'll be ready in a few minutes," Babs said.

"Don't hurry," I offered weakly.

Bob introduced me to two other guests, his neighbors, Jane and Dick Lieberwitz. They were also staying for dinner and, as it turned out, boasted that they had selected the snails.

"Things will work out wonderfully," Jane said. "We were each going to have five snails, so, if we give up one apiece, that'll be four all around."

"Plenty for us," Dick said, patting his round belly.

"Honestly," I said, "I'd be the last one on earth to take another person's snail."

"Glad to do it," Dick said. "We picked up this dish in Europe. Ever been to Europe?"

"A couple of times."

"The French call it *escargot*," he said.

"They also rave about Jerry Lewis," I remembered.

"True." Dick balled up his fist like a shell. "Most Europeans devour loads of gastropods. That's the true name for them. The French mainly eat whelks, periwinkles, and ormers. In 1922, for example—" He vigorously smacked his lips. "—some 889 tons of whelks and 3,245 tons of periwinkle were delivered at Billingsgate in London."

"Is that where they keep the crazy people?" I asked.

"No, no. Billingsgate's a market. You're thinking of Bedlam."

"Why the fact about 1922?" I asked.

"Oh, I did a research paper in college, back in 1972." He shook his head at the stupidity of ivy-covered life. "Professor Darymple said I should have used more recent facts, like at least something from 1962."

"The utter fool," I said. "*Tsk-tsk*, madness in Academe."

"I know," he agreed, "but what—?"

Bob interrupted us and motioned for me to come into the kitchen. "Here's how you fix snails. You buy them in a small jar or can. Mix them with spinach, butter, and garlic."

"Don't forget the parsley," Babs called.

"That, too, my dear." He glanced quickly at me. "You don't object to spinach, garlic, and parsley, do you?"

"No, not to them, I don't."

"Good," he said. "You mix them and put them in shells, which you keep as miniature pots and pans. You don't throw the shells away. So, after putting them in the shell, you place them in the oven to bake." He cracked open the oven door and inhaled deeply. "Ahhh, let's go into the dining room. They'll be out in a jiffy, just ten minutes."

At the dining room table, we settled in as Babs placed the food on the table. Then Bob said a prayer over the snails, though he expressed thankfulness to the King of the Universe, whereas I would have opted for forgiveness for the transgression.

"How's the writing coming?" Bob asked me.

"At a snail's pace," I said. "I never seem to have enough slime...or *time*."

Bob pointed to the plates. "Since you've never eaten escargot, this ought to be an enlightening and cultural experience. You *are* what you eat, you know."

"I've heard," I said, trying not to look at the plates.

But there they were: four of them, the biggest and fattest snails I had ever seen. Everyone else's snail seemed puny and emaciated in comparison. I studied the plate and sipped my glass of iced tea.

"You use the little fork." Dick demonstrated by flicking the fork around like it was a baton or scalpel. "Stick in the fork, and dig out the little beggar, and—*voilà*!—there it is, the little forker." He slurped as he popped it into his mouth. He closed his eyes and seemed to have an orgasm as he tried to let it melt on his palate.

I sipped my iced tea again, cleared my throat, and studied the plate again: still four of them, each still bigger than anyone else's.

At that moment, I knew deep down inside (in the stomach area, to be precise) that, regardless of what everyone says, I am not a debonair, urbane, worldly wise sophisticate. A small voice kept saying, "You just ain't got no cooth." I knew my wonderful food column would never make it to print.

Another look at the snail shells and their buttered and garlicked inhabitants brought out the country in me. I drawled, "No rush in getting to these."

"Go on," Bob coaxed. "They won't crawl away."

So I extracted with the little biddy fork the first snail in the whole wide world that I was to eat, and popped it into my mouth without looking at it, because, if refined I'm not, then stupid I'm not either.

I could taste the spinach and parsley.

I tasted garlic.

Butter, too.

And then I bit down with a taste-defying crunch and swallowed. Three crunches later, it was over.

Thirty minutes later, it was time to go and to escape the ritual of back-slapping comments.

"It wasn't so bad, was it?" Bob said.

"Admit it: You loved it," Babs insisted.

"Isn't it great?" Dick and Jane chorused.

As I vowed never to borrow a book or even a pencil from the Suches, I smiled weakly as I struggled to open the front door.

Babs called, "Oh, you must come again next Friday."

"No snails?" I asked.

"None, we promise." She looked at Jane and Dick. "We're still voting about what to have next."

The next day, Bob e-mailed me: "It's a toss-up between squid and kidney pies."

That's why I've decided to do an automotive column, if I can ever figure out how to pop open the hood of our family's really neat '59 Edsel Ranger. It's a cool car and easy to park if you have spent your life practicing parallel-parking with nuclear aircraft carriers.

HARD WORK, BUT SOMEONE HAS TO DO IT

Yes, I told a friend, a sports writer does have a heart, and mind, and soul, frequently all three of them. Moreover, if you hang around newspapers enough, you'll learn that most sporting writers look forward to going to, and reporting on, historic games.

When they are writhing in ecstasy as they babble about the benefits of satellite TV, with 122 games going on at once, they moan about not being there even when memorable games occur: e.g., this grand-slam, that touchdown play, this thirty-foot putt.

However, there's one game that no sports writer would want to go back in time to cover, although it might have been fun to watch. It was in Atlanta on October 7, 1916, when the Georgia Tech football team met Cumberland College from Lebanon, Tennessee.

If a game is a game, what was the big deal about that contest in 1916? That was the highest-scoring college football game of all time. Coach John Heisman's Georgia Tech team beat Cumberland College by a score of 222 to 0.

To entice Cumberland to play the game, Tech had offered a $500 guarantee, and, although $500 would not cause Jimbo Fisher or Nick Saban to lift the phone today, keep in mind that a good weekly salary for an adult then for a Southern male was $15 to $20.

Grantland Rice reported the game and wrote, "Cumberland's greatest individual play occurred when fullback [George E.] Allen circled right end for a six-yard loss."

Allen disputed Rice's report, since "there were several plays in which we only lost three yards."

Allen was normally the Cumberland manager (and a future friend of FDR, Truman, and Ike), but against Tech he had to be a substitute player. He said Cumberland had stopped in Nashville on the way down and tried to borrow a few players from Vanderbilt University, but Vandy had a difficult game coming up and couldn't spare any.

(Yes, Virginia, the NCAA of today would have trouble with some of the practices early in the past century.)

To make things worse, three Cumberland players got lost in Nashville and missed the train. That left sixteen players for Cumberland, including their manager.

Even though Heisman was building a football powerhouse, Cumberland took pride in its skills on the gridiron. It felt smug about its "classy set of signals."

"Each player was named for a vegetable," quarterback Morris Gouger explained. "If I wanted to send the right halfback through left tackle, I'd call 'turnip over cabbage,' or a pass from QB to left end, 'tomato to carrot'! The trouble was, Tech made vegetable stew out of us." (Instead of becoming a chef or veggie farmer, the QB eventually practiced law in Mississippi and Indiana, probably because he wanted a higher celery.)

Today, a sports writer would have a sports information director and staff doing a play-by-play print-out from a PC and photocopy machine, with the scribe perhaps using a laptop unit for his or her running notes and story. In 1916, though, the sports writer in the press box needed to log each play using a pencil and notepad. I suspect Grantland Rice only jotted down the actual scores, since the first quarter score ended up being

63-0. That score included nine TDs with Jim Preas kicking nine points after (he had 18 consecutive PATs for the day, one of the many records established in the game).

Those 63 points were also scored in only twelve and a half minutes, since Cumberland had figured it might not prosper if the full fifteen minutes were played in each quarter.

The second quarter featured another 63 points from Tech, so the halftime came with Cumberland trailing 126-0.

Apparently, Heisman's inspirational locker-room speech did not rank up there with Knute Rockne's "Gipper" talk, but he noted: "You're doing all right, but you just can't tell what those Cumberland players have up their sleeves. They may spring a surprise. Be alert, men! Hit 'em clean, but hit 'em hard!"

The Cumberland coach wasn't able to use the appropriate line in his talk: "Men, we've got Tech frightened. They're petrified because they may be charged later with first-degree murder."

Georgia Tech was not as overpowering in the second half, mainly because Cumberland had gotten Tech to shorten the quarters from twelve and a half minutes to ten minutes.

In the third period, the mighty Cumberland players yielded only 54 points and then 42 points in the fourth quarter.

This game of the era was also a comedy of errors, which can unbalance the conscientious scribe trying to follow the bouncing ball. For example, Allen punted once and the ball hit his own center in the back of the neck, bowling him over.

By contrast, when Tech punted once, the ball hit a Cumberland player in the back, bounced back to the punter, who carried the ball in for a touchdown.

A Cumberland back fumbled in the fourth quarter, and the ball was rolling toward Cumberland halfback "Bird" Paty. The fumbler shouted, "Pick it up!" But Paty glanced up at the Tech players thundering down on him and yelled back, "Pick it up yourself! You dropped it!"

The most experienced player on the Cumberland team was R.E. (Pete) Gray, who had played football for several seasons at Oklahoma and was one of six Cumberland athletes to play the entire game.

Some Cumberland players sought refuge in strange places. For example, in the final quarter, Tech players noticed a Cumberland player wrapped in a blanket sitting at the end of their bench. One of them called, "Hey, you! You're on the wrong bench!"

Said he, "No, I'm not! I'm not going to get sent back into this game again."

A sports writer obviously would have had to hit the highlights in such a game, since only *The New York Times* Sunday edition would have had room for all of the particulars. Similarly, the skills of a statistician would have been whetted enough for him to measure the sands in the desert.

The stories, however, should have mentioned several records that stood through the years:

—Biggest score;

—Greatest number of TDs and PATs;

—Highest score for one quarter;

—Most PATs by one player;

—Greatest number of players scoring TDs (13);

—Greatest number of yards gained in one game (978).

But the Second Battle of Atlanta had a couple of omissions, or records of another sort. Neither Cumberland nor Tech made a first down. Cumberland simply could not do it, and Tech wound up scoring touchdowns instead.

To wrap up the where-are-they-now department, let's mention that the Cumberland Law School was moved in the 1960s to Birmingham, where it became part of Samford University (formerly Howard College). In 1958, its football coach was Bobby Bowden. A couple of decades plus later, the Samford Bulldogs were coached by Terry Bowden (later at Auburn, of course), but their fortunes have never been as grim as CC's back in 1916.

In closing, yes, although sports writers do have souls, it is also correct that they do not cast shadows and that they are unable to see themselves in mirrors, but that relates to their habits of hanging around sports bars at night and generally being as glass-cracking homely as wart-hogs.

And, although their job looks like fun, sometimes it would be easier to dig ditches than cover some games.

THE RITUALS OF BASKETBALL

The first thing you must understand is that EVERYTHING is symbolic of something. I vividly recall a time near the end of a weekend drunk that Salvador Dali said to Sigmund Freud, "You know, Siggie: Sometimes a cigar is just a basketball."

The remark, as is often the case, meant little because Dali was speaking in Spanish and Freud was listening in German.

Later, I turned my life's work to analyzing that which others have neglected to study and latched upon the quandaries and perplexities of basketball. I perused the volumes outlining what supposedly was a history of the sport and quickly realized that past experts had missed the true significance of the so-called sport.

Basketball, I realized, is not a game of territorial acquisition and penetration, symbolic in its way of one army raiding the treasure-house of another country. No, basketball is a religious ritual that comes from the Old Testament and has been modified by several faiths through the centuries.

Basketball is based on the ritual of offering sacrifices.

The ball has taken over the symbolic significance of the former lambs or goats; the baskets have replaced the altars of old; and the courts are used as the sanctuary or nave. It is not accidental, therefore, that many boys and men claim to "worship" during the time of March Madness.

Each group of worshippers corresponds to one of the ancient tribes of Israel. (Consequently, most conferences have ten or twelve members.) Each team is charged with the task of out-offering the other tribe so that the first Tribe can receive the greater blessing.

You detect that this is related to the Cain and Abel struggle, but the fratricide is avoided by having a neutral tip-off, during which a priest throws the sacrifice into the air and the two tribes strive to gain possession of it. The more blessed tribal head (often the tallest) gets the offering.

Then the tribal head dribbles or throws the offering down the sacred area and approaches the altar (from the Latin *alta* for "high" since the net is higher than the worshippers and priests).

Formerly, the worshippers offered burnt offerings, but they slam and dunk to "burn" the net metaphorically. If the chief worshipper with the offering is touched by an opposing worshipper, he gets to make an unhindered offering, which was once called a peace offering, but is now known as a free throw.

If a tribesman violates a technical rule of the service, the other tribe gets to make either a trespass offering or an offering for the sins of ignorance, depending on the offense.

Since the advent of Christianity, the game has been modified to include both Gentile and Hebraic offenses. Christian decisions are settled in one of three circles, representing the Father, the Son, and Holy Ghost, while Hebrew disputes are decided from the side of the sacred area.

The two tribes, wearing the holy garments of Aaron, exhibit greed much in the same manner as the Spanish Conquistadors, who plundered the Americas and contributed the spoils to the Church. And again, stealing the sacrifices is proper, as long as no one is touched, probably because the other tribe is unclean. If a tribesman touches another, the abomination is atoned at the sacrifice line.

The two priests, their loud jaws reminiscent of the jaw bones of an ass that Samson used, blow whistles instead of trumpets, as at Jericho. They do not permit a tribe to wander in enemy territory for forty years. They also penalize worshippers for traveling, since that is symbolic of Moses' forty years of wandering before reaching the Promised Land (e.g., the sacred court). These offenses give the other worshippers possession of the offering.

Even as the congregation joins priests, rabbis, and ministers in modern worship, so do the congregations at the ball sacrifices. The tabernacle is filled with pews lining each side of the nave, and the congregation is seated after offering tithes at the door. During the sacrifices, the congregations stand and pray loudly how much their contributed: "Two bits, four bits, six bits, a dollar."

The priestesses or Vestal Virgins of old are represented by about six young ladies who suffer from St. Vitus Dance. There is now a peculiar custom in the ritual. Often these vestally once-virgins shout one prayer and the congregations rebel by shouting a different one.

The congregations are eternally faithful to their tribe of worshippers. At Florida State University, just for one example, the congregations will pray, "FSU, all the damn time!" or "Go to Hell, Gators."

During the service, the patriarch of each tribe (the coach) may disagree with the decisions of the priests. If he is unwise, he may leap to his feet and shout heresies, whereupon the priests penalize him with a technical foul (as opposed to former punishment of stoning him and scratching the flooring).

The tribe of worshippers that sacrifices the most receives the most blessings, and, at the end of the service, the congregations find out which tribe is the greater blessed by looking at a lighted sign, which represents the handwriting on the wall.

During the whole affair, a voice from heaven (now coming from a loud speaker) tells who sacrifices each offering or who must be punished.

Clearly, then, James A. Naismith has received too much credit for supposedly inventing the game in the 1890s. The game goes straight to the Bible and teaches us about cardinal and venal sins (three- or two-pointers from the field and one-point free-throws respectively), along with sins of omission or commission.

Sadly, due to the restrictions of the First Amendment about there being no state-established religion, it is only a matter of time before the U. S. Supreme Court rules the game unconstitutional at state-supported schools and colleges.

Until then, as the priests say, "Pray ball."

All Hail My Dictatorship ...or Else

I realize it came as a shock this morning when you woke up to discover that I had declared myself Dictator and Grand Hot-Stuff of the Simplified States of America (SSA).

You don't need to be alarmed because I've been judicious with my early edicts. I understand that, if the individual is weak, absolute power corrupts absolutely.

You see, *moderation* has been my watchword, and, as a wild-eyed moderate, I have ordered all immoderate people to be shot.

Already, I hear protests from a few knee-jerk critics who claim that I want to solve all problems with a hail of bullets and a brick wall.

These charges hurt me deeply, since I, as the Great Simplifier, find walls of wood, cement block, stone, coquina, or adobe to be equally satisfactory.

No doubt, you have already noticed several improvements in our country (or "my country," to be exact). For example, the TV news staffs who once engaged in on-camera "happy talk" have been shot.

Although the remaining TV reporters seem to be a humorless and apprehensive lot, let's acknowledge that they dash through the news in no time and are covering three times as many stories as before.

We no longer have to read reporters and columnists who have been gassing on about pre-season rankings in football or basketball. Their replacements have agreed that they can delay stories about rankings until a few weeks into the season.

Be forewarned: The Brick-Wall Brigade (BWB) is making appointments with any college graduate who says, "How 'bout *them* Dogs, Noles, Hogs, or Gators?" I am reasonable enough to let high school drop-outs misuse *them* and *those*, but not college students or graduates.

Yes, it's true that the B-W Brigade has probably taken care of many of the politicians in your state, but only those who thought that they were elected to line their pockets and massage their egos.

We note there are hundreds of vacancies in some state legislatures, where lawmakers sat through three or four months of dithering, only to pass everything in the last seventeen minutes of the final session, by having a blindfolded pizza delivery boy play pin-the-legislation.

In the future, their replacements will have to take the blindfolds off the delivery boys and give them a few weeks to read the bills.

Hollywood has been transformed. Those having "taken a brick wall" include the producers, the directors, nonliterary stars who insist on endless rewrites, and, of course, the accounting officers who were declaring that a film that has made $216 gadzillion has lost money and can't pay the promised percentage to a writer, actor, or investor.

The new kings and queens of Hollywood are now the writers, since they have thought of all the lines that Ted Bimbeau and Terri Bimbo have mouthed in their films.

Many Hollywood stars are defunct (Madonna, Sean Penn, Roseanne, and all actors better looking than I am; space does not permit me to list all of the latter). However, my main elimination was the terms *foley artist* and *gaffer* in film or TV credits. I'm not sure what either term means, but I suspect it's making fun of the Great Simplifier.

Cable company executives have some vacancies in their ranks. In the future, customers will only pay for the cable stations they actually watch. It came to me that, if I go into a bookstore to purchase a $20 book, I don't expect them to say, "It'll be $200,000 because Tomes-a-Gadzillion allows you access to a gadzillion books."

Speaking of ads, the S.S.A. is a quieter world. You will notice the absence of radio and TV pitchmen who used to SHOUT, SHOUT, SHOUT about DEALS, DEALS, DEALS at this or that car lot.

On the other hand, I am not an unreasonable tyrant. Media announcers have been given twelve months to be retrained so that they no longer refer to "low, low prices." One *low* will suffice unless they wish to stand in front of a brick, brick wall.

New cars will now come with a label telling when the smell of wet dogs and kids' vomit will overcome the new car smell.

I have ordered new endings or scenes for several movies, using computer representations of various characters, if necessary.

For example, at the end of *The Sands of Iwo Jima,* Sergeant Stryker (John Wayne) will no longer be shot in the back after taking a drag on a cigarette and saying he never felt better in his life.

Next, the shower scene in *Psycho* will be changed to a bubble-bath, and Janet Leigh will sing "I'm Gonna Wash That Psycho Right Outta My Hair." She will scare Norman Bates away with a rubber ducky.

Finally, *Chinatown* will end with a custard-pie fight, during which John Huston's wicked grandfather character will slip and wind up in a body cast. As the final credits roll, Jake Gittes (Jack Nicholson) will pour itching powder into the body cast.

It's been a busy day. If you disagree with any of the Great Simplifier's edicts, I encourage you to express your viewpoint in writing. Be sure to include an address where my associates may contact you. Oh, and let us know if there is a nice solid wall close by.

No Carols? Goodbye to Civilization

Some critics argue that Americans started pumping a hand-cart to hell when "The Lord's Prayer" was removed from public schools. Such poor reasoning suffers from what Roman logicians called *post hoc; ergo propter hoc*, which may be roughly translated as "the rooster on the post thinks he crowed the top off of Vesuvius."

Today's critics argue: The schools had relative peace up till the 1950s. Then prayer was abolished, and here we are today.

The argument, of course, is silly nonsense.

In truth, I realized back in the Hydrogen Bomb days of the 1950s that American civilization was being destroyed by the most powerful device known to humankind. I speak, of course, of the hula hoop.

Anyone who would put a hula hoop around his or her waist and wiggle it all about would stoop to other disgraces: smoking multi-leafed plants, holding up convenience stores, and listening to people claw at amplified guitars. (I will save my discussion of the Hokey Pokey Syndrome for a less trifling monograph.)

However, the removal of prayer and Christmas carols from the public schools did cause substantial damage, and it has ruined the word skills of many decades of students.

Early in this new century, an essay in my college composition class had only a vague mention of Christmas carols, and I said to the students, "We could have some specific carols mentioned, such as 'Silent Night,' 'We Three Kings,' and 'Joy to the World.'" I erred when I added, "You probably even know the school kids' parody of 'We Three Kings.'"

Not one head nodded.

Shocked, I asked again, "Are you *sure* you haven't heard the parody?"

That class had not, and I struck out when I checked with other classes.

In panic, I eventually started babbling, "I know they're not Politically Correct, but did you have Little Moron jokes when you were kids? Like, 'Why did the Little Moron live in a round house?' 'So he couldn't pee in the corner.'"

The students weren't so tasteless, though a couple had recently watched *Forrest Gump* on video again and wanted to prattle about that. Others were trying to guide the conversation toward such irrelevancies as whether Shemp was as good a Stooge as Curly.

To get them back on task (as we say in the chalk-and-talk biz), I turned to non-verbal areas. "How about mumbly peg? Did you do that?"

What's that?

"You take a pocket-knife and flip it off a finger, a knee, and elbow, competing with a friend to see who can make it stick in the ground most often. You can read about it in Robert Paul Smith's book, *Where Did You Go? Out. What Did You Do? Nothing.*"

They hadn't, and thought it was a stupid game, and the book had a dumb title, too.

"How about gross stuff? In the seventh grade, to gross out the girls and make the teachers wince, did you say 'great green greasy gobs of gory gorilla guts'?"

Only one or two smiled that they had, or would probably do it that afternoon. Most thought it was stupid, and gross.

Then it hit me: Kids aren't practicing Christmas carols, as each class prepares to sing one or two songs at a school concert. They aren't hanging around and playing with the words, and nobody is there to start them singing:

We three kings of Orient are,
Puffing on a rubber cigar.
It was loaded, it exploded,

BANG!

[Pause]

We two kings of Orient are,
Puffing on a rubber cigar.
It was loaded, it exploded.

BOOM!

[Another pause]

I one king of Orient are
Puffing on a rubber cigar.
It was loaded, it exploded.

BANG!

[Pause and all sing]

Si-lent night, Ho-ly night...

The parody enables a kid to explore grammar, particularly in the third stanza, where it stumbles into a subject-verb disagreement (e.g., "I...are" to rhyme with "rubber cigar").

You debate with your friends about changing it to "I one king of Orient am," but another pal notes it only ruins the joke.

One friend suggests, "Okay, let's work in 'Munching on a can of old Spam,'" but that's not satisfactory either.

A buddy wins the argument by saying that you could sing, "We one king of Orient are," which could at least refer to the lone singer and the bits and pieces of the other two, especially gobs of gory guts.

The parody trains the three singers to sing the words clearly and then bang out the explosion. They learn to wait a proper beat or two before starting the next stanza. Finally, they learn how to go from a rousing "We Three Kings" to a soothing "Silent Night" before snickering at their prowess.

A buddy may discuss the surrealistic elements in the parody: "I've never seen a *rubber* cigar."

"There are *bubble-gum* cigars," another observes. (Our setting is a small town, and not one in the group has even ridden on a city bus yet.)

"But no one would put a fire-cracker in a bubble-gum cigar."

Says another, "Then who'd put one in a rubber one? And who'd be stupid enough to try to smoke rubber?"

The stink of burning rubber naturally leads to a catalog of other gross smells and disgusting armpit noises before *rubber* reasserts itself and causes the group to challenge each other in rapidly repeating "rubber baby buggy bumper, rubber baby buggy bumper, rubber baby buggy bumper."

Alas, my buddies *could* have gone off and written Great American Novels, Plays, and Poems, but someone came by with a hula hoop and Caroler No. 1 tried it and became, in order, a drug-addict, a John Kerry Democrat, a C.P.A., and a Dubya Republican.

Caroler No. 2 wiggled it all about and drank himself to death while scheming ways to tie H-Bombs to himself and blow up Phil Rizzuto.

And Caroler No. 3 (i.e., yours truly) only spins circles with words, never ever with plastic hoops, no, sirree.

LET'S HANG THE WRITER

If you write consistently, you will make someone angry. That point was driven home again when someone hit the ceiling merely recalling a piece that I knocked off a year or so ago.

It started me thinking, but not about apologies, of course. That's because our family coat of arms features a pig sty, our ancestral slop bucket, the pig in a tartan, and the motto in English *Close Enough for Jazz*. Actually, the motto should be in Latin or French, but everyone in the family thinks the English is close enough for jazz.

More than a fiction writer, playwright, or poet, you will find that a journalist is likely to Offend Someone. We members of the general public may wish to burn a sexually titillating book, but we have to fight our mob instincts to keep from hanging reporters and disemboweling columnists.

We take offense so easily. For example, when I was a smart-aleck sports editor for *The Florida Flambeau* (a/k/a the *Flamboyant*), the student newspaper at Florida State, I referred to the Seminoles' team physician as "the sawbones."

Oddly enough, this man who went through medical school and cut up cadavers, hadn't learned to ignore disrespectful kids on a student newspaper.

A journalist learns early that there will *always* be people wanting Respect to be shown.

Another tempest at FSU occurred in the early 1960s (still the age of segregation), when Bob Hayes of Florida A&M was competing against athletes throughout the country, but not against the Seminole runners, who practiced only across town.

At my manual typewriter in the dorm, I wrote a pitiful first draft while nibbling on some take-out of grits, chicken-fried steak, a glob of sho'nuff, and a mint julep sans alcohol, suh. The piece would have made for some mighty fine readin' in *The Bugtussle Bugle*, but it was backward and provincial.

My paternalistic column, however, did make the valid point that our guys should be able to compete against Hayes.

My consciences (and fact-checkers), future attorney Vic Comolli of Santurce, Puerto Rico, and restaurateur Mel Keller of Clifton, New Jersey, shouted at me until I excised the Old South paternalism and produced a more enlightened and sensitive column. When it appeared, the campus had petitions from students, and a fair amount of debate and controversy. (Hayes and FAMU weren't invited, and the tournament wasn't held the next year.)

As a full-time journalist after graduation, I often covered high school football games on Friday nights in my home state. Since I lacked the heart, mind, and soul of a sports writer (not an oxymoron, by the way), I did not mind covering an inconsequential game between the Podunk High Yellow Jackets and the Hayseed High Tigers.

Since I had not been to either school and did not know any student or faculty member at either place, I could produce a totally objective story about Poduck's 15-9 victory over the Tigers. The story would have been equally objective if the Tigers had prevailed.

Yet Saturday would bring a phone call to the sports department from some girl from Hayseed High wailing, "Who wrote that *awful* story about Hayseed High?"

Being perverse, if I was working in the department that day, I would say with a cheerfulness that would torture the devil, "Why, I wrote that story, ma'am."

"Didn't you even *see* the game?" she would shriek. "How *could* you write that?"

And the conversation went on and on like that.

Long, long ago, a friend wrote a gentle, teasing column in which he joked mildly about his teeth and his dentist. He did not say that the dentist dressed up like Queen Victoria and went around saying, "*We* are not amused." But his dentist was not entertained and did not add up the free advertising that the gentle remarks in the column yielded. Instead, the sourpuss pouted because he felt he was not being shown Proper Respect.

A few years back, a North Florida friend wrote a column in which she joked about the chaos in the cafeteria of a day-care center. Day-care people reacted as if they had been accused of making lamp shades out of the rugrats in their care.

Moral: Bureaucracies and businesses are *not* amused about anything, even if you concede that a rug-rat will barely make a decent shade for a night-light.

A final example: A very long time ago, a police chief in my home state was not amused by a comic piece I did about an actual jail-break. Two or three prisoners had escaped from the old jail. That is embarrassing enough, but they did not overpower guards, did not break out through an air-duct, and did not slip away while working as trustees.

Instead, they dug out with (get this now) a spoon.

It does not matter how you ask, "Chief, what caliber spoon *was* that?" Write the story any way you wish, and the chief and city council will look like buffoons.

So, with a demolition course before you, how do you negotiate a safe path away from the pits that explode with Great Offense?

If you write humor or present an opinion, you have to wear armor. People often complain because of self-interest (*à la* sawbones, tooth-yankers, and little girls who date losing football players).

If you are writing with a mean or backward spirit, you may want to see if you can grow beyond it.

If you are reporting and freelancing, then make sure your facts are as correct, objective, and balanced as possible, then put your fingers to the keyboard and fire away.

'TAIN'T FUNNY, MCGEE

One of my wife's biggest disappointments came when she discovered that I am an Alabama-style Milton Berle, someone who has stolen his best jokes and lines from the Masters of My Generation.

Her second disappointment came when she found out that the one-liners didn't stop. As she complained about living twenty-four hours a day with a comedian, I even began mumbling in my sleep, "Take my wife, please," which only brought hard looks over the morning muffins and yogurt.

Keep in mind that each generation has its own purveyors of humor, and mine included Mark Twain, James Thurber, Don Marquis, Robert Benchley, Will Cuppy. These are the most important ones. But I also loved Josh Billings, Petroleum V. Nasby, Mr. Dooley, H. Allen Smith and Thorne Smith. You will note that my so-called generation read books, since only Thurber and H. Allen Smith were still alive when I began attending Rim-Shot U.

Thanks to the X-rated comics on cable comedy-club shows, Rim-Shot U. now relies on punching up a stand-up comedian's bland statements with obscenities. A movie comedy thrives on flatulence and masturbation. *Tsk-tsk.*

That's not at all what I heard on radio courtesy of Freeman Gosden and Charles Correll ("Amos & Andy"), Edgar Bergen and Charlie McCarthy, Jack Benny, Fibber McGee and Molly, the Great Gildersleeve, Abbott and Costello, and in the waning days of old-style radio Stan Freberg and the records of Tom Lehrer.

The original *Mad* magazine came along about the time of Freberg, and their sophomoric humor appealed to me as a tenth grader and gave me cryptic phrases that I still pitch in conversations whenever there is a lull: "Potzeebie?... By the way, Ed. How's your mom?" (Don't ask me to explain.) While you were leaving the scene with a couple of friends, *Mad* gave you some practical exit lines: "Hup, hup, hup" (well, you really did have to be there for that). They seem to mix well with Spike Jones' recordings, especially the impressive "Beetle-BUM," which, properly delivered, can set an archbishop to cussing.

Despite the power of television in the mid-1950s, I reserved Friday night to listen to the radio high-jinks of Phil Harris, but, when I skipped it a couple of Fridays, the show betrayed me by going off the air, permanently.

The big eye then trapped us.

In mornings, we were hypnotized by that Indian chief test pattern until our only station came on at seven o'clock. The boob tube, however, did offer Ernie Kovacs and Steve Allen (the latter with Don Knotts, who was the nervous man; Tom Poston, who didn't know his name; Bill Dana, whose name was u-no-wot; and Louie Nye, who was "Gordon Hathaway" and greeted Allen with "Hi ho, Steverino").

If you were like me, all of the Masters' work got stirred together, and you found yourself using their lines, sometimes at inappropriate times:

A woman might come up to you and ask, "Is Chloë here?" That only causes you to turn and holler, "Chloë! Where are you, you old bat?" (Spike Jones)

And she asks, "Would you call Leroy instead?" And you go "Leeee-roy," with a falsetto vibrato because that's the way that Gildersleeve called his nephew.

"Would you taste this?" someone asks, handing you a spoonful of stew being prepared. "Don't bother. My taste buds were shot off in the war." (Tom Lehrer)

You need to rendezvous with someone at noon at the mall. "Okay, let's Simonize our watches." (Amos and Andy)

Being philosophical to an unhappy friend, you say, "Life is like a sewer: What you get out of it depends on what you put into it." (Again, Tom Lehrer)

Sometimes jokes back-fire. For example, Jack Benny had a routine in which Mel Blanc could not pronounce *cinnamon.*

He kept saying "Cimarron."

Then Benny would correct him with "CIN-na-mon," whereupon Mel would say, "I know: Cimarron."

The routine was a cousin to the routine with Blanc, as a Mexican, answered "*Sí*, Sue, Sy, sore" when Jack asked questions requiring the following respectively: a yes answer, his sister's name, his uncle's name, and the state of his bottom after a long ride on a burro.

When I began asking my parents to pass the Cimarron toast, they gave each other Worried Parental Looks ("Is this the sort of thing John Dillinger did just before he went bad?"). They corrected me, gently, to protect my tender ego.

So I delivered the punch-line again, "Right: Cimarron."

Thirty years later, my father was rocking on the front porch and reminiscing about when we boys were boys. He said in the confessional tone that a parent uses to admit that, yes, at one time you seemed destined to become an ax murderer or the village idiot: "For the longest time, you couldn't pronounce *cinnamon.* We were down-right embarrassed for you and hoped you didn't say it out in public anywhere."

Similarly, the joke, "Nine out of ten people mispronounce *liberry*," simply won't do if you are a teacher. Not only will (some) students do double-takes and gasp, "And *he's* a teacher," you also find that you get so fond of the joke that you inadvertently say, for example, to a visiting team from an accrediting association, "The next group of faculty you want to talk to is in conference room in the liberry."

Before you can say, "Did you know that nine—", you overhear someone whispering, "You should have heard him order cinnamon toast this morning."

In writing or doing humor, however, always be conscious of the critics out there. My wife, for example, says, "You have been doing that line for nearly forty years."

"Hey," I protest, "Jack Benny based an entire career on stinginess, poor violin playing, and age thirty-nine."

"*He* had better writers!"

NO PARLEZ-VOUS FRENCH ...AND IT SHOWS?

Despite America's emphasis on multi-culturalism, God forbid that the U.S. should really stress the learning of other languages. We Americans are not like the elite of previous centuries and in the early part of the 20th Century. They were schooled in Latin, French, sometimes Greek, and German.

Rather than risk a caning from the headmaster, these students spent their nights translating Cicero, having learned already from Caesar that all of Gaul was divided into three parts.

For centuries, Latin was the International Language. In the 17th to 19th Centuries, it was French. Now the International Language is English.

Students and graduates plowed through Gibbon's *History of the Decline and Fall of the Roman Empire* well equipped to handle the passages in Latin when Gibbon discussed the perversities of Caligula or Commodus. (However, sometimes after wading through a Latin dictionary to see what delicious horror Caligula was getting up to next, you found that Gibbon was only gassing on in Latin about the weather or the price of pumpernickel in ancient Rome.)

It's handy that, since Americans won't learn other languages, we are best served by obeying George Orwell's admonition to avoid foreign words and phrases altogether. Orwell wanted things said in English.

When reporting on high school sports years ago, I learned the wisdom of Orwell's advice. Despite my not having had French, I used a dictionary to check my phrase and wrote something like this: "With 1:57 left in the game, quarterback John Jones executed the coup de grace with a 15-yard touchdown pass to halfback Sam Smith."

It was risky business to attempt such erudition for a mere sporting page. While I was writing the story, I let a juggling challenge overcome my better judgment: One hand juggled the container developing a roll of film; another hand juggled the statistics; the right foot juggled the play-by-play I had chronicled along the sideline. So the left foot (the sinister one) needed to juggle a French expression.

All of this juggling went on while I was battling an 11 p.m. deadline.

Finally, I turned it all in, knowing that the French phrase should have been underlined or italicized. However, in the "hot metal" days, you dared not to require the linotypist to take off the heavy case of regular type to load the heavy container of italics.

In addition, the phrase needed a hat on it: *coup de grâce*. Headgear notwithstanding, only a psychopath would have demanded an accent mark from the composing room.

"You want a hat on the 'a'?" an irritated linotypist would have asked.

"Yes, sir. That's what it looks like. It, the phrase, means 'stroke of mercy.'"

Long suffering sigh and a call to the foreman. "Smitty! Get your butt over here. The fool kid wants a hat on the 'a' and probably a corset and petticoat on the 'p.'"

So that scene never occurred because of my natural wariness: Even then, I knew never to play cards with a guy named Doc, never to date a girl named Bertha who has a snake tattoo on her face, never date a girl who can cuss better than you, and never to ask a printer to put hats on lowercase vowels. These rules have served me well in life.

The next day when our afternoon paper came out, I compared with satisfaction my statistics with those of the rival, now defunct *Birmingham Post-Herald* (whose sissy stringer probably relied on the guys up in the pressbox keeping official score). I skimmed my own story, admiring the way I had worked in names of a runner who had gained so many yards and (this is impressive) the name of the *defensive* player who tackled him (you didn't find that in the *P-H* story).

But then I blanched: Some agent of the devil, some regular sports writer editing copy, some proofreader, or even an enterprising typesetter, had put an "e" on *coup*! My story referred to a *coupe* and not a *coup*! As far as the world knew, the dummy with the byline was the only one stupid enough to conjure up a "coupe de grace," which (what *would* they think?) would be a two-door automobile of mercy.

In the decades since that shameful episode, I've learned that French is also dangerous to others.

Voilà, for example, has maimed many writers, though an English speaker, thanks to a gesture, can get away with exclaiming, "*Voilà*!" Listeners will understand that he or she means "and there," "it's done," "I'm satisfied," or "Bob's your uncle" (though mine was Joe).

However, in writing, even if you type it correctly, the word may have to go through an editor or another typist, and it may come out as "Viola." That only causes the readers to ponder all the Violas in the their lives: There's Saint Viola, who stood only eighteen inches tall and had six strings, and there was Viola Poovey in my third-grade class in Vidalia, Georgia, who could knock a dragonfly out of the air with a stream of tobacco, and others, of course.

Even worse, perhaps someone relies on phonetic spelling (risky at best with the way Americans pronounce French), and he comes up with a sentence like this: "Then you put the cake batter in the over at 400 degrees for 30 minutes. When it's done, walla, you will enjoy the best cake you've ever made." *Walla*, Viola?

So what have we learned, besides useful information about cards, tattooed women, and printers? Never use a foreign word when an English word will do.

Sacre blew!* Got through *that* without another error.

(*Yes, I know.)

WENI, WIDI, WECI? GET SERIOUS, JULIE

Many years ago, my worst fears as a student at Pensacola High surfaced during period four's Latin I class. As in a Hitchcock film, the 10th grade class opened innocently enough, with Miz Mona Durge teaching us our first sentence: "America est patria mea" (which means "America is my country").

With that easy sentence, we learned that in Latin the modifying possessive pronoun follows the noun. This was a harmless enough insight, but hardly the clue as to why Rome conquered almost every camel, haberdashery, and barbecue joint in the Mediterranean.

Gradually, we struggled through our early lessons on declensions and conjugations. We even found that Latin words have gender. A bird (*avis*) and a bee (*apis*), for example, were feminine, while an elephant (*elephantus*), a horse (*equus*), and a lion (*leo*) were masculine. A lamp (*lucerna*) was feminine, but its light (*lumen*) was neuter.

We discovered that Latin also had cases for nouns and pronouns. One had a familiar name, but the others had been renamed. The nominative was the same in English grammar, but Latin grammar referred to the possessive as the genitive. It also had a dative case for indirect objects and objects of prepositions and an accusative case for direct objects. Don't ask about the vocative case. You really don't want to know. The Latin cases differed in their singular and plural endings, or they did *not* vary, lest we detect some order and feel like trusting Cicero (meaning "chickpea" and probably pronounced *KEE-ker-o*, by the way).

Then the Latin translations dragged us into swamps of strange and obscure sentences, especially for those of us too lazy to learn the vocabulary for each lesson.

A decent Latin sentence at this stage might be translated into this: "The spears flying and striking the shields, the phalanx marched forward, the Gauls ready to flee."

That awkward sentence should have tormented an English teacher, say, Pretty Miss Wilcox in period five English, except for two reasons. First, Pretty Miss Wilcox devoted her career to perching on her desk and hypnotizing us boys with the swinging of her movie-starlet legs. Second, Pretty Miss Wilcox suffered nicotine fits and would have slit any throat in the class for an unfiltered Lucky Strike.

Such sentences always seemed to verge on dangling modifiers, although things that dangle, such as the limbs of Pretty Miss Wilcox, definitely had their allure.

In first-year Latin, I should have brought the linguistic peculiarities of the old tongue to the attention of Miz Durge, but, like Medusa turning the ancients to stone, she neutralized my best intentions.

With her strands of blue hair hovering like a wicked aura in a cheap sci-fi film, Miz Durge wielded potent weapons: the largest, saddest eyes in the Florida Panhandle. Her glasses magnified her blue headlights until they were the size of Pontiac hubcaps. She could make Stone Mountain feel guilty for not being a mound of mashed potatoes and gravy. These hypnotic eyes even intruded into any dreams about the remarkable legs of Pretty Miss Wilcox ("Howard, how *could* you think of legs, when you could be thinking of phalanxes?").

So, torturing each of us in turn, Miz Durge worked her way down the rows and finally called upon me, as I hid behind the

Latin I Mountain, left guard Maynard Tagwell III in the sixth seat in the second row from the window. She fixed those sad-and-blues on me and asked sweetly, "And how would *you* translate this, Howard?"

Poorly, I quickly proved. I knew I had betrayed her; then I writhed in her gaze and twitched in my seat like a sophomoric Count Dracula struggling to escape the sun.

Thanks to a transfer from Uncle Sam, our Navy household soon relocated to Norfolk, where I entered Norview High's Latin I class. Miz Lipschitz and her students were also studying John Flagg Gummere and Annabel Horn's *Using Latin* from Scott Foresman, but they were two weeks *behind* Miz Durge's spirited pace.

This newcomer from Florida, therefore, reveled in the glory of Natural Scholarship and Genius. Can you believe such genius in this shy, goofy kid with the monocle and top hat? Alas, the Academic Halo was knocked loopy when we caught up to where I had left Pensacola.

For consistency's sake, I found that Miz Durge and Miz Lipschitz both emphasized that the "v" in Latin was pronounced as "w." Thus, we discovered that Gaius Julius Caesar's manly "I came, I saw, I conquered," was *not* pronounced in a hairy-chested manner as "Veni, vidi, vici," as you might intone "victor, viewer, victorious."

No, no. Julie-baby—this hard-nosed conqueror, this thug (according to some bitter historians)—was actually saying, "Weni, widi, weci."

We guys exchanged glances and rolled our eyes about that Roman weenie. No self-respecting Roman thug was going to talk like Peewee Herman or Ed Grimley, Jr., I should say.

Ages and eons later, I learned that German scholars of Latin had insisted on the *v*-to-*w* pronunciation. In German, a Volkswagen is pronounced as "Folks-vahgen."

Back to the story.

During that year at Norview, Caesar taught me about putting sentences together. The principles about Latin frequently applied to English sentences. As you struggle to decide what is the subject, its modifiers, the verb, and tense, you automatically develop skills to use in English sentences.

Moreover, you build a body of words that you find valuable in figuring out English. The names of our relatives, of course, give us *pater* and *mater*, along with *frater* and *soror* (all pretty obvious), and you understand why your Uncle Al is called avuncular (*avunculus* for "uncle") and whom you may have bumped off if you are arrested for *uxor*icide (the wife).

As the years rolled by, we ex-Latin students corrected others' misuse of Latin, and, then as our knowledge faded, we began to make atrocious mistakes ourselves.

For example, some people transform *etc.* into *et. cetera.* There's no period after *et*, which is the entire word for "and," while *c.* is the abbreviation for "the other, the rest of, the others" (reserved for objects, not people).

Then, if you write the old gag that *Antlers in the Treetops* was composed by Hoogoose D. Moose and others, you may wish to stay with English. But if you say "and others" in Latin, you will need to write it *et al.* (the shortened form of *et alia*, "and others," referring to people). It is never written as *et. al.* or *etal.*, although Madonna's cones won't fall off if you do.

Recently in a dark alley, the Latin Goon Squad slapped me silly and pummeled me until I promised to use *e.g.* (*exempli gratia*) only in place of "for example." They made me stop misusing *i.e.* (*id est*) and shouted that it should only be used for "that is," when something needs to be explained.

At first, the beatings I suffered over *qv* and *cf* prompted condemnations from Amnesty International. Unfortunately, their chief investigator was a Latinist, who glared at my error, denounced me, and, while chanting, "*Amo*, *amas*, *amat*," rabbit-punched me senseless for twenty-seven instructive minutes, though I felt that "*Odo, odas, odat*" would have been more appropriate (*amo* = love; *odo* = hate).

Sometime during this love-chant, I'm afraid I scribbled a confession about stealing Wrigley Field and snuffing out Julius Caesar, James Garfield, and Jimmy Hoffa.

Anyway, *qv* comes from *quod vide* ("which see") and would refer a reader to another work.

Now trust me on this next one, since I only lie about RRBTs (i.e., Really, Really Big Things):

One *Cf* refers to "centerfielder," meaning a Christian who hightails it to the center of the Coliseum to delay his being eaten by the lions. It's true, really.

A second *Cf* is the symbol in the sciences for "Californium," the main ingredient that causes bad acting in made-for-TV movies.

In addition, *CF* (in caps) has nothing to do with Latin. In English, it only refers to "carried forward," "centrifugal force," "cost and freight," and "cystic fibrosis."

I hope you took notes on the above, since it reflects half of what I learned at Florida State and everything from my six years in the Army National Guard protecting Bessemer, Alabama, from the atheistic hordes of communism.

All right. I hear you. I'll 'fess up.

In Latin, *cf* comes from the imperative form of *conferre*, meaning "to compare." Therefore, you would use *cf* if you wanted the reader to compare one book or essay with another work.

In closing, I must admit that *et al* could be used in another context. Let's say that you and some friends were camping in the mountains during a time of poor visibility, and you were all making a giant pot of Mulligan stew, and your Uncle Al fell in while you were all distracted trying to decide whether to pitch in kumquats or rutabagas, and you all stirred the pot and then slurped and gulped down your entire culinary creation.

If all of the above did occur, someone might then ask, "Holy heartburn, what have we done?"

At this point, some gourmand would naturally answer: "Et Al."

The avuncular stew, at a minimum, would certainly make you cry "uncle."

HIGH TECH LAYOUT VS. PURE HOGWASH

"Aarrgh!" I've just thrown two magazines across the room and convinced Panda Cat that the day has come when I turn psychotic and do in all the black and white cats in the household.

The old ladies are wiser. Granny Mo opens one eye and then resumes her drooling on the new couch. Princess Maddie ignores me, probably realizing that some magazines have once again infuriated me with something in their layout that's stupid, stupid, stupid.

She's right. A science-fiction entertainment magazine has put its page numbers over graphics like the left/right arrows you find in a Microsoft program. Another magazine has laid out its table of contents as if it were the menu page for Microsoft for Magazines, and both magazines have incorporated the little headings and options that you find in a Windows-type program.

And, of course, I'm infuriated because I am apparently the only person in North America who realizes that magazines and newspapers are NOT computer programs.

Listen to me, you high technoids who work in the print medium. Listen to my revealed truth because I am armed with a loaded rubber chicken and a seltzer bottle, and, by God, I am dangerous:

- If it is on paper, you do NOT interact with a newspaper or magazine, except by reading it, thinking about it, and discussing the articles or artwork with others.
- You do not need little icons to click your mouse on so you can turn the page or go to the front or the back of the publication. That is because (pay attention, since this is revolutionary) you just flip the pages, or even turn them one by one. Sometimes, if you are lying in a hammock, even the wind will turn them for you.

Ironically, the technoids looked at the generally difficult world of computers and figured that Joe Sixpack would not know what to do with programs that required typing in such commands as

"c:\ razzledazzle/ipsoquid|do|wop|a-|lula/yomama2."

So, they devised a system where folks like me (known as morons to the professionals) could click on icons or images of what we want to do. Their shortcuts eat up a lot of memory, but they do make the computers user-friendly.

However, a magazine or a newspaper is as user-friendly as you can get. A child can turn the pages and admire the pictures. Once the child learns how to read, he or she can even comprehend what the magazines and newspapers are saying.

Unfortunately, many in the print medium really do not believe in their product, so they steal layout ideas from *USA Today* (which is trying to be like television). They steal from *CNN Headline News* or *Fox News* (which suffers from Macintoshosis, with a rash of on-lineitis). And they steal from the ad world, which has been purloining visuals from inept snapshots and home movies of Aunt Martha and Uncle Boyd (jiggle that camera, aim left, aim right, keep everything out of focus, make everyone swallow a Dramamine and reach for a barf bag).

Another magazine has fallen in love with color on its pages. The story type is probably 10-point (a little smaller than what you are reading); the type is black, but the mag has put the black type over a dark red on these two pages and over a dark green on two others.

From a distance, it LOOKS GOOD, but (and I maintain that this next observation reflects a serious deficiency) YOU CAN NOT READ the type.

You will understand the effect if you will take a page of a newspaper and, before reading it, pour on some gravy or raspberry yogurt.

Back in the 1960s, a silly Canadian academic, Marshall McLuhan, lucked up when the media liked his axiom, "The medium is the message" and then his later ten-cent pun, "The medium is the massage."

Never mind that he spent eighty percent of his writing quoting such visual medium whiz kids as William Shakespeare, Andrew Marvell and William Wordsworth, the media put him on the mountain-top and crawled up there for his pronouncements and wisdom. The whole decade and much of the next one were devoted to people grappling with the notion that the fast-paced images of television would revolutionize the world. And we'd be astounded at the Wonder Kids from the next generation because, like, wow, they'd pick up exciting new mental capabilities, man.

Unfortunately, we have found that this basically meant a ten-second attention-span.

Prodded by McLuhan, MTV, and advertising's spastic hand-held cameras, the print medium tries to become more NOW.

However, I have spread out before me a couple of magazines and newspapers. The newspaper has jagged edges on its columns (to "give it white space" and "let the page breathe"), color in the headlines and subheads (anemic red and barf green), and a New Look.

And, guess what?

The page is gray and boring. Once you step away a bit and ignore the ineffective color, the page looks like something laid out by Rufus Slickpants for the weekly edition of *The Two Egg Chronicle.*

TV, movies, and MTV have brought us some powerful images over the years: Cary Grant running across the cornfield, the Kennedy cortege, the Robert Palmer girls (*pant pant*). In the print world, *Life* magazine and others have given us outstanding images, from such eminent photographers as Robert Capa and even Weegee.

But just what are you doing, Marshall McLuhanites? Look at the excuses for photographs in typical papers today:

Page 1 may have lucked up with a so-so photo. Page 2 strikes out, all gray matter, mug shots, and weather graphics. Page 3 strikes out; page 4 ditto; in fact, the first section lacks a single memorable photo.

The second section, though, has a photo on its page 1. But what's this? It's a plaque presentation, two men standing side by side grinning like idiots. Page 2 is text, and so on. You can go through entire magazines and newspapers without seeing one photograph worth looking at for more than one to three seconds.

Ah, you ask: What's the point of all this ranting, or am I only having a bad freckle day?

Magazines and newspapers exist because they *print* articles, stories, and columns. Cartoons, photographs, headlines and graphics exist to make it easier to read the publications. Sometimes photographs of accidents or disasters complement the stories. At other times, they help a page to stay visually alive.

However, when the headlines and graphics take over, the editors have lost sight of their job. When they think that the print medium is obsolete and doomed, they have lost their professional souls.

Oops! Maddie the Princess is interrupting my ravings by rocking her head back and forth, mouth open and gagging, but, thanks to a subtle shift of the magazine with my foot, something slides beneath her mouth when her lunch and the hairball are disgorged.

Hmm, interesting effect. Perhaps I should send it to the magazine. The blob works so well with their layout.

KNOW THE NEEDS OF YOUR CHARACTERS

When the actor David Niven turned from writing excellent memoirs to attempting a novel, he asked advice from a prominent novelist (perhaps Graham Greene). The old pro said, "Well, it'd be helpful if you'd have a beginning, a middle, and an end."

Niven produced a competent piece of work, but others have hit a wall when trying to complete a novel manuscript.

For example, the late Ed Bradley of *60 Minutes* remembered when he was a young man in Paris: "One day, I saw this stunning woman standing in a doorway, and I got very excited and began writing this wonderful scene. Except that I didn't have a plot or characters or dialogue or any notion of where I was going. And that was the end of my writing novels."

One aspiring novelist tells me that she sits at the keyboard, perhaps thinking of herself. She tippy-taps on the keys for 1,000 words, then 2,000, and finally hits a wall at 5,000 words.

How does an Ed Bradley or any others learn to break through this barrier?

First of all, the trick is in knowing the characters so that the writers understand what each one wants or *thinks* he or she needs. Second, the writers have to understand why other characters don't want the protagonist to get what he or she is after.

Let's look at MGM's version of *The Wizard of Oz* by L. Frank Baum and be sure to credit the scriptwriters, Noel Langley, Florence Ryerson, and Edgar Allan Wolfe.

Each character in the story wants something, but each also has someone else who wants to prevent him or her from getting it.

Dorothy (on the farm) needs someone to listen to her b&w problem, but Hunk (Ray Bolger), Zeke (Bert Lahr), Hickory (Jack Haley), and Uncle Henry (Charley Grapewin) all need to finish their chores.

Auntie Em (Clara Blandick) finally listens and learns that Dorothy needs someone to rescue and protect Toto from the hard-hearted Miss Gulch (Margaret Hamilton).

The adults feel they need to obey the law when Miss Gulch produces a court order, but Dorothy doesn't want to go along with legal mumbo-jumbo that will destroy her dog.

Miss Gulch needs Toto put away for revenge against Toto's being a nuisance.

After the tornado and Dorothy's arrival in Oz, almost everyone in the kingdom needs something:

—Dorothy needs to get home and, like Odysseus, goes on a journey that has complications at each stage.

—The Scarecrow needs a brain; the Tin Man, a heart; and the Lion, courage. They all believe they need to get to the Wizard (Frank Morgan), the solver of all problems; in order to thrive, the Wizard, of course, needs distance, respect, and illusion.

—The Wicked Witch of the West, by contrast, needs revenge and justice. After all, the fall of the house of Em and Henry snuffed out her sister. In addition, she wants her late sister's ruby-red slippers. She rightfully believes that Dorothy would have trouble in a probate court claiming the shoes are hers, despite the claims of that busybody Glinda the Good Witch of the South. She is also tormented by the obstacle posed by Dorothy and needs to undercut and torment Dorothy at every turn.

What is so excellent about the lines given to Margaret Hamilton's Wicked Witch is that we understand what she wants and why she wants it. A sublime villain, she is only on the screen for about twelve minutes. She is like Lugosi's Dracula in that, even when she's not on the scene, we feel her presence. We know what she would say and how she might react.

We understand the needs of effective villains, even though we may hope that the protagonist will dash water on them or drive a stake into their hearts.

Similarly, in *The African Queen* (screenplay by James Agee and John Huston from C. S. Forester's novel), we can trace how each character wants something and frequently is denied that desire. Some examples:

Rose Sayer's brother needs respect and recognition, but the church relegated the Reverend Samuel Sayer (Robert Morley) to missionary work in an obscure section of Africa. He is thwarted by the Kaiser's soldiers, who even burn the village and his church.

Rose (Katharine Hepburn) has needed a life of her own and a meaningful relationship, but she has followed her brother to Africa. There, she perceives that she needs to care for her brother, but he succumbs to injuries after being clubbed by the Germans. Then she needs to relocate since their home has been burned down. On the boat of Charlie Allnut (Humphrey Bogart), she needs to exact revenge on the Huns, but is almost checked by German gunners and seemingly unnavigable waters.

Charlie has only needed something to smoke, something to drink, and, no doubt, someone to have sex with. The war changes his universe and leaves him without a safe harbor. Now, he needs to escape from the Germans and to get Rose to safety. Trapped with her, he needs to keep her from pouring out his liquor and, when she tames him, he needs her physically.

Finally, having taken on her vision, he needs to help her sink the *Louisa.*

Plotting, therefore, begins with effective characters. Some characters want something specific, but they are opposed by those who don't want them to have that something. Once writers think out these "needs," they should strive to end up with the following:

1. A lead character is introduced at the start of the manuscript and dominates the action. The reader needs to be able to identify with this character, whether a Dorothy, a Rose, or a Hamlet.

2. The character is immediately faced with an urgent problem (e.g., get home to the farm or make it to a lake to sink an enemy ship), something that must be done or dealt with; however, there doesn't seem to be a way that he or she can do it.

3. The lead character faces a series of complications (field of poppies and crabby apple trees for one; waterfalls, a broken prop, and leeches for the other). Each difficulty frustrates his or her efforts to solve the problem or deal with the problem. Tension builds up with each complication.

4. The character finally reaches a crisis point, an emotional and dramatic high point of the action (capture by the Wicked Witch or the Germans). Defeat looms on the horizon despite his or her best efforts.

5. Finally, the lead character resolves the problem and brings about one of two outcomes: success or defeat (but a defeat in which some new insight emerges).

If manuscripts have frozen in place, the writers should see if the protagonists have anyone disagreeing with them and thwarting them. If not, the writers need effective antagonists to drive the action forward.

Finally, if aspiring writers are still searching for direction in life and, in an aimless way, pop a flash drive into their laptop, they want to avoid making the protagonists too autobiographical. Often, such protagonists spend their days drinking adult beverages and flirting with characters who appear in the manuscript, but to little purpose, since there is no story.

But even an aimless protagonist becomes effective when, as with Luke in Donn Pearce's *Cool Hand Luke* (screenplay by Pearce and Frank Pierson) or Ken Kesey's Randall Patrick McMurphy in *One Flew over the Cuckoo's Nest*, he fixates enough to fight authority or normality. If there is Nurse Rachet or the Captain constantly arranging for a lobotomy or saying, "What we have here is a failure to communicate," the narrative will often write itself.

WHAT PRODUCES A PIG'S BREAKFAST?

The television program ended, and the female writer in our household turned to me and sighed, "Well, THAT was a pig's breakfast."

Since I like science-fiction, sometimes the offending show was an episode of the often well-done *X-Files*, but it could also be *Star Trek: Deep Space 9*, that big muddle called *Star Trek: Voyager* (in its first two seasons), *Torchwood*, or perhaps a film.

Frequently, competent actors delivered their lines, an adequate director set up the shots, and a reasonably skilled editor assembled the whole package.

But the teleplay or screenplay had gaping holes, or it was just stupid, or, if it was a sequel, it violated the ground rules laid down for the series.

Hollywood frequently takes the position that the people out there in the boonies won't notice the problems. That attitude, of course, enables Lala-land to continue writing some sloppy lulus, or to go through enough rewrites of a once-sensible script until asininity emerges.

Harlan Ellison believes the latter occurred back in the 1960s when Gene Roddenberry gutted a plot element from his *Star Trek* episode, "City on the Edge of Forever": drug peddling on the *Enterprise* (in the episode, an accidentally wired Dr. McCoy ended up in 1930s America).

I maintain, however, that Ellison (a/k/a/ The Archon of Eccentricity) was being self-indulgent, since Roddenberry never intended that the *Enterprise* was to be a Microcosm of Social Problems. It was not a hard-boiled *Naked Space* following in the footsteps of *Naked City*, but a *Wagon Train for Space*.

To use computer lingo, certain stories have specific defaults, certain facts, that are not changeable. For example, if you were writing a Road Runner-Wile E. Coyote cartoon, you must keep it in the desert (sorry, having alligators in Florida chase Road Runner won't do), you may not have the characters talk (too bad, only *beep-beep* for the bird, not "To beep or not to beep, that is the beeping question"), and you must not have the Coyote capture the Road Runner (alas, a final gag with Wile E. Coyote's Arizona Fried Road Runner franchise won't do).

Of course, sometimes these defaults are not present at the creation, but evolve over time: Mr. Spock's stoic intellectualism and the Vulcan neck pinch did not emerge until several episodes after *Star Trek* first aired.

Orders from above can create pigs' breakfasts. One movie sequel, for example, referred to the first movie as the film "that set the rules," the second film as the film "that bends the rules," and the third film as the one that "breaks all the rules." In effect, they argue that they are too lazy, or greedy, to keep consistency in their universe.

Idealism can also deep-six the rules, as we can see with Gene Roddenberry's Star Trek franchise. He ordained that *The Next Generation* crew would not squabble, but would have learned to Get Along With Each Other. We are supposed to forget that the classic series was supposed to have taken place a mere seventy years earlier (warp speed for evolution).

Since CONFLICT is the alpha, omega, and wormhole of good fiction and drama (human vs. human, human vs. self, human vs. God, human vs. Them), Roddenberry gutted that on *TNG*'s *Enterprise.*

Aliens 3, on the other hand, ignored the defaults laid down in the two earlier movies and became a general all-around pig's breakfast. In the second film, the humans used flame-throwers to fight, with some success, against the double bicuspid monsters. However, in the third film, an alien is submerged in molten metal and—guess what, dear heart?—springs out of it *à la* the ending of *Carrie*. The film opened with two key characters from the second film already killed; thus, it wasted many dramatic possibilities. (There is much, much more wrong, but let us move on.)

On the plus side, the often superior writing on an old British series, *Blake's 7*, helped the viewers to overlook the series' two-bit FX. One refreshing change involved a handsome anti-hero, Kerr Avon (Paul Darrow), who looked out after Numero Uno first and his shipmates last, and then only if their survival would help *him* stay alive. When Roj Blake (Gareth Thomas) and some crew members teleported down on a dangerous mission (a typical James T. Kirk affair), Avon took the sensible position: "I'm not expendable, I'm not stupid, and I'm not going."

The second season opened without the noble and idealistic Blake, since Thomas wearied of playing the space freedom fighter. Eventually, the front office pressured the writers to take the edge off Avon and to make him more heroic—never mind consistency.

Similarly, the second season of another old British series, *Space 1999*, featured a disturbing change-about. The writing in the first year appeared to emulate the serious demeanor of *2001: A Space Odyssey*, but apparently someone objected to their detachment and icy professionalism. The second year opened with John Koenig (Martin Landau) joking and laughing with Dr. Helena Russell (Barbara Bain). Apparently, having "mooned" half a galaxy, they acquired a sense of humor.

Sometimes scripts become the morning fare of our porcine friends because the concept is so formulaic that it exhausts the writers. A British comic, for example, made fun of a typical classic *Doctor Who* scene by shouting, "Quick, let's run down the hallway!" Why? Because that seems to be what the Doctor and the companion spent most of the mundane episodes doing.

Frank Gorshin (though doing a competent job with what he had) appeared in one of the silliest of classic *Trek* shows. Thanks to very obvious make-up, half of his face is white and half is black, and, of course, his people dislike others on their planet who are black and white on the other sides (on an off-week, that was Deep Thinking for *ST*). Gorshin spent much of the episode running down the corridor of the *Enterprise.*

The Voyage to the Bottom of the Sea from Irwin Allen's slop-bucket had a couple interesting episodes, but it essentially employed three story-lines, actually two of them:

1. Admiral Nelson turns into a werewolf and terrorizes the *Seaview* until he's changed back.

2. A giant something (e.g., seaweed or jellyfish) attacks the *Seaview.*

3. A variation on #1: Captain Crane turns into a monster and terrorizes the ship until he's transformed back.

Although the great villain in films and TV has been the Maw of that Monster Success that demanded script after script, regardless of whether a particular story worked, we find a pleasing number of stories that succeeded because the characters had clearly defined desires, fears, joys, and obstacles.

Okay, quick examples: "A Piece of the Action" on *ST*, almost any script by Charles Beaumont on *Alfred Hitchcock Presents* or *Twilight Zone*, any of the *Fawlty Towers* episodes by John Cleese and Connie Booth, most episodes of *Frasier*, and early, but not late *M.A.S.H.*, when the original heavies such as Hot-Lips wanted to be depicted sympathetically.

In closing, let's admit that there has *never* been a Golden Age of Excellence in Film or TV Writing. Select any period, from the 1920s, through the 1930s, up to the present, and you will always find more slop than fine cuisine for the mind and soul.

So, do we watch Callie Kinky interview the transvestites who have meaningful relationships with pigs ("They bring home the bacon, and kiss it, too")? Or should we tune in a prime-time soap ("A blow to the head reveals to Rodney that he's not a kind-hearted ecologist, but a serial killer who has been masquerading as a male stripper in order to trap and murder ex-nun Rhoda")?

Oink, oink.

"It's Copy, Stupid," Says Psychotic Editor

It has happened again. The members of a writers' group are complaining about what magazines and newspapers have done to their stories, columns, and articles. Little do they suspect that a psychopathic copy-editor is in their midst.

One growls, "When I send my story in, I've worked on it a lot, and I don't like it one bit when they change my wording."

"I don't even like it when they add or take away commas," snaps another.

"I put 'copyrighted' on my stuff—you see?—so that means they *can't* change anything," asserts a third, quite in error, by the way.

They do not know that, if I were editing their submissions, I would change or delete wording or punctuation because that is what an editor does. I learned this years ago, on the student newspaper at Pensacola Junior College, when I sat with our advisor, Dr. George H. Goodwin, and winced as he went through my precious copy.

"Necessary requirements" became "requirements." His pencil transformed "postpone until later" and into "postpone."

Eventually, my wincing decreased until I anticipated some of the improvements when the pencil hovered over a word or phrase: Yes, "fall down" could simply be "fall," since no one falls up.

When I was a cub and writing some stories for *The Pensacola News-Journal*, I felt neglected when a news editor simply slapped a head on my story and sent it to the composing room. Part of me was pouting that he didn't *care* enough even to read my stuff closely, as did Leo Coughlin, their assistant sports editor. Leo always found spots where my copy could be tightened.

If you go through stacks of copy with someone, you learn that copy is copy…and it probably can be improved.

Actually, of course, some editors decide more about whether or not to accept stories and do little actual editing of the copy. Once they and the publication have bought into the concept (and "purchased" it, even by paying in copies), the story finally goes to a copy editor who, in theory, makes everything right.

A newspaper copy editor may wrinkle his or her nose and wonder who was foolish enough to agree to print, say, Homer Harvester's agricultural column. In trying to explain hog inoculations, Homer may fight, and lose, his weekly bout with the English language.

A staffer may entirely rewrite Homer's copy, or a copy editor may transform the story by turning passive verbs into active ones, by shortening sentences, and by using the exact words that were eluding Homer.

The copy editors have a near-mystical obligation to (let's have some transcendental music, Maestro) *Become One* with the reporter or freelancer. They attempt to divine the spirit of a piece and to write what the writer wants to say, even though the copy falls flat here or there. The story editor of a literary magazine has an even greater duty, needing to stay close to the writer's vision. By contrast, copy editors at such magazines as *Time* or *The New Yorker* may need to see if the writer has stayed close to *their* vision. If not, they will edit in the correct "sound" or tone.

Besides searching out errors of fact and grammar, the editors help keep writers from looking like fools in print. Anyone who writes enough will write something stupid, and dissenters to that view are either fibbing or they don't write much.

Nearly a half-century has separated me from the stupidest line that I permitted to survive. On the now defunct *Bessemer News* weekly section of *The Birmingham News*, our women's pages editor, Frances Thames, had finished her stories and column and gone home. About an hour later, with the deadline long past, a harried woman rushed in with a handwritten story about her daughter's baby shower.

Being helpful, courteous, kind, and efficient, I grabbed the account, typed it, quickly read through it for any spelling errors and slapped a head on it. By that deadly time of the day, I didn't have someone to check my own work.

When the weekly section came out on Thursday, Mrs. Thames read through the stories and started laughing. She had spotted this throat-cutter of a line in that story: "**The centerpiece for the table was an arrangement of daisies and a yellow and green baby.**"

Aarrgh! A spray-painted baby perhaps? In the haste of typing the story, I had understood that the mother was referring to a yellow and green doll, to a figurine, or even to a cake in the shape of a baby. I rightfully endured the horse-laughs of my colleagues since I had let the error slip through. (Oscar Wilde was right: No good deed goes unpunished.*) (*See next piece about this quotation.)

A year or so later on the copy desk for the main paper, I spotted a story that was about to say: "**The defendant was convicted of manslaughter by a jury of half men and half women.**" After every copy editor enjoyed a good laugh, my editing pencil quickly changed the hermaphroditic jurors to "six men and six women."

That gender-baffled reporter, however, may have deserved some compassion for his silly sentence. In reality, in those pre-FAX, laptop, and modem days, perhaps he dashed from a courtroom as a verdict came in, called the city desk, was assigned to someone to take dictation, and read out the story off the top of his head, all that with a deadline fifteen minutes away. He may not have even *seen* the offending sentence on paper.

Editors may stop such sentences as these:

"They were a trilogy of American heroes — Armstrong, Aldrin, and Collins." (Not *trilogy*, but *trio* or possibly *triumvirate*.)

"Fashion is belt happy this year. It seems that everyone is getting a little drunky with joyee over rediscovery of the feminine waist and are grabbing at anything to encircle it. Anything, that is, which is pretty, handsome, fun, surprising." (Any reader should hate this irritating attempt to be cute. It also has a problem in subject-verb agreement, a fragment, and an unintended sexual innuendo.)

"The Governor said he concurred with the thinking of the senator that future facilities must be planned for the retarded that are small, compassionate, and within reach of all educational, vocational, medical, and religious resources of the community." (Perhaps the lazy reporter is paraphrasing the bureaucratic jargon from a state agency. The sentence also has a parallelism problem. Most seriously, it makes us wonder about what's being planned for "the retarded [who] are *large* and *un*compassionate." And with "retarded," we have a politically incorrect word.)

On the other hand, an inattentive editor may damage correct copy. For example, a freelancer may have written,

"The museum will purchase $527,000 worth of *objets d'art*," but the sentence may emerge "corrected" as a *objects d'art*, even though the French expression is not spelled with a *c*.

Sometimes a sentence is spelled correctly and has correct grammar, but the editor realizes a perverted reader will snicker at the wording. In closing, decide what you would do, if anything, to this sentence:

"During World War I, Murphy joined the Army and was sent abroad to fight. He got hit in the Dardanelles."

No Good Quotes Go Unattributed

Since there is nothing worse than arrogant academics who think that they can walk on water, I want to assure you that I am fallible, very much so.

However, I do have a confession to make. Several years ago, when I was feeling a little on the omni-side (i.e., omniscient, omnipresent) and hankering to engage in some aquatic pedestrianism, I parked my Dodge Omni near the St. Johns River, and, with firm jaw and determined eyes, stepped out onto the surface of the river and began marching my merry way to the other side.

Halfway across, with the water already nearly up to my knees, I had to turn around in great humiliation and slosh back to the shore, soaked to the skin all the way to my waist. It taught me humility and gave me a terrible case of diaper rash.

I was also recently humbled to receive an e-mail message from journalist and teacher Michael Ray Fitzgerald, about an article I wrote several years ago for the Florida First Coast Writers' Festival's *Penchant*. The article was mentioning how, during the administration of Warren G. Bush or Lyndon Bush (they all run together), I had done a favor for a woman who had brought in a handwritten piece about a baby shower. Even though she was past the deadline for our newspaper, I retyped the piece, slapped a headline on it, and sent it in, only to have a throat-cutting gaffe left in the piece because I had been in a hurry. I remembered that Oscar Wilde had said, "No good deed goes unpunished."

Except...

Mike was saying that Oscar didn't say that.

Stunned because of my tenderness of my ego, I called Dr. Foxwhistle to schedule an additional month of therapy sessions and then quickly searched Google and Yahoo to discover what I could learn about the quote. I found that many writers attribute the quotation to Oscar, but books about quotations attribute it to such folks as Claire Booth Luce, Gore Vidal, and Thomas Brooks (among others).

Mike said he too researched the origin of the quote in an effort to find authoritative evidence that pointed to whom the line was first attributed. "Just as you," he wrote, "I found a number of unsupported claims naming a wide variety of people," adding, "The quote you indicated in your article should have read: 'No bad deed goes unpunished' - Wilde. This may sound like semantics, but, in fact, this particular claim is one of those that is unsupported by tangible reference."

Mike had researched *Brewer's Dictionary of Phrase and Fable*, which says of the quote, "...[It] is a consciously ironic rewriting of the older expression 'No bad deed goes unpunished' and has been attributed to Wilde, but remains unverified." The book noted:

> Joe Orton recorded it in his diary for 13 June 1967: 'Very good line George [Greeves] came out with at dinner: "No good deed ever goes unpunished" 'and "James Agate in Ego 3 (for 25 January 1938) states: '[Isidore Leo] Pavia was in great form today: "Every good deed brings its own punishment."

Even Claire Booth Luce was not the first great mind to make this observation, Mike said.

As I was pondering this peculiar problem, I remembered recent articles about quotations that have been misattributed to Mark Twain. (You can find such websites by typing in "misattributed quotes" and "mark twain" in your favorite browser.) One of Mark Twain's clever lines was "The coldest winter I ever spent was a summer in San Francisco."

Except...

As you are probably guessing, it can't be proved that Twain ever said that. Such scholars as Kim A. McDonald, Shelley Fisher Fishkin, Barbara Schmidt, Robert Hirst, Ralph Keyes, and Stephen Goranson have spent portions of their professional careers tracking down these quotations. If they can't find a line in a book, diary, letter, newspaper article or interview, they mark the quotation as suspect or misattributed.

I think I know partly what is going on with the supposed quotations by Oscar Wilde or Mark Twain. Our culture has created a Wilde Persona or an Übermensch Twain or the Writer as Overtone.

Let me explain:

If you are deep in slumber, you may dream that Jerry Seinfeld, Gore Vidal, and Fanny Flagg get on the elevator with you. You may even carry on a conversation with them. Jerry may say something humorous ("Why do they call this an elevator if it's going down? Shouldn't it be called a descendor then?"); Vidal, something caustic ("Stand-up comedy itself is entertainment's equivalent of Burma Shave signs"); Flagg, something apropos for a Southerner ("my best friend in Birmingham is such a bad cook that her fried green tomatoes taste like they were made with Burma Shave"). *You* are dreaming the dream, of course, creating the dialogue and action, but the personae are saying what sounds right for each to say.

Several personae could say, "No good deed goes unpunished." It resonates with Oscar, even cynical Mark Twain, Oscar Levant, Luce, or Alice Roosevelt Longworth ("If you can't say anything nice about someone, sit next to me").

A few years ago, a political columnist attributed to Mark Twain the line, "I'm not a member of an organized political party. I'm a Democrat." That was a reasonable mistake, but I knew that it was said by Will Rogers. Again, the cultural persona of a cracker-barrel philosopher could have the line said by Josh Billings, Mark Twain, Will Rogers, or even the piano-plunking satirist Mark Russell.

Oscar muddled the water a bit by going to parties and hearing clever lines from lords and ladies, barristers and bankers, and scholars and scamps. He'd work many of them into his plays or stories. Once when he heard something clever, he said, "I wish I'd said that," and his friends (looking to his next play) replied, "You will, Oscar. You will."

Or was that said by Oscar Meyer?

COMMON SENSE: ALL EVENTS AREN'T EQUAL

An oral historian complained once that academics often tell the poorest stories. He was having better luck interviewing truck-drivers, plumbers, and sales clerks. The ivy-covered professors apparently had become so immersed in their ocean of facts, disclaimers, and equivocations that they lost the ability to make their stories interesting.

That loss would unhinge news reporters, who must try to make the first paragraph give the five W's and make you want to read the whole story. Usually, they focus on the MAJOR event, and we seldom notice the prioritizing of important information.

However, flaws emerge especially in stories appearing in weekly newspapers and in some newsletters, where you may encounter reports about community news or garden clubs. In these reports, the amateur writers may have presented everything equally.

Years ago, I read a column in *The National Observer*, an excellent weekly newspaper then published by Dow-Jones Inc., which put out *The Wall Street Journal* until it was purchased by Rupert Murdoch's empire. When the *Observer* died, I mourned by wea

ring a black armband for a month.

A writer for the *Observer* quoted a story from a minor New York newspaper about 1947, when the citizens of

Dutch origin were interacting with Italian-Americans. (I would give credit to the author, but, unfortunately, the writer's name crumbled off the clipping after some cough drops melted in my desk drawer during the Nixon Administration.)

Since I like to read the story aloud to all those whom I find in dire need of enlightenment, I have inserted some Dutch and Italian names a little friendlier for the classroom than what the *Observer* reprinted.

> The Parent-Teacher Association of New Amsterdam School held its regular monthly meeting Tuesday evening in the school cafeteria, for the election of officers for the coming year, with Mrs. Noah de Witt, president, in the chair. The nominating committee proposed Mrs. Douwe Talema for president, Mrs. David Demarest for vice president, and Mrs. Laurens de Geer for secretary-treasurer. It was moved and seconded that the nominations be closed.
>
> Mrs. Gianello Birnisi arose and said she wanted to nominate Mrs. Katrina Gardino, Mrs. Giuseppe Romano, and Mrs. Maria dal Vapore. Mrs. de Witt ruled Mrs. Birnisi out of order. Mrs. Birnisi appealed to the parliamentarian, Miss Sarah Kierstad, who sustained the chair.
>
> Mrs. Birnisi took a small automatic pistol from her handbag and shot Mrs. de Witt between the eyes. Constable Abraham Brinkerhoff came and escorted Mrs. Birnisi to the county jail. The body of Mrs. de Witt was removed to Van Emburgh's Funeral Parlor.
>
> There being no further business, the meeting adjourned for refreshments, which were served by Mrs. Adrian Blauvelt's committee. The next meeting will be held on Friday evening, Sept. 9, for the installation of officers.

The *Observer*'s writer admitted that he had lost the original clipping but had memorized the story. He used it to emphasize that the good old days of journalism often weren't so splendid.

To make his point, he also noted that the night editor only read the first paragraph and slapped a headline on the story saying something like "PTA Debates '46-47 Slate."

However, I want to take a different slant and focus on what went wrong with the PTA story.

1. The major event was not in the first paragraph. When you have covered an event and are about to write the first graph, you need to follow the advice of Susan Cheever, who was once told by her city editor: "Imagine that you have asked someone, 'Guess what happened today (at the meeting or whatever)?'"

That person will probably ask, "What?"

When you answer that question, you have the material for the opening.

2. The story was merely the minutes of a meeting, but minutes are rarely structured correctly for a story.

3. For routine meetings of most organizations, a newspaper is probably not interested in all those nominated for any positions. Instead, you want to focus on the ones who were elected. Exceptions include officer elections for major organizations, say, the NAACP, boards of major corporations, and major political positions.

4. The opening sentence was overloaded and difficult to read. Instead, a good sentence in journalism needs to focus on one major thought.

Undoubtedly, your club meetings lack the drama of someone slinging hot lead. Even so, your meeting may have featured one interesting bit of information that deserves to be in the first graph.

If you say, "No, it was pretty much the same old same-old," then you probably do not need to pester your daily or weekly newspaper to print an article about the meeting.

Let's acknowledge that the New York newspaper helped to create the silliness in the story. It decided to help the secretaries of clubs and organization by giving them a form to use in reporting events in a meeting, whereupon the secretary dutifully filled out each blank and converted it into an article. No doubt, the newspaper had neglected to tell the secretaries to rank the most important event at a meeting, and (the worst of all failures) both the secretary and the editor failed to use common sense.

THE GOOD OLD DAZE

Everything, of course, was better in the good old days, but, even as a kid, I had doubts about that. In the middle of the rock 'n' roll years, an older friend, for example, gassed on at length about Glenn Miller's recording of "The Big Noise from Winnetka."

"It wasn't recorded by Glenn Miller," I announced with the irritating certainty of a Moses handing down Ten Commandments to his followers. "It was Bob Crosby and the Bob Cats."

"It most certainly *was* by Glenn Miller," my friend retorted. The smile disappeared from his eyes, and we faced each other with the hard eyes of gunslingers in the streets of Dodge City. He fired off, "*I* ought to know. *I* was around back then."

His retort missed me by a country mile. "Look, 'Big Noise' was written by Ray Baduc and Bob Haggart. They played drums and bass for Bob Crosby."

"Glenn Miller," he insisted and turned away, firm in the knowledge that a funny farm would cart me off for masquerading as trumpet player Wingy Manone.

Then I started hearing old-timers talk about how well newspapers were proofed in the olden days, when they had multiple copy-readers, one reading the copy to another. "If there was a typo," asserted the grumpy Tobe Misseldeim, a printer, "the foreman got out the galley proof and tracked down who was responsible."

His good friend, Johnny (Goon) Myers, agreed and shook his head sadly at what the composing room was having to make do with.

By and by, I came across a stack of old Alabama newspapers from 1908, and, granted, these were weekly issues of Jasper's *Mountain Eagle* and not one of the big city papers. The good old days of printing seemed to have a glitch or two.

You notice that weeklies (and many dailies) back then borrowed freely from papers across the nation to bring their readers all the news that would fit.

On one page, for instance, the Jasper newspaper reprinted articles from *The Marion Standard*, *The Birmingham Age-Herald*, *The Carbon Hill Weekly*, *The Reflector*, *The Southern Democrat*, *The Dixie Manufacturer*, and *The Huntsville Tribune*.

The Northport Breeze noted in a reprint: "An effigy of Carrie Nation, the famous temperance lecurer [sic] and Kansas saloon smasher, was put in front of the defunct dispensary in Tuscaloosa.... The live ones are what she's after."

The *Eagle* informed its readers: "Rev. Leroy Williams of Boldo was in town yesterday, as bad as the weather was, as lively as usual." Who? The weather or the preacher?

The Cullman Tribune told of a man being bitten by a "maddog at Joppa last week." The *Trib* said, "The dog's head was shipped to Auburn, where examination by state experts proved that it was a case of genuine rabies." You can only wonder what would have happened if the Joppa man had gotten artificial rabies.

In an obituary, the *Eagle* commented, "The deceased was a Confederate veteran and a harmless, hardworking old man." I deduce that, if you have lots of harmless men, you are more likely to lose a War of Yankee Aggression.

In 1908, words were different. For examples, cows "estrayed" from their pastures, and folks "removed to" another town.

"Blind tiger" was an earlier name for "white lightning" or "bootleg liquor," and Mrs. Jones would "happen to" a serious accident and perhaps be "right seriously hurt," whatever that meant.

After telling the readers that someone "burned to bear [sic] bones," the 1908 papers make the skin crawl of anyone familiar with libel suits in this excerpt (I'll use fictional names rather than rekindle old sorrows):

"John Brown, who returned Sunday from Winfield, reports a killing that took place near there Saturday. As Mr. Brown heard it...John Smith delibertly [sic] walked up behind Tom Jones and fired two shots from his pistol into his victim, who lingered until an early hour next morning and died."

That was the year when the community of Manchester got an electric light plant, when former President Grover Cleveland died (made page 7), and when a "cyclone" destroyed the community of Bergen. This "greatest calamity that ever visited Walker County" wiped "this little town... completely off the face of the earth."

As far back as the 1880s, Birmingham's leaders and newspapers jealously predicted that in due course their city would surpass Atlanta. This rivalry was reflected in 1908 in a reprint entitled "Atlanta Journalism":

"Birmingham may entertain some hopes of becoming greater, when she can exhibit a photograph of her jail without anyone in it."

Three pages later in the same edition, an item redundantly said, "Feb. 10 is the day that will go down in history as the first day in the history of Birmingham, in which not a single person was locked up in the city jail."

Sixty or so years later, I was listening to complaints about the typographical errors, spelling mistakes, and grammatical transgressions in various papers that employed me as a flunky emeritus.

We reporters, editors, and copy-editors came up with alibis (e.g., deadlines, distracted printer, etc.), but we were too diplomatic to jeer at our critics about the grammar of articles-to-be being submitted by club correspondents or P.R. people.

One news release, for example, came in referring to "Mr. and Mrs. John Smith, the formula Jane Jones," who was probably a fetching little thing who worked in a laboratory.

A club secretary wrote that a speaker practiced "peiaditrics." Obviously, she had a vague idea of how to spell *pediatrics*. The word has an *e*, a bunch of *i*'s, plus a *p*, a *d*, and a *t*.

Coaches invariably leave "roosters" on the desk of sports writers wanting to know the names of team members (a bit of a cock-up, you might say).

During Christmas season, a club wants everyone to drive by a church and see how the "spot-lots" have lit up the decorations.

You learn too that Mrs. Jones had delivered a "dovation" at church, while Mrs. Smith was elected as the "tresure." Another club reports that Mrs. White is to be "congradulated" for her "meny" trips to "Montegomery" (or "Tallyhassee" for a story in the Sunshine state) on behalf of the group.

Many successful people in business will send in news releases saying:

"Mr. Smith was formally with Jones Manufacturing."

"At a chapter meeting, Mr. Jones was elected sentenell."

"The meeting closed with Mr. Smith delivering the apprication."

In the good old days, they had spelling bees, and people *cared* about proper spelling and grammar. They—

Sorry, fellow. They were just as lazy and spacey in the good old daze as they are now.

QUEEN VICTORIA'S SCRAPBOOK

I am thumbing through Queen Victoria's scrapbook from the 1880s and, of course, thinking about the transitory nature of life.

I should make two clarifications:

First, it's not the actual scrapbook since my brother David had wonderful copies of the original made at UPS and sent them to selected members of our allied families. The brittle pages of the original make you nervous when you turn the pages since little pieces drop off like lonely snowflakes.

Second, it's not a scrapbook from the British queen, but from THE Queen Victoria in my family's life: Queen Victoria Lollar O'Rear, my great-grandmother.

To think of her is to contemplate our mortality. Queenie (as her family called her) began her scrapbook when she was about fourteen, and she kept it up until she was about eighteen. I suspect that her attentions then shifted as four babies arrived to complicate her life.

On the first page is a six-inch-long lock of brown hair, and I don't know if she cut her own lock metaphorically to meld her DNA with the old pages or if a family member took the lock when she died of throat cancer at the age of twenty-eight.

The family oral tradition is precise about her painful last days in a particular room in a house on Sixth Avenue in my hometown. Because of the terrible pain, she could not eat any food but could only manage to swallow some beer, and near the time of her death she met with her four children, daughters Clare and Lucille and sons John B. and Ezra, and told each one how much she loved them and, no doubt, prayed they would have good lives. Inevitably, she also grappled with a dying parent's fear of what would happen to her babies and who would look after them.

A natural progression from those thoughts is to count the number of people who owed their existence to this young girl/woman and her erratic husband, James O'Rear. These include her surviving granddaughters in Clare's line, the classical pianist Sarah, 94 at her death; the stalwart Marjorie, 98 today; and the baby Jane, now her 90's. Other grandchildren died at ages 60 (Joe, from diabetes), 71 (Mary Clare, possibly from a stroke or a reaction to a shot), and 84 (Victoria, from a confluence of ailments). Clearly, Queen Victoria would have loved to reach any of those ages and to have lived to the late 1920s or the early 1960s.

When individuals in any family care enough to assemble scrapbooks, collection of poetry, portfolios of drawings, and packets of letters, they are affirming the importance of the creative spirit and the strength of the word or image. They are saying, "I thought this," or "This thought appealed to me."

As I write this, I am listening to a CD of Queenie's granddaughter Sarah Stephenson Westbrook playing on the piano Chopin's "Polonaise, Op. 26, no. 1." She is striking notes to be heard as long as those particular CDs exist, just as Faulkner said a writer labors to speak to those seventy years in the future. (Why only seventy? Homer is speaking after nearly 3,000 years.)

I grew up with examples of Sarah's paintings around Mammy and Pappy Stephenson's house. (When the grandbabies started coming, Clare would ask to kiss one of the grandbabies under the chin: "Let me have some Mammy sugar." That expression may have gone back to Queen Victoria's time, but the joke stuck; she became "Mammy Sugar" and then half of "Mammy and Pappy.") At age fourteen or so, Sarah had painted a robin on a terra cotta pot and painted reproductions of turn-of-the-century paintings. These announced, "I saw this" or "This image appealed to me."

Family letters can tell a lot about an era and the people in it. In the Middle Ages from 1422 to 1509, the Paston family exchanged letters that survived and that instruct us about the attitudes of that age and family. You discern matters in those letters that you don't discover in typical histories of the period.

Sometimes letters and such material in a family don't survive. A few years ago, a poet speaking to the North Florida Writers was asked about when he became interested in poetry. He said his father wrote poetry throughout his life. After his father died, his mother wanted to get rid of clutter. It made me sick to hear that she had thrown out his father's notebooks and poems. Each family has its archivists and historians, along with those stuck in trashcan mode.

Sometimes life eradicates things for us. For example, my grandparents dated two years before they first kissed, and during their several years of genteel courtship, they exchanged letter after letter with each other. After they married, they went out of town and rode the train on a dog-leg line to a nearby community to a friend's wedding, and, while they were gone, their little frame house went up in smoke. Gone were many letters and other items precious to a family archivist.

As they got back on their feet, moving to an in-law's farm in the country for several years and then back in town, they saved batches of letters, mainly from the late 1930s and 1940s through the early 60s. These eventually were put in a storage outbuilding that developed a leaky roof. With thoughts of the Paston family in mind, I replaced that roof one summer and looked forward to sorting the riches of the letters into valuable stacks, perhaps letters of the Roaring Twenties, letters of the Depression, letters of World War II, etc. Alas, the rain had gotten into the boxes and foot lockers, and, instead, I had the gloomy task of sorting the letters into three different stacks: readable, partly readable, and mushy pulp.

Although collections of letters (and genealogical information) can be given to library collections, some families are so prim and proper that they wouldn't dare let others know the dark secrets of their lives. Some families no doubt let their letters go the way of mushy pulp, but other families, somewhat reserved, restrict access of their letters in library collections for twenty or thirty years.

In looking at Queen Victoria's scrapbook, you notice that she didn't go to a store and purchase a blank scrapbook. Instead, she took a book entitled "Memorial Addresses: Life and Character of Fernando Wood, February 28th, 1881." The first question is who was Fernando Wood, and resources reveal he was a controversial mayor of New York City. No one in Alabama would have cared about that, until a little research reveals that he was a leader of the Peace Democrats (a/k/a the "Copperheads") during the Civil War. He even suggested that NYC secede from the Union so it could continue trading cotton from the South. Opponents said he was probably the most corrupt of mayors, but posterity can thank him for keeping Central Park from being turned into a business district.

That book may have helped validate the service of several Lollars in the Confederate army, but it was of little interest to the young girl, so she began pasting in items that she had collected over the years.

She loved poetry, and, as she read the weekly newspapers, she clipped out dozens of poems that had appealed to her. Except for a small poem by England's Charles W. Lamb, you won't find any poems by the American giants of the 19th Century: Poe, Whittier, Whitman, and Emily Dickinson. About the time that Queen Victoria was working on her scrapbook, the Belle of Amherst had died unrecognized and largely unpublished (Emily's first collection wasn't published till 1890, with critics in general noticing her excellence by the 1920s).

Browsers occasionally yield hits about the authors of the most of the poems in the scrapbook: a New England poet Mrs. E.O. Jewell; Thebon Brown; Paul Hamilton Hayne; Cecil Moore; D. Brainerd Williamson; Mary Mapes Dodge; Edward S. Creamer. Some poems are only identified by their newspaper or magazine of origin: *Harper's Young People*, *Boston Transcript*, *Harper's Bazaar*, *Congregationalist*, and others.

Queen Victoria loved poems that we would term didactic or at least life-affirming. She first pasted "Things That Never Die" by Mrs. Jewell: "It never dies—a mother's holy love / strengthens with every ill that may betide, / every phase of life its waters move...."

Newspapers back then frequently reprinted poems and articles from other papers. Weeklies, in particular, had no news or wire services. Occasionally, Queen Victoria saved tiny "fillers"; these are small blurbs of one to three lines used in the "hot metal" days when a column of type runs a little short. A makeup man in the composing room of a newspaper could spend maybe five minutes sticking in thin blank leads to expand the type or simply pop in what became known as a "factoid," a filler that would close up the space.

One filler was obviously a popular saying of the day: "Touch that water-melon lightly, darling, touch it lightly."

Another filler came from another newspaper near Jasper: "The [Mountain] Eagle say's [sic] that Jasper has more than its prorata of girls. We will ship a car load of boys in a few days, and hope the Eagle will hand them around."

Fillers could even be verse, as in this sentiment: "When a girl can read her title else / To matrimony's share, / She craves no fruit of any kind / But one delicious 'pair.'"

The scrapbook also contained a signature book about the size of a playing card, beginning around Nov. 1883 (when she was fourteen). The pages are filled with beautiful Spencerian handwriting, to remind us that penmanship mattered once upon a time.

One page says, "Little friend, a long life with a happy end, is the sincere wish of your friend, N.B. Haney."

Another says, "Miss Queen—'Bright be the years before thy friend of my childhood day of peace weave her live o'er thee, and joy attend thy ways.' Your real friend, Arba L. Lamillin Jasper March 14 1884."

Her "affectionate" sister, Fannie Lollar, wrote what was a popular refrain, "My Dear Sister, May your life be long and happy...."

Her book contained helpful advice that we may only need to know today during hurricanes when our lights are out. "To Prevent Fire" gave twenty-one tips with "sound advice" about old-timey kerosene lamps, matches, etc. A sampling:

1. Always buy the best of oil.

2. Never make a sudden motion with a lamp, either in lifting it or setting it down.

3. Never put a lamp on the edge of a table or mantle....

6. Never blow a lamp out from the top.

7. Never take a lamp to a closet where there are clothes....

19. Be sure there are no curtains or shades that can be blown into a gas light.

20. Never examine a gas meter after dark.

Strange as it may seem, at one time, Americans criticized their Presidents, and Presidents would have their defenders. Queen Victoria had empathy for former President Chester A. Arthur, who succeeded the assassinated James A. Garfield in 1881. She included a poem "Chester, Farewell!" It opens with "Soon gentle, genial Chester A., / Your manly form shall pass away / From politics. / In peace you may your soul posess [sic], / No longer in the muddy mess / To move or mix..../ Your party rotten to the core / Exalts its noblest men no more / In this our day; / So close to decency you stood / That you were clearly much to [sic] good / For such as they...."

The Republicans dumped him on the fourth ballot in 1884, preferring James G. Blaine, and Arthur died two years later at the age of fifty-six.

Her scrapbook doesn't contain any photographs, as you would find with wealthier families. A typical family at that time managed perhaps a group school photograph or a bridal portrait. Her graphics consist of a cartoon and a line drawing of an eight- to ten-year-old girl braiding her doll's hair into a pigtail while her kitten watches. The drawing is sweet, but not sentimental.

Queen Victoria had saved a cartoon of a prim young woman and a disappointed suitor with bowler hat, monocle, cane, and a moustache:

"He (After proposing and being rejected).—'I suppose in the end you will be marrying some idiot of a fellow—'

"She (Interrupting).—'Excuse me; but if I meant to do that I should have accepted your offer.'

"Oppressive silence."

Not surprisingly, when we have scrapbooks, letters, poems, stories, music, and paintings, we aren't left with a silence, oppressive or otherwise. Instead, these items symbolize individuals' creativity and their time here on earth.

On Orwell, Elephants, ROVP, and the Schoendienst Curve

I came up with Denson's Rule of Verb Percentages (ROVP) because we August Linguistic and Philological Authorities (ALPAs) always offer advice backed up with statistics and acronyms. It encourages people to give us easels, posterboards, and pointers, plus healthy consultants' fees.

I am still waiting for any fees, although I have gotten an easel and a posterboard saying "Take a hike." I also have the pointer. It's only temporarily in my possession since a note contained a cryptic message about its disposition. I will need to confer with a weatherman to find out where the moon never sets.

Despite that lack of appreciation, I need a drum roll and a trumpet fanfare as I present Denson's ROVP:

> **An article or essay should contain 85 percent strong or action verbs, 10 percent linking verbs, and 5 percent passive verbs.**

I heard the commandment one evening from a burning bush in the backyard, although I will confess that I coaxed the Celestial Pronouncement with a cheap portable tape-recorder, a can of kerosene, and a Zippo lighter.

Since I had the splendid rule, I applied it to George Orwell's "Shooting an Elephant." While some students were grumbling through a final exam, I went through the seven pages of the essay, fully convinced that Orwell would validate my formula. What did I find? The essay, surprisingly enough, threw me a curve, causing me to adopt what the late Jon Wood Patton called the Schoendienst Curve Corollary (SCC).

The essay took up four pages when photocopied, so I will list the verbs and their categories in four rows, since numbers in columns and rows convince readers that the writer is an ALPA whose pronouncements matter. My hasty tabulation revealed 389 verbs and helpers:

Action Verbs	Linking Verbs	Passive Verbs
25	15	3
92	28	4
82	34	3
80	19	4
279 (71.7%)	96 (24.6%)	14 (3.5%)

If your life is empty enough, you may wish to go through the essay yourself to validate, or refute, my count. Perhaps the essay actually had 395 verbs or 350. I would go back through again myself, except for the pressure of another big project in my life: finding a new first name for the 1950s Tab Hunter, since no man in his eighties needs to be confused with a diet cola.

Whatever the verb count (or new name, for Tex Hunter—how's that?), Orwell violated my ex post facto requirement that he use the 85-10-5 formula. Almost 25 percent of Orwell's verbs fell into the pathetic category of linking verbs.

When I examined his essay more intently, I saw the reason for his deviance from the norm that I had so expertly established. Orwell was focusing on the condition of the Burmese under the British colonial rule and especially on his own condition; hence, the Schoendienst Curve Corollary permits a limited use of linking verbs to establish the state of an individual or society.

Orwell frequently employed the Schoendienst Curve Corollary to use linking verbs: "The young Buddhist priests *were* the worst of all. There *were* several thousands of them in the town and none of them seemed to have anything to do except stand on street corners and jeer at Europeans." (*Stand* and *jeer* are really infinitives of action verbs.)

However, when Orwell settles into the narrative about an elephant after an attack of *must,* he relies more and more on action verbs: "It *had* already *destroyed* somebody's bamboo hut, *killed* a cow and *raided* some fruit-stalls and *devoured* the stock; also it *had met* the municipal rubbish van and, when the driver *jumped* out and *took* to his heels, *had turned* the van over and *inflicted* violences upon it."

In that passage, Orwell, the former sub-divisional police officer, teasingly uses police jargon, with "inflicted violences." Police reports often show that some law enforcement officers had rather die than use *cuts*, *bruises*, and *scrapes*, when they can wallow in *lacerations*, *contusions*, and *abrasions.*

If you examine the last paragraphs of the essay, where Orwell finally forces himself to pull the trigger, you will find a wonderful narrative passage that is also pure process (here is how to shoot an elephant ineptly) and cause-and-effect (a bullet here results in this change of behavior and health). It also contains two different similes for the elephant ("he seemed to tower upwards *like a huge rock toppling*, his trunk reaching skyward *like a tree*").

When you study this essay, as I have been doing since the Eisenhower Administration, you may notice that skilled writers do a variation on Hamlet's advice to the players. Hamlet tells the players to "match the action to the word." (Shakespeare apparently was encouraging his own thespians to cut down on excessive gestures, unnecessary shouting, and other forms of scene chewing.)

If Hamlet had been giving advice to fiction writers and freelancers, he would have advised the opposite. If we are trying to put words on blank paper that will let others know about, say, an elephant's rampage or about a skier's accident, we ask ourselves what actions we are describing. Once we have a fluid and vivid image in our mind (or a shadowy image on paper that can be nudged, coaxed, and revised in that direction), we match the words to the action.

In "Shooting an Elephant," Orwell uses short sentences as he fires the rifle; hence, a sentence with a bang needs to be short. However, when he takes us through the effect of the shot, the sentence becomes longer, with the frequent use of strings of three verbs (see the rubbish van sentence quoted earlier).

Denson's rule argues that a first-rate piece of writing relies heavily on the strong action verbs. The rule does *not* outlaw all passive verbs ("President Kennedy was shot today") or linking verbs ("The Lord is my shepherd"), but demands that they justify their presence in a sentence.

To demonstrate the power of action verbs, let's close, not with a prayer, but with King James version of the "23rd Psalm":

> The Lord is* my shepherd; I shall not want**.
>
> He maketh** me to lie*** down in green pastures; he leadeth** me beside the still waters.
>
> He restoreth** my soul; he leadeth** me in the paths of righteousness for his name's sake.
>
> Yea, though I walk** through the valley of the shadow of death, I will fear** no evil, for Thou art* with me; Thy rod and Thy staff, they comfort** me.

Thou preparest** a table before me in the presence of mine enemies; thou anointest** my head with oil; my cup runneth** over.

Surely goodness and mercy shall follow** me all the days of my life, and I will dwell** in the house of the Lord forever.

*Linking verbs (2)

**Action/strong verbs (13)

***Infinitive of action verb (1)

Passive verbs (0)

So, if you write like Orwell or like the old Hebrew bard, you should do just fine.

A POST-SCRIPT ON BURMA: One person from Burma is called a "Burman." Three, four, or forty of them jeering and irritating you are called "Burmans." All of the people in the country are called "Burmese." But what do you call a child from there? Simple: "He's a cute little Burma shaver." (Trust me on such trifles. I only lie about really, really big things.)

ANOTHER P.S. ON BURMA: Burma, of course, has been called Myanmar for a couple of decades, possibly to avoid the Burma Shave joke.

POST-SCRIPT ON ACRONYMS: An ALPA is an August Linguistic and Philological Authority. You should not confuse ALPAs with retired educators reduced to eating dogfood, better known as ALPOs.

ONCE MORE INTO THE BREACH, DAG-NABBIT

As I pack my bag to get my gear together for a trip to a desert island, it is comforting to know my role in life. Dubya's job was to keep the nation's reporters out of trouble. Mel Gibson's job is to show his nekkid derriere in *Lethal Butt XIV* or metaphorically to traffic cops. And my job is to fulminate and sound alarums about American civilization going to hell in a Hyundai.

What am I ranting about? Okay, look at these course registration booklets from the colleges and universities in Northeast Florida. Look there under English or Literature. See? While you flip through the booklets for each term, I will just stand here and grind my teeth down to the gums.

Through?

Spot it?

Nothing on Shakespeare, except now and then.

Almost zero!

If the Planet Earth is to hold onto its atmosphere and keep the polar ice caps from melting, our colleges must be offering at least three regular courses on Shakespeare: The Comedies, The Tragedies, and The Histories. Each term, one of them MUST be taught.

Instead, what do we have? There is the Literature of Intercultural Cuisine and Metaphors of Menus, featuring "a meaningful and in-depth look at the haute cuisine from each culture and continent."

All right, I lied about that.

The above course is not being offered, but it could be. I am just too lazy to list all the trendy junk courses in the booklets. You will easily find lots of multi-cultural courses, and you'll see that these have pushed aside the world's greatest English writer and the greatest synthesizer of the cultures of his time.

Actors, of course, need to know Shakespeare, but any writer of fiction and serious non-fiction, especially as it relates to historical pieces, needs to be thoroughly immersed in his plays. Why?

He had a wide-ranging interest, and reading him stretches the reader and the aspiring writer. Discovering Shakespeare, for example, transformed Herman Melville and helped to temper the work that became *Moby-Dick*.

Though Shakespeare often did not think that well, he knew the human heart better than any other single writer. Reading Shakespeare will not cause aspiring writers automatically to understand presidents, senators, and governors, along with pimps, grocers, and preachers, but writers will be alerted to stretch their empathies to the limit.

In addition, Shakespeare gives us exciting and intricate stories, which, like life itself, frequently have loose ends that cause us to ponder and deliberate about drama-as-life or life-as-drama: Who was the third murderer in Macbeth? (Who was on the grassy knoll? Why didn't Grant go to the theater that night? Does hot air from Rush Limbaugh really cause the polar caps melt faster?)

Shakespeare's plays, despite their apparent wordiness, are outstanding examples of concentrated language (that is another way of calling it poetry). Moreover, this language is essentially the same language that you will find in what snickering gossips call the Queen James Version of the Bible.

So, to read on the desert island, I am taking the collected plays and poems of Shakespeare, the King James Version of the Bible, Homer's epics, Herodotus' history, and the October 1962 issue of *Playboy* (mind you, not for the fold-out who loved nude sky-diving and who was lusting after Rock Hudson, but for the really deep essay by Hef on selecting pipe tobacco, ridding oneself of repressive attitudes, and practicing group intimacy).

After aspiring writers read Shakespeare and the other works above, they (or just a civilized human being) will not find anything new in the human heart. It is all there.

I will close by saying the magic words of grumps such as myself: "By cracky, they're destroying civilization today, and people won't be able to screw in a light bulb if things continue, and food doesn't taste as good as it used to, especially since the choppers are ground down to the gums."

Dag-nabbit.

(Now, let me flip to the sonnets and wonder what was the second major disappointment in the life of Miss October 1962.)

SOUTHERNERS AND CROAKING IN THE BIG POWER POND

In the old film *Bananas*, Woody Allen's nebbish character, Fielding Mellish, struggles vainly at a banquet to get through a disastrous joke that alienates the listeners.

The agony of the speaker is periodically recreated throughout the country when, say, a golfer or a white member of the City Council misjudges and tells a relatively mild modern parable that dies, and dies, and dies as the joke-teller struggles through the parable about the races. Along with other complications, such jokes shoot down endorsements and prospects for the presidencies of city councils, colleges and universities, and major corporations.

Since I have spent my adult years in journalism (in Birmingham during the turbulent 1960s) or in education (teaching about communication and humanities), let me share a few insights that may help other Southerners.

I have developed some rules about using the Power Dialect and croaking in the Big Power Pond:

Rule 1: White Southerners cannot tell any joke about African-Americans, cannot use an Uncle Remus dialect, and cannot attend cook-outs that jest at being coon-hunts.

Rule 2: White Americans from any region cannot tell such jokes, if they wish to prosper in the politics of government, athletics, the military, or business. Ditto for dialect and race-theme cook-outs.

Rule 3: Ambitious whites (in politics, public service, or the military) cannot even use the word *nigger*, since the word forks lightning and electrocutes the user. (Few sober whites would be so silly as to use the high-voltage word in public.)

The Bill of Rights may provide for freedom of speech or association, but whites may not speak freely regarding the above. That may be unfair; however, it only re-adjusts the scales that so long permitted us whites to be condescending, paternalistic, or even malicious in speaking to, or about, people of color.

Let me illustrate the restrictions with "The Garbage Truck Story," which I first heard in my home state:

> Two men are driving a garbage truck to the city dump, but, since they forgot to bring a tarpaulin, they notice that trash is blowing onto the highway. The driver says to his African-American co-worker to get in back of the truck and lie down to hold down the trash. He explains, "If you don't keep it from blowing off, we're going to get a ticket, and the fine will come out of our pockets." The co-worker climbs in back and spreads himself out until he covers the maximum trash. The truck passes two Pollacks working on a telephone line, causing one to shake his head and say, "Someone's thrown away a perfectly good nigger."

Now, besides the insensitivity of the last line, I assumed the joke originated in Chicago, Philadelphia, Pittsburgh, or New York. I knew that many of my fellow Alabamians vaguely knew a Pollack was someone from Poland, but it was not natural for Southerners to stick that element in a story.

The Garbage Truck Story next surfaced in a film, *Better Off Dead*, a 1985 dark comedy in which the teenaged protagonist tries repeatedly to kill himself. He ponders jumping off a bridge over an expressway, but is knocked in by a passerby, and, instead of being reduced to a pulp on the asphalt by big rigs, he lands on the back of a truck hauling trash. The truck passes beneath two African-American linemen at work on a telephone pole, and one delivers a variation of the line, "Someone's thrown away a perfectly good white boy."

The exact joke appeared in a second film, *Men at Work* (1990), once again with the punchline using "a perfectly good white boy."

What is happening here?

Clearly, the concept of the original story was not racist (what was supposedly thrown away, after all, was "perfectly good"), but it used ethnic overtones and a racist term in the punch line. However, two black characters, social underdogs, could safely deliver the punchline about someone from a more secure and powerful social class.

Long before I came into the world, white Southerners had few penalties when they told jokes about blacks and whites. Genteel Southerners did have rules about when to say "colored people" or the Southern form of "Negro." Ignorant people or trash, of course, said "nigger." When Stokely Carmichael, Eldridge Cleaver, or Dick Gregory began referring to "black is beautiful," Genteel Southerners resisted since *black* might be "too impolite" to use. We could digress that it wasn't too impolite to keep the colored people from using the same water fountain, restroom, lunch counter or café, or movie theatre. Contradictions in human behavior are built into our psyche so that the angels will have something to laugh about.

After a decade or so of everyone adjusting to saying "blacks" or "black people," the grander term, *African-American*, came in. With its seven syllables, the term has its defects:

—Are Egyptians who move to the U.S. African-Americans?

—Do white Afrikaners immigrating here become African-Americans or European-African-Americans?

Yes, there are problems with the simpler terms, too: Blacks are often brown, tan, or even lighter than some outdoorsmen in my family. We whites may be pink, though tan or "pink, freckled, and liver-spotted" more exactly describes many of us.

Many terms, of course, have gone out of fashion. White racists may spout off about a *nigger*, but no white says *darky*, *pickaninny*, *Negress*, *quadroon*, or *mulatto*, all quite common in the 1800s and in the early 1900s. Several recordings from the 1930s can make us wince. For example, in the Paul Whiteman recording, "Mississippi Mud" by James Cavanaugh and Harry Barris, Bing Crosby and the Rhythm Boys sing the lyrics about "When the darkies beat their feet on the Mississippi Mud." In the Tommy Dorsey recording of the 1940s, that phrase was changed to the more euphonious "When the people beat their feet."

If you have surfed through the cable system or listened to various radio stations, you have heard rappers, athletes, and black comics regularly use the word *nigger*. These African-Americans may safely use the word because they have announced themselves as small frogs satisfied with their Small Power Ponds.

With some exceptions (Ronald Reagan, Arnold Schwarzenegger, George Murphy, Sonny Bono, Fred Thompson, and Al Franken from entertainment and Bill Bradley, Jack Kemp, Jesse Ventura, J.C. Watts and Steve Largent from sports), actors and athletes, regardless of race, do not get to be frogs in the Big Power Pond.

Michael Jordan, Roger Staubach, and Whoopi Goldberg would thrive in the Big Pond, but Bill Cosby drops from the

A-list and joins Richard Pryor, Dennis Rodman, the late Michael Jackson, Howard Stern, and Andrew Dice Clay as those who would not thrive in the Big Pond.

Nigger, we see, may only be used by African-Americans who are *not* ambitious and who announce themselves as socially or politically second-rate.

That means one thing. My Rule 3 above applies to everyone. *Nigger* (though it derives from the Latin *niger* for "black") has become a 100 percent racist term, which we do not permit Serious People to use. Serious People among African-Americans include Colin Powell, Condoleeza Rice, Clarence Thomas, Jesse Jackson, and others.

When you look at the word and study why it has become so odious, we realize that it is not the sound itself. Skimming through the alphabet, we have similar words: *bigger*, *chigger*, *digger*, *figger* (colloquial for "figure"), *Gigger* (proper name in Kipling), *jigger*, *ligger*, *rigger*, *trigger* or *Tigger* (Christopher Robin's friend), and *wigger* (proper Dutch surname and possibly someone who works with wigs). Ironically, then, when we refer to the "n"-word, we are referring to the most abhorrent part of the word. Clearly, we do not object to the mere sound of the word, but to its connotation: It represents the horror of Jim Crow laws and cruelty masquerading as vigilantism to protect the peace.

In the mid-1970s in London, I attended a variety show at the Palladium and was shocked by comics' open use of racist humor. The five comics (two of them black or half-black) did not tell "The Garbage Truck Story," but they told the "Hitchhiker Story." I had heard this version in my home state:

> Two blacks are hitch-hiking but not having any luck. One says that a car will stop if one of them lies down on the highway. While he reads out the tag of the approaching car, the joke ends with "bump bump" since

> Governor Faubus of Arkansas or Wallace of Alabama is the driver. In London, the story involved two Pakistanis, and this time the car was driven by the late Enoch Powell, the great opponent to unlimited immigration.

That taught me that the world will always have ethnic and social humor, but ambitious people avoid such terms if they wish to advance in politics, business, the military, athletics, or public service.

What about the case of the District of Columbia officials from a decade or two ago who fired a white employee for using the word *niggardly*? The African-Americans to whom he was speaking were certain that he was dissing them, and they complained to officials. An uproar swept through the country and provided op ed columnists and newspaper editorialists with a topic *du jour*. Most of the columns and editorials *tsk-tsk*ed at the ignorance of the D.C. workers who wouldn't even look up the word, which had nothing to do with race.

Instead of standing four-square with education and the search for truth, let me suggest another perspective: Whenever we write or speak, we have a primary responsibility to consider our audience's strengths and weaknesses. We have an obligation to use words that will best communicate what we want to say. *Niggardly* simply fails to rate very high. If we mean that budget constraints will require our agency to be stingy, then we can take comfort in the fact that most listeners will understand the word *stingy*. *Parsimonious* probably would not be as effective as *stingy*, but it would not unintentionally offend as *niggardly* would do, unless the audience included a parson or a parsnip.

THE WEARING OF THE OLIVE DRAB

Some time ago, a conservative columnist was defending the non-military background of Newt Gingrich when he first became Speaker of the U.S. House of Representatives. It is sort of embarrassing when you have been lambasting your opponent for *not* having worn the olive-drab, only to find out that one of your own prominent leaders has had similar wardrobe deficiencies. (And, yes, they wear jungle or desert camo now.)

Such can be the stuff of which schizophrenia is made, as a columnist asserts, in effect, "Suh, there's a danged big difference between Yo' Cowardly Civilian and Our Stead-fast and True Civilian Patriot." So, the columnist wrote, "Abe Lincoln was one hell of a hawk back then [during the War of Energetic Northern Tourism in the South], although he never himself saw action."

Presumably the columnist meant that President Abe did not strap on a sword and try to lead troops at Manassas. He certainly did not. By the same token, George Washington during his eight years as President did not go into combat, and Dwight Eisenhower managed to resist the temptation to storm a hill in Korea or the beaches of Lebanon.

However, Abe had been in the military, particularly 1832's Black Hawk War. Abe enlisted as a volunteer but was elected captain of his company. Years later, Abe joked that he had seen no "live fighting Indians" during the war but had had "a good many bloody struggles with the mosquitoes."

At some point, in looking at the gray-haired crowd, we see it is futile to discuss the military careers or non-careers of American males when in their twenties. In fact, in between the Korean Conflict and the Vietnam Confusion, we had males in each high school graduating class facing the draft.

If we were drafted after high school or after college, we faced four likely scenarios:

THE BEETLE BAILEY SCENARIO: We would dig fox-holes in continual maneuvers or bivouacs in Kansas, or maybe Iowa, but some place where the only point in digging the fox-hole was to kill two years of time and satisfy Sergeant Snorkel.

THE ELVIS SCENARIO: We might luck up and get stationed in Germany, which could be like having two years of digging fox-holes in the Black Forest on Monday through Friday (though Elvis got to be a jeep driver) and perhaps time to see the Old World on the weekend. We could not count on our own Priscilla, however; considering her age at the time, that is just as well.

THE FROZEN BUTT SCENARIO: Instead of freezing our derrieres in Germany, we would freeze them off in Korea on the barren rocks that made such depressing news reels.

ENLISTMENT SCENARIO: We actually might enlist in something. We could enlist in the U.S. Navy for six years and barf out our hearts and souls for the Good Old USA. Or we could enlist in the Army for four years and perhaps still wind up digging your fox-holes. Or the Air Force recruiter could tell us how peachy keen it would be to be a jet pilot, although he would admit, "Now that you mention it, pilots don't get a chance to say 'oops' a lot." (We omit the U.S.

Marine option without comment.) Or, there was the home-grown option of enlisting in the "Nasty Guard."

So it was that I also did not see action in the Vietnam War when it came later, but I served as a company clerk for an Army National Guard unit. General Schwarzkopf is proud of his service in Vietnam and in the Gulf War, but I must emphasize that I was so successful in defending Bessemer, Alabama, from the atheistic hordes of communism that even today there are thousands of people in Bessemer who do not even know the meaning of the word *communism*.

Democrats and Republicans will use any weaponry against each other in political campaigns, but it does not hurt for the electorate to remember that the Vietnam Confusion was NOT World War II. At any time, President Lyndon Johnson and the Democratic Congress could have called up guard units, could have said that caring for children or working as a flunky journalist did not exempt one from service. LBJ could have said that college enrollment was not sufficient; he could have said that conscientious objectors could at least be medics, and so on.

World War II is about the only war having America's near total support, but even that support materialized only *after* the Japanese were foolish enough to bomb Pearl Harbor. The rest of America's wars, from the Revolutionary War, to the Black Hawk War, to the War against Southern Contrariness, to World War I, and Vietnam, had substantial opposition.

Since Congress and Presidents Johnson and Nixon did not commit the U.S. completely to the Vietnam War, we need to get off the backs of Newt and Bill Clinton.

FARLEY AND THE RIGHT ENDING

As an admirer of cartoon art and story-telling, I noticed the day that Lynn Johnston's strip, "For Better or Worse," added a puppy named Edgar.

When Edgar showed up to irritate his old father, Farley, it signaled to me that Johnston's model for Farley had probably died. In addition, since she writes and draws a realistic strip (and an excellent one, at that), I figured Farley's days were numbered.

By contrast, Daisy in "Blondie" has been a canine Greek chorus to Dagwood's foolishness since 1930, while Ruff has been with "Dennis the Menace" since the lad began menacing his neighborhood in the 1950s. The Bumsteads aged enough for the kids to be teens, but then time stopped. Their Daisy has never aged, unlike Farley.

Johnston had featured panels about Farley's sleepiness and inability to hear or see as well. Assuming that Farley was a real long-time family dog, I wondered how she would handle his death.

She could have let him die in his sleep, as probably happened to the real Farley. Perhaps the old dog stepped out in front of a truck or car. That happens far too often. Perhaps she would have Elly Patterson take him to the vet as I had to do with my old Cholly, his back legs useless due to hip dysplasia, and have him put down. Would Elly cry all the way home, as I had done, or would the pet-executioner have to be John, her husband?

One day, with Elly's mother visiting, little April (who was about four years old) discovered a toy boat that the melting snow had revealed. Delighted, she was looking for a place to float it, and she remembered the river. As the bright idea crossed her face, young Edgar and old Farley were looking on, both a little worried.

"Uh oh," I called to my wife, "Farley's about to buy the farm."

She snatched the paper out of my hands and scanned the day's panels. "She wouldn't do that! It'd be cruel and sadistic."

In the next day or two, the adults in the strip talked about the weather and the dangerous river, and April got closer to her destination.

"How do you *know* Farley's going to drown?" my wife challenged, becoming increasingly upset.

"Well, I don't think April will drown, but the currents may prove too much for Farley. He may save the little girl, but not be able to save himself. Or maybe hypothermia will get him."

Finally came the day when April slipped into the river, and the last panel that day showed her underwater, her eyes wide open.

Each day on the way to work, I was stopping to buy the paper, checking "For Better or Worse," and then driving on, knowing that I wouldn't mention the day's happenings when I got home.

Meanwhile, like Lassie running for help, Edgar was hightailing it to April's house, barking and trying to get John, Elly and Elizabeth to come.

Farley, of course, had jumped into the river and was holding onto April for all he was worth. Eventually the

Pattersons figured out she had gone to the river, and they got there, and, working like a team, managed to pull out April and Farley, who promptly collapsed of "exhaustion."

I thought I was wrong for two days, while the adults chorused relief that April was safe and sang their praises for the wonderful Farley. But their accolades sounded a bit like a eulogy. Then Elizabeth noticed that Farley wasn't breathing. As their vet confirmed, the strain had proved too much for the old dog.

I should not have doubted the direction of the story because Johnston draws and writes truly. A dishonest and immoral writer will fudge at the crucial moment, perhaps rewriting the ending of *Romeo and Juliet* so the lovers get together or cheating death to bring back Bobby Ewing, Spock, or Sherlock.

As Farley was holding onto April, Johnston had drawn April's eyes wide open and Farley's eyes closed. An excited animal, of course, will open its eyes as wide as possible, perhaps in panic, but Johnston was telling us that Farley had used up his regular energy, plus the energy from the adrenalin in his system, and was doing all he could to hold on for just a few seconds more, and then he collapsed.

Perhaps it is not realistic to let an old dog die such a heroic death. Going Farley's way is better than watching a plunger in a hypodermic needle go down in one second and life go out the next. Yes, and it is better than seeing some growth on a pet's belly and watching it eat away at the life-force. It is also far better than what happens to millions of little creatures who meet death on highways or in the supposedly humane chambers of animal shelters.

I wrote to Johnston up in Canada and learned that I had been guilty (once again, of course) of committing the biographical fallacy: assuming that Farley had lived with them to his less dramatic death.

Johnston wrote back: "The real Farley story is—we used to live in a house in Drundos, Ontario, overlooking a ravine. We bought an O.E.S. (Old English Sheepdog) puppy, but, when our son was born, the dog, Farley, was jealous, became a threat, and we gave him to a childless couple in the country. The river in the ravine was always on my mind. I worried about Aaron and then Kate going down and falling in—but we moved to Northern Manitoba, where Rod was a FLYING DENTIST for six years (the arctic run), and the kids grew up, and the worst fears never happened. I saved my 'imagined scenario' for the strip."

Fiction writers, of course, take bits and pieces of "real life" and put them together to tell stories. A little bit of Aaron and Kate have gone into the fictional Michael and Elizabeth, as Johnston demonstrates that artist-writers for comic strips have much in common with playwrights, novelists, and screenwriters.

A final thought: Ms. Johnston eventually let her strip come to an end, although it is still going on in re-runs. It is comforting to learn that even a story-teller in ink can make you shed tears for a character, even for an old dog that neither you nor anyone else has ever petted.

LOOKING AT THE BIG PICTURE

Various forms of narrative today seem to prove that an imagination, a mind, is a terrible thing to waste, but, waste it, we will. Centuries and millennia ago, story-tellers used their memories to preserve stories of struggle, triumph, treachery, and debauchery. Today, despite SAT scores and high-sounding babble about technology, we have moved more and more towards minimal use of our brains and discipline.

To prove this point, I want to focus on some symptoms that on the surface may seem dissimilar, but, to those of us with mosaic minds, are key pieces in the big picture.

Let's begin with one of the tempests that may erupt in the journalistic teapot of your choice. Our first piece in the mosaic does not rank high, but it has its significance.

For much of a year, the main newspaper in Northeast Florida was featuring irate letters about the paper's choice of comic strips. Many readers complained about the absence of the "story strips," while a few readers (subversives no doubt and probably Communists to boot) maintained that comic strips are only supposed to be funny.

Naturally, as an expert on popular culture, I have weighty opinions about what belongs in newspapers, and I am a particular authority on comics and the funnies, having acquired impressive credentials as a kid.

To establish these credentials for this forum, I need to put it on the record that, in 1946, while we briefly resided in

Gadsden, Alabama, my father introduced me to some man at the circulation building of *The Birmingham News*. "Son, I want you to meet Popeye."

Although much of what my father said needed to be sifted carefully, he had, nonetheless, gained my immediate attention. Popeye was high on my list of personalities to meet, but even my five-year-old mind knew that Popeye only appeared in the funnies or on the movie screen along with Gene, Roy, Bugs, and Tarzan. Clearly, that slightly overweight gentleman before me was not the Sailor Man. He looked as if he might live down the street from us and might wave at us as he grilled hot-dogs in his backyard.

Later, I understood that I had shaken hands with Tom Sims, the writer for "Thimble Theatre" (a/k/a/ "Popeye the Sailor") and other newspaper features. Sims came after the Great Era of E.C. Segar, for the cognoscenti.

Then, a decade later at a conference in Orlando for high school newspaper staffers, I met one of the giants of the cartooning field when I conquered the latent insecurity of a zit-ridden ninth grader, walked to the front of an auditorium after an address (where *people* still in the hall could, and probably *would*, look at me!). I forced myself to ask (and receive) the autograph of Roy Crane, the creator of "Buzz Sawyer" and "Wash Tubbs and Cap'n Easy," the latter then being drawn by Leslie Turner. (Crane and Turner were adept in the use of washes…for those who don't know.)

Keep in mind that, in the Pantheon of the Great Ones of the 1930s to 1950s, you had the late George Herriman, Alex Raymond, Milt Caniff, Roy Crane, Hal Foster, and a few other skilled artists. Others in the Pantheon, such as Chester Gould of "Dick Tracy" and Harold Gray of "Little Orphan Annie" couldn't really draw worth a flip, though their strips often told potent stories.

Now, these are heady credentials, and, if you are not sufficiently impressed, you should stay away from me at parties. I will not know, nor care, anything about deconstruction, the best mileage for today's automobiles, mutual funds and stock options, or the latest trysts of Brittany with the Society for Minor League Shortstops. Moreover, you probably won't know of James Thurber, writer and "third-rate" cartoonist; Dashiell Hammett, novelist and script writer for "Secret Agent X-9," artwork by Alex Raymond; e.e. cummings, poet and painter; Benjamin Franklin, Master of Everything, plus creator of a key political cartoon; and others.

Having established my credentials and crankiness, I will return to the Northeast Florida paper that was being roasted for having dropped most of its story-strips. I would delight in criticizing this newspaper for this misjudgment, especially since Article I of The Bill of Life says, "All Americans shall lambaste their daily newspaper every day and every way." To digress slightly, I note that it is grossly unfair that Article II says, "Each American city or town gets the newspaper that it deserves."

Mix all the above together, and you have my mindset on a spin through much of Florida, some of Georgia, and Alabama, when I decided to study other newspapers and found that (dramatic fanfare and drum roll) Jacksonville's *Florida Times-Union* actually merited high marks for having three daily story strips: "Gil Thorpe," "Mary Worth," and "Steve Roper & Mike Nomad." It has since dropped all three, generally replacing them with strips by cartoonists who can't draw. ("Alley Oop" lives in the Valdosta and Ocala papers. In *The Gainesville Sun*, The Ghost Who Walks still puts jungle villains in their place in "The Phantom." Elsewhere, Uncle Walt, Skeezix and others still go on in "Gasoline Alley.")

Many Florida newspapers don't have *any* story strips, while a few will only have "Mary Worth." The *T-U*, although keen enough to follow journalistic trends, once deserved some congratulations for being conservative enough to hold onto three story strips. It also merited a pat on the back for holding onto Lynn Johnston's brilliant strip, "For Better or Worse," even though some short-sighted readers were complaining a few years ago about Mike's friend discovering his gayness. I knew this was nothing, since it was only a matter of time before friendly old mutt Farley had to be put down. I also predicted correctly that the warranty on Elly's mom would play out by and by, and, of course, both of those events came to pass.

Out of curiosity, I wondered what the *T-U* was doing back in the 1960s. Mr. Microfilm Machine informed me that, in 1963, the daily *T-U* had twelve story strips: "Gil Thorpe," "Laredo," "Mickey Finn," "Dick Tracy," "Mary Worth," "Mary Perkins On Stage," "Terry & the Pirates" (originally by Caniff, but drawn since the early 1950s by George Wunder, who executed bottom lips in a unique way that both disturbed and intrigued me), Caniff's "Steve Canyon," "Steve Roper" (with the emphasis then more on Steve instead of Mike Nomad), "Annie Rooney" (a "Little Orphan Annie" clone, but better drawn), "David Crane," and "Buzz Sawyer." The Sunday issue added "Walt Disney's 'Son of Flubber'" (rotating the Disney spot as it went through each of their films), "Lil Abner," "Tales from the Great Book," and "Judge Parker" (then more about the Judge and not so much about Sam Driver).

Later, as I had the melancholy duty of sorting out the junk and intrinsic treasures in the attic in our family house, I opened a trunk and found dozens of copies of newspapers from the 1950s and 1960s, mainly from Pensacola, Birmingham, and Norfolk. As I noted that the vivid colors of the Sunday sections were undimmed by time, bright light, or dust, I saw that the trend was the same: Story strips regularly outnumbered gag strips.

Today's gag strips, to be fair, may not tell stories, but a few of them may do the equivalent of, say, TV sketches: Blondie starts up her own business; "For Better or Worse" deals with the death of a beloved old neighbor, the aging of parents, peer pressure of children, and the loss of pets; and "Doonesbury" played out various narratives.

So what is happening in newspapers, other than the infection of the worst features of *USA Today*? Story strips require some coherence, skill in plotting and story-telling, and some thinking; they bear a distant relationship to the works of Homer. Alas, the goal of newspapers today is to "dumb down" for their readers. For example, on the news side, snippets of news stories replace the fuller treatments of yore. The complete addresses of, say, U.S. presidents to Congress were appearing only in the papers that viewed themselves as national "newspapers of record." Newspapers were becoming as much as possible like TV (while C-Spans 1 & 2 and YouTube become the medium of record).

Lately, the speeches, statistics, Wall Street stocks, and the like receive links on newspaper web pages, but get almost no ink space.

Uncle Walter used to say that television news could never cover stories with the thoroughness of newspapers. Cronkite noted that a TV news story might take up one or two minutes of air time. By contrast, the newspaper stories, he was saying in the 1960s and 1970s, would be much more extensive.

The ethos of newspaper editors from the boob-tube era, however, now argues that papers don't need to give extensive coverage to what has already been on the network news shows. They will also assert that their readers don't *want* long stories or can't follow them anymore (an odd position portending no confidence in the future of daily journalism).

Regarding the comics, editors allege that they must reduce even the sizes of comics (to conserve space). Oddly enough, they simultaneously enlarge weather pages, house ads, photos, and artwork, and they set stories in large type with ragged ends, flushed left or right, to "open up" the pages with white space.

It is strange that, if "stories" in comics are passé for newspapers, why isn't television filled with variety shows with comics, jugglers, and something different every two minutes? Where are today's versions of "Laugh-In" and "Hee-Haw"? But the national networks mainly have shows that "tell stories," slight though many of these may be. Notice also that cable TV relies very much on the old "story" programs, thanks to their re-runs of "Alfred Hitchcock Presents," "Twilight Zone," even "The Dick van Dyke Show."

Moreover, newspapers in the hot metal days just didn't do surveys about the funnies. The editors themselves decided which strips appeared, or disappeared. Today's newspaper editors (like Pilate washing his hands) use surveys, supposedly to involve their readers, but apparently designed more to come up with demographic data to dump story strips and blame the deed on somebody else.

Of course, it is helpful if newspaper readers will quickly forget that the *story* strips that were dumped. That way, the readers can enjoy the newspapers' biting editorials and columns that decry TV networks' refusal to support quality shows that may have low ratings or poor demographics (a case of the Print calling the Pixel black).

Another popular culture expert may observe that newspapers of the 1920s and 1930s (and before) regularly printed short fiction and poetry. The story comic strips, no doubt, helped to kill off this area of fiction writing.

Although we know that the Road to Cultural Oblivion is paved with inattention, We Caretakers of Civilization remember the glorious jewels that we once enjoyed. For example, while my brothers and I emptied our deceased parents' attic and house, I felt my melancholy lifted by the brilliance of a Sunday comic section from the early 1960s: the beautiful, dynamic, and exciting draughtsmanship of Milt Caniff, George Wunder, and Hal Foster as areas of black competed with the primary reds, blues, and yellows.

Pope Julius II must have felt the same when he first espied the ceiling Sistine Chapel by Michelangelo: "What beautiful colors, what lines and visuals!" No doubt, he looked at the image of God creating night and day, at Adam and Eve standing next to the tree, and at God punishing our progenitors for their sins, and he probably added, "And what a wonderful story they tell!"

THE HAPPINESS FROM A COLUMN

I started thinking about a co-worker from long ago, when I heard a discussion about heart bypasses and the big C.

Several decades of calendars have been used up since the time I was rotating flunky duties for *The Birmingham News*: copy editor, makeup editor, sometimes writer, Friday night high school football sports writer, and continual grumbler. However, it seems as if it was only a couple of years ago.

One of my two favorite complainers was Richard Pitner, a transplant from Idaho whose horn-rim glasses and tight curls reminded me of jazz pianist Dave Brubeck. Pit, however, played puns, not piano keys, and could out-pun me ten puns to one, leaving me sputtering obscenities at him because he would use the two or three that I *would* have thought of if he hadn't been sharper.

None of us, neither Pit, a friend I'll call Sam, nor yours truly, liked the way that *The News* was being run and published. Surprisingly enough, *The News'* top execs paid no more attention to me than did the top brass in the Alabama National Guard, nor the executive officers of any other organization I've been involved in. (That, plus the fact that I was lazy and immature, was a grievous problem.)

One day, *The News* created a magazine section called *Saturday Punch*, which was to contain the TV schedules for the upcoming week, columns and articles on restaurants, pop music, the arts scene, Hollywood personalities, and the like.

They suggested that some staff members rotate on a column, and Pit was contributing every other week. He worked over and polished his piece, and, since he was an excellent copy-editor, he wrote a column that seldom required any additional editing. He wrote gentle, sometimes teasing pieces about home life, dentists, and neighbors.

Oh yes, and he gleefully called the column, "Pitner Patter," and grinned evilly when you winced at his audacity.

During a coffee break, Pit told Sam and me that he was going to win out and be the sole columnist. Sure enough, after a while, "Pitner Patter" was the weekly feature.

Pit met the challenge of the weekly column, which balanced nicely with the mind-numbing routine of editing that he had to handle. Writing a column three times a week (as Bill Buckley, James Kilpatrick, Ellen Goodman, and others have done) is daunting. Someone, maybe the late Mike Royko or Lewis Grizzard, once noted that column writing is fun, for the first seven columns; then the tyranny of the task sets in.

Pit, by contrast, handled a different tyranny: our regular baskets of copy, plus the "redline" financial edition each weekday. As he used a portion of his mind to process the stocks, he devoted most of it to thinking of something amusing for his column.

During this time, I noticed that his carping about the idiocy of *The News* editors declined, though his remarks about the managing editor, the late John Bloomer, maintained their edge.

However, during one coffee break, fellow grumbler Sam described an editorial meeting at which the top editors evaluated the pluses and minuses of *Saturday Punch*. Someone had suggested dropping Pit's column, but the managing editor jumped to its defense. "Many readers look forward each week to Pitner's column," Bloomer said. "We've got to keep it."

Pit had the strangest look on his face when he processed that his supposed nemesis was one of the strongest supporters of his belovéd column.

Eventually, I wearied of the tedium of working at one spot from 5 a.m. to 1 p.m. (or 6 to 2 on other days), and I left for graduate school and a classroom where I could talk about Shakespeare and Michelangelo and get paid for it, but I followed Pit's writing whenever I vacationed in my home state.

One day my father mailed me a clipping about Pit's death. Apparently he had been having pains in his legs and went to his doctors for a check-up, and, whatever physical problem it was, it took him out quickly. For years, I thought it was the curse of cancer. Lately, though, a social media site for former employees of the *News* mentioned Pit and one of his humanitarian acts. Pit had a very rare type of blood and regularly received calls that his blood was needed. He always responded, and apparently one of those donations resulted in an unclean needle giving him Hepatitis C or HIV/AIDS.

When I think of this good man, always fondly and with an appreciation for his humor and for his tightly written columns, I also think of how lucky some people are to have jobs that they absolutely look forward to, not the whole job necessarily, but at least to a significant part of that job. When I remember the satisfied joy in his face for a job well done, I feel sorry for the poor soul who goes ten, twenty, or thirty years in a job without praise or fulfillment.

Writing, believe it or not, can bring meaning to a life and can make jobs and routines tolerable. If you write as cleanly as a certain puckish punster did two or three decades ago, you will have reason to be pleased with your accomplishment.

"LIGHTS, CAMERA, ACTION, SCRIBBLE!"

Filmmakers in Hollywood and Britain have often used writers as characters and have labored to come up with exciting visuals as the scribes create their novels, plays, or poems.

Writers pace the seashore and wrinkle their brows to come up with ideas, and the 100-piece orchestra saws its strings a little off camera while the waves lash against the shore.

The movies usually do not show what writers actually do, which is read a lot, scrunch over and write with a quill or a keyboard, grimace at what they have written, frown at rejection slips, smile occasionally at an acceptance, and revise, revise, revise.

So, film buffs everywhere, let's quiz you on movies about writers, but we make a few restrictions:

The movies in the quiz have to be theatrical films about real poets, novelists, or playwrights; and they shouldn't include any films by Ken Russell.

Okay, on second thought, we will let the late Ken Russell play, too, even with the nudity, drugs, and rats he likes to use.

First, a warm-up: What American writer is most likely to appear as a character in a film set before 1900? That, of course, would be Mark Twain, who even appeared twice on *Star Trek: The Next Generation.* (Don't ask.) Edgar Allan Poe, of course, comes in second, thanks to walk-ons in various horror flicks.

A second warm-up: Until recently, what major British writer is *least* likely to appear as a character in historic films? Among the titans of Brit Lit, William Shakespeare was seldom used until *Shakespeare in Love.* In *Anonymous*, Roland Emmerich tried to make the case that Edward de Vere was the true author of Shakespeare's plays.

Now let's go for the questions that count:

1. Two poets are enjoying themselves in Switzer- land, making up spooky stories and swapping ideas. One poet's new wife is only eighteen and has a yearning to write. Name films involving any of the three main writers. (10 points for each film named)

2. A woman with an unhappy marriage leaves the North and settles in a swampy area of Florida, where she realizes the story potential of the rustic setting. (10 points)

3. The Irishman is immobilized by cerebral palsy, but finally gets movement in a foot, so he paints and even writes a novel. (10 points)

4. He's witty, but also the social conscience of France in the 18th Century. Knowing the danger of dissent, he lives next to the Swiss border in case he needs to make a run for it. In his old age, the Parisians finally celebrate his work. (10 points)

5. Although continually fighting and being arrested for theft, he was well-beloved by Parisians during the reign of Louis XI. (10 points each)

6. A British science-fiction writer is chasing after Jack the Ripper in a time-machine. (10 points)

7. A British poet lives with her maiden aunt in the 20th Century. (10 points)

8. The French woman uses a male penname for her novels and stories and is in love with a pianist-composer. (10 points for each)

9. An old bachelor in Britain has spent his life with his writing until an American divorcee comes along. They marry and live happily until illness strikes her. (10 points)

10. This film is about the last years of a British writer of "dirty novels." (10 points)

11. Inspired by the example of sports writer Paul Gallico (who boxed with Jack Dempsey to see what it was like), this Ivy League writer talks a professional football team into letting him take some snaps in a game. (10 points)

12. Karen Blixen marries for convenience and moves to Nairobi, where she falls in love with an Englishman and pursues her writing career. (10 points)

13. A playwright, novelist, and all-around wit defends his reputation in a libel suit, but loses and winds up in jail for sexual deviance. (10 points for each)

14. The Persian poet gave us the lines "a loaf of bread, a jug of wine, and thou" and inspired a silly film, even though he was a great mathematician, astronomer, free thinker and epigrammatist.

15. He made it through the Civil War, wrote lots of weird short stories and devilish definitions, and then disappeared in Mexico in 1913. Perhaps Pancho Villa's troops got him. Or maybe it was an *X-Files* case that would have interested Mulder and Scully. (10 points)

16. This fabulist and long-time slave from Samos in the sixth century B. C. goes a-wooing in a film that will tell you more about Hollywood musicals than about the Greeks. (10 points)

17. Controversy and a passion for art followed this Japanese writer after World War II. Also, an actor,

playwright, director, and militarist, he commits a ritual suicide in 1970. (10 points)

18. While in a Spanish prison, the author wiles away the time by writing, supposedly prompted by prisoners to come up with an entertaining tale. (10 points)

19. He writes hard-boiled detective stories and novels and is in love with a playwright. (10 points each)

20. A mathematician-logician is afflicted with a stammer and is drawn to the society of children, especially little girls. He writes two famous books for a Miss Liddell. (10 points for each)

Answers to the Movie Quiz

1. *Gothic* (1986), with Natasha Richardson and Julian Sands, shows the danger of turning Ken Russell loose with undeveloped film and a script supposedly about Lord Byron, Percy Shelley, Mary Shelley, and Dr. John Polidori back in 1816. The film is a mess historically since it is doubtful that any woman in the party crawled around nude with a rat in her mouth, and Russell probably had a bad trip, too. Polidori was inspired to write *The Vampyr* (which some want to credit to Byron), but Mary's creation was more powerful.

Haunted Summer (1988), with Phillips Anglim and Laura Dern, does a little better job of telling about that encounter. However, *The Bride of Frankenstein* (1935) is a better all-around film than *Gothic* or *Haunted Summer.* It opens with Mary getting ideas for what became *Frankenstein: A Modern Prometheus.* Elsa Lanchester played Mary and the Bride. Other films: Lord Byron is featured in *Lady Caroline Lamb* (1972) and *Bad Lord Byron* (1951).

2. *Cross Creek* (1983) starred Mary Steenburgen as Marjorie Kinnan Rawlings, with Malcolm McDowell doing a cameo as Scribner's legendary editor Maxwell Perkins.

3. *My Left Foot* (1989) features Daniel Day-Lewis as the Dublin author Christy Brown.

4. *Voltaire* (1933) features George Arliss playing the author of *Candide* and finally being feted in the capital when he is an old man. The parties prove too exhausting and kill off the old fellow.

5. François Villon, poet and scoundrel, was the subject of *The Vagabond King* (1956), with Kathryn Grayson, Oreste, Rita Moreno, and others, and *If I Were King* (1938), with Ronald Colman and Basil Rathbone.

6. Not very biographical or historical, but generally fun, *Time After Time* (1979) features Malcolm McDowell as H.G. Wells, with David Warner playing the Ripper. Wells, author of *The Time Machine*, has become as useful as Mark Twain to some SF story-tellers and even appeared several times as a character on ABC's *Lois and Clark*.

7. *Stevie* (1978) featured Glenda Jackson as Yorkshire-born Stevie Smith, with Mona Washbourne playing the aunt. The diminutive Florence Margaret Smith was nicknamed "Stevie," after a jockey. The film is based on the play by Hugh Whitemore.

8. Merle Oberon plays George Sand in *Song to Remember* (1945), with Cornel Wilde as Frederic Chopin, but a better version may be *Impromptu* (1991), with Judy Davis, Hugh Grant, Mandy Patinkin, Emma Thompson and others.

9. Anthony Hopkins played long-time bachelor C.S. Lewis in *Shadowlands* (1994), whose script was by playwright William Nicholson. Debra Winger played the love interest, and Edward Hardwicke was Lewis' brother Warnie.

10. Ian McKellen portrayed the ailing D.H. Lawrence in *Priest of Love* (1985), with Janet Suzman playing his wife Frieda during his last years when *Lady Chatterley's Lover* was published.

11. Alan Alda played George Plimpton in *The Paper Lion* (1968), which also featured Alex Karras and Sugar Ray Robinson.

12. She adopts the penname Isak Dinessen and is played by Meryl Streep in *Out of Africa* (1985).

13. That's Oscar Wilde, of course, who often crops up in films: e.g., *Oscar Wilde* (1960), with Robert Morley in the title role; *The Trials of Oscar Wilde* (1960), with Peter Finch as the Wilde man. Oh, and someone let Ken Russell loose again, so we wind up with *Salome's Last Dance* (1988), which has Oscar lounging in a knocking-shop, where his play is about to be performed (and where he will be arrested by and by). Stephen Fry portrayed the title role in *Wilde* (1998), which also starred Jude Law and Vanessa Redgrave.

14. *Omar Khayyam* (1957) featured Cornel Wilde as the author of *The Rubaiyat.* It also starred Debra Paget, John Derek, and Raymond Massey. (10 points)

15. Ambrose Bierce, played by Gregory Peck, is the subject of *Old Gringo* (1989). It also featured Jane Fonda as an American spinster.

16. *A Night in Paradise* (1946) was supposedly about Aesop of fables fame. It starred Merle Oberon, Turhan Bey (as Aesop), Gale Sondergaard, Ray Collins, and Ernest Truex.

17. *Mishima* (1985) is a stylized drama about Yukio Mishima.

18. Miguel de Cervantes, of course, was the creator of Don Quixote, and the film is *The Man of La Mancha* (1972), with Peter O'Toole playing Cervantes and Quixote.

19. Jason Robards plays Dashiell Hammett in *Julia* (1977), with Jane Fonda as Lillian Hellman and Vanessa Redgrave as her radical friend in the 1930s. *Hammett* (1983) is a piece of fiction about Hammett's involvement in a real-life mystery. It stars Frederic Forest, Peter Boyle, and Elisha Cook.

20. Ian Holm played the Reverend Charles Dodgson, or Lewis Carroll, in *Dreamchild* (1985), which features Alice (Coral Browne) coming to America in the 1930s in her 80s and remembering some scenes that make today's viewers uncomfortable.

Scores: 250-290, You do not watch any network TV, you do not read, and you are going to too many Ken Russell films; 210-240, You have an excellent memory and you are probably avoiding Ken Russell flicks; 150-200, You are probably reading more than the average bear; 50-140, You are either reading a whole lot or you only go to the movies to see *Star Trek Degenerations*; 10-40, You only go to Ken Russell films, or you *are* Ken Russell.

WHEN HELL FREEZES OVER

A colleague saunters into the faculty lounge, spots me sipping my decaffeinated stomach lubricant, and stiffens instead of amiably passing the time, as he would have done a year earlier. He frowns, sits nonetheless, and, with exaggerated concentration, maneuvers the lid off his thermal food container.

I become fascinated at the change in the formerly versatile colleague. Once he was able to feed his face, flirt with the women in the lounge, and overhear and comment on his male friends' battles with generators and errant students, all simultaneously. Now, he musters all his powers into making sure his lukewarm carrots negotiate the distance from thermos to his mouth. He is too absorbed to speak.

What is the reason for the transformation?

Simple. To his way of thinking, I had picked up a social disease: unionism.

It is not hard to understand the reaction, for I remember the attempts of one history instructor to bring the American Federation of Teachers to our campus. "I'll tell you what," I taunted. "I'll join your AFT when a man in a red suit, with cloven feet, and a pointed tail, stops me and says, 'Howard, old buddy, it's frozen over.'"

But things started happening: unwise administrative decisions; portents that our college might turn into a mere high school, filled with the faults of the worst of the country's schools; students steadily dropping in quality, with no college officials willing to state publicly that the high schools were not doing their jobs ("So you think I'm stupid enough to ruin my career?"); and so on.

There came a decision: I could hope that the situation did not worsen, since I could endure the ordeal at that time; or I could fight to prevent further deterioration, since most of my teaching career lay ahead of me.

Then one day I handed a dues' check to the late John Kolesar, geology instructor and treasurer of the local. I did so secure in the knowledge that Dante's *Inferno* should now be called Dante's *Icebox*.

When I entered the union along with many conservative colleagues, I shared their vows: We would *not* become firebrands interested only in recoiling at some offense and declaring war; we would be suspicious of the word *strike*, especially because the 1968 fiasco in Florida; we would use our dominant strength to keep any malcontents from ruining our school and profession.

Satisfied that the majority of my new allies felt the same way about protecting themselves and the non-union members, I managed to see how the new alliance could offer strength to education and how it could even help administrators to endorse educational reforms ("I'm sorry, man, but Johnny's got to improve his reading level. As a school official, I can't just let anybody into a regular college class or I'll have a platoon of faculty firebrands in here trying to run me out of town. You understand, don't you?").

Behind my new faith, however, I still had remnants of the old anti-union religion, which had been dutifully taught to us by Southern editorialists, ministers, and Chambers of Commerce.

During the depression in my hometown, a certain barber took it upon himself to paint his house. The painters' union heard about his atrocity and gathered in force to picket his house. They paraded back and forth, glowering at the barber on his ladder. Finally, the barber noticed their attitude was becoming nasty, and he ambled over, only to hear them complain, "You're costing us a job and taking money out of our pockets."

The barber weighed the matter a minute, nodded in agreement, and said, "That's true, but how many of you shaved yourself this morning?"

They all did.

"Well, I cut hair and shave men, and *you're* taking money out of *my* pocket." With that, he turned around and splashed more paint on his house. The pickets disappeared.

In the same town, my uncle, Joe Stephenson, and his partner Jim McClain came back from the war and opened a cafe called Jim & Joe's. They had one cafe and even managed to open a second one. However, they learned that the restaurant and cafe business is rough, and they were only making enough money to support one family, but hardly enough for two of them to stay at it indefinitely. The original cafe, however, needed to be painted, and, after closing on Saturday, they painted the place themselves.

So Monday morning, they opened with shiny, fresh enamel on the walls to greet the hungry citizens. On Tuesday, Jim & Joe's opened to the usual business, but with two pickets out front. For the next couple of days, Jim & Joe's remained "unfair" to local labor. On Friday, one of Joe's quail-hunting friends dropped in for lunch and returned the shotgun he had borrowed from Joe.

During a lull, Joe lounged at a table near the front window and noticed the gun was dirtier than he liked. He disassembled the gun and cleaned and oiled the parts.

Only later did he notice that the pickets had disappeared. After a while, he laughed when he figured out why they left.

As rock 'n' roll was coming in, I was discovering a stack of old 78s and realizing that the Big Band Era had once existed. To my horror, I also found that Big Bands had been fatally weakened, not only by such major wartime restrictions as gas rationing and the draft, but also by a musicians' strike. George T. Simon recounts how James Caesar Petrillo of the American Federation of Musicians ordered his members to stop all recording on August 1, 1942:

> If the record companies couldn't devise some system whereby musicians were paid for the use of their recordings on radio programs and in jukeboxes, then he wouldn't let them record at all. The big band leaders almost to a man disagreed violently with Petrillo's actions. They recognized far better than he the importance of records to their future. The strike did not end until November, 1944.

After the strike ended, the world of music had moved on, leaving big band music behind. The singers now prevailed, and the glory days would be no more. To this day, I select August 1, 1942, as the day that Western Civilization capitulated and surrendered to the forces of darkness.

Once there was a great newspaper called *The New York Herald-Tribune*, but the *Herald-Tribune* was sinking in the quicksand of ineffective organization, obsolete equipment, high salaries, and a unionism that refused to permit streamlining and modernization.

The *Herald-Trib* was sold and became the *World Journal Tribune*, but the old ailments still prevailed and finally killed the new creature. Read *The World of Jimmy Breslin* for a fuller account.

So, the old religion had much validity and was not founded on superstition and myth, but *new* truths do emerge.

One summer, I was telling one of my aunts about life in the junior college classroom: "...and I finally joined the union, if you can believe it."

"Oh, you were forced to join," she said. "Well, my neighbor's daughter had to join the union to work at the department store where she was hired."

"No, I wasn't *forced* to. It was the only logical thing to do." I recounted the growing deficiencies and showed her the stack of student papers that I had been sending my grandmother.

Unfortunately, my exact description backfired. "This is not even third-grade work," she declared. "How can you put up with this? I believe I'd look for a job somewhere else, in a *real* college."

"Well, I *do* have *some* good students."

Her husband interrupted, "If that's as good as the schools can do, then we ought to close them down...that is, if they don't change."

I said, "They won't change, not until some professionals gain enough strength to make it politically expedient to change."

These staunch Republicans, probably to be polite with one of the youngsters, said, "Yes, I guess so."

The moral of these digressions?

1. Unions have their place, but they ought not to try to conquer the world.

2. Unwise actions, such as the one Petrillo took after reading the report of an "expert," can be disastrous. Just as union leaders should have consulted the big band leaders, so should any teachers' union, and all educrats, listen to all of the teachers.

3. Featherbedding ought to be spurned, as with the one-to-four ratio of administrators to faculty in most of higher education.

4. The main spur for employees to form a union is poor management and bad supervisors. When employees are treated fairly, it often doesn't occur to them to form a union.

These digressions also imply that the institution and the profession are to be protected, promoted, and improved at all costs. To do otherwise is to invite professional damnation.

And hell is a very cold spot.

Igor and a Few Warm Bodies

Q. You are probably asked this a lot, but let me bring it up anyway. Did Hollywood and the books get any of it right?

A. About me and Dr. Frankenstein? Nein, they always seemed to miss the whole point.

Q. Could you explain that?

A. They usually make me look like some idiot. Sometimes they call me "Igor"; other times, "Fritz."

Q. What is correct?

A. I've got one of those wallet-sized diplomas. If you can see in this light, check out the name on the diploma. See? "Igor Fritzenheimer."

Q. So it is. Now you claim Dr. Frankenstein was simply trying to run a school.

A. Exactly, prep school, college, university, it didn't matter to the Doctor. Once he got an idea, you just had to stand aside. You know how those people are.

Q. So you and he opened the school, and what happened?

A. Nobody came. We had spent a year at it. I was busy putting up chalkboards and making desks, and the Doctor was writing lesson plans, but zilch.

Q. What did the Doctor do then?

A. Oh, he pitched a holy fit, of course, and, when he calmed down, he sent me out to get a few warm bodies, speaking metaphorically, as I realized later when I deposited all the fresh corpses in the science lab.

Q. Did that please him?

A. Good Lord, no. He came in, saw the corpses, and hollered, "Do I have to do *every* damned thing myself?" He'd say that sort of stuff. He'd go on, and on, till you wanted to pull your hair out.

Q. What did you do with the bodies?

A. Well, we put them on ice until we could figure out a use for them. Then we put an ad in the Sunday paper asking for students with a temperature of 98.6 degrees.

Q. Did that help him attract any pupils?

A. Nein, not a one.

Q. Did he ever think about opening a charter school and using tax monies to put all students online and pay himself a salary of half a million?

A. It seemed like a sweet deal to me, but the Doctor had his principles: "I'm no educational crook," you see? I may only have a freezer full of corpses, but it's honest.

Q. What happened next?

A. That's when he began tinkering with the bodies.

Q. What, if anything, was correct in the movies?

A. Well, let's see. The basic experiment was okay, I suppose, but, when the fingers first moved, the Doctor didn't shout, "It's alive! It's alive!"

Q. What *did* he say?

A. "Professor Fritzenheimer! Take this one to testing and placement!"

Q. Do you remember the name of the first one?

A. The Doctor wanted to call him "Adam," which seemed sort of egotistical to me, but the first creation wasn't a scholar. No, sir, he never was meant for the schoolroom. Called himself "Boris."

Q. Boris? Now, that's the one that started all the troubles, correct?

A. That's the one.

Q. How did that really happen?

A. Well, I got him through the Kruder Preference Test and then the Strong-Campbell Interest Inventory. You know, basically about what he wanted to do in life. He kept saying he was more concerned about what he wanted to do in death.

Q. I see.

A. Next, I gave him the Myers-Briggs Personality Assessment test, to see whether he was Introvert / Extravert, Sensing / Intuitive, Thinking / Feeling, or Judging / Perceptive. I'm an INTJ myself, meaning Introvert, Intuitive, Thinking, and Judging.

Q. What was this Boris?

A. I really don't know. Before we could test him, he went rampaging out the door after snapping the neck of a counselor.

Q. That must have upset the Doctor.

A. Not really. It was only a counselor. The Doctor always had a hard edge as far as management was concerned. But then Boris rampaged through the village and tore down the school there.

Q. That must have terrified the children.

A. Are you crazy? Weren't you listening? He *tore down* the *school.* Get it?

Q. Oh, I see. Didn't he throw a little girl into a lake?

A. Well, yes, he sort of did that, but it was Frau Schmidt's third-grade class. He threw them *all* in, but they all got out. Thought it was great fun and wanted him to do it again. Oh, now that I think of it, Boris probably was an ESFP, him being so impetuous and all that.

Q. What would ESFP be?

A. Extravert, Sensing, Feeling, and Perceptive.

Q. I don't understand *Perceptive*.

A. That mainly means "spontaneous."

Q. Why isn't it just called *Spontaneous*? That could drive you to distraction.

A. That's what Boris said. Anyway, the village was all upset and chased us out of the castle and over the hillside. Things settled down by and by, and we turned out some fine graduates. Now I spend all my time grading papers, going to departmental meetings, and listening to excuses like "my grandmother died…the dog ate my homework…my hard-drive crashed."

Q. You sound a little melancholy.

A. Ja, I guess I am. The old days were rough at times, but they also had their blessings, you know. Back then, you'd go into a tavern, and the villagers perked up. They were interested to see you: "Güten Tag, Igor. What's new? Hey, Fritzenheimer, *who's* new?" Of course, now and then, they might feel the need to go after you with pitchforks and torches, but at least there was some gawdamned Respect, you know what I mean? But, now, if you try to tell them about kids turning in their papers all late, their eyes just glaze over, you see.

Q. Is the Doctor still active?

A. Oh, yes.

Q. He's the president, or principal?

A. He prefers to be called the "Headmaster," given his interest in fresh brains and minds. Still teaches a class now and then, mainly Anatomy and Ethics. Dry stuff, but the students don't dare go brain-dead on him, not with him just dying to pop a fresh one in their craniums, or *crania*. He's exact about his Latin, you know.

Q. If you had to do it all over?

A. I might go into Mortuary Science.

Q. Why's that?

A. It'd be easier to pump embalming fluid into dead bodies than knowledge into dead brains.

Q. Would you like a clipping? I can email it to you or send it by snail mail.

A. My computer's frozen up, so just mail it to me.

Q. At the Frankenstein Academy?

A. He changed the name to Second Chance Academy.

Q. I saw your billboard on the way here: "You'll graduate with a better brain than you came here with."

A. And who has to read the obits and keep up with the deaths of rocket scientists and geniuses? Who has to dig them up? Fraulein, bitte ein weiteres Glas Bier!

Q. Auf Wiedersehen, Igor.

THE PARABLE OF THE "BLUE NECKTIE RULE"

Once there was a college where many believed that true-blue professionals wore blue neckties or scarves. The college did not actually have a rule that specified that a faculty member must wear a blue necktie or scarf, but, during chit-chat at meetings and around the coffeepot, you often heard:

"He's a good man in the classroom and wears a fine blue necktie, too."

"She's very competent, relates well with students, and I love her blue scarf."

Not all faculty or administrators wore blue neckties or scarves. Some wore brown neckwear, or plaid, or even none at all. And nothing was said, because, after all, the college did not have a dress code.

In the Widgetry Department, a Professor Mann was one of many faculty members who did not wear blue neckties.

One day, a student complained to his supervisor about not understanding him, and the supervisor, having been to a marketing seminar on Students as Customers, announced, "The student is *always* right." He promptly transferred the customer to Miz Lovely's class because the last time she failed anyone was during the administration of Bush the Elder and Wiser.

After the next test in Professor Mann's class, other students complained about This and That, since they knew a way to get out of having to learn material on tests.

The supervisor looked up "This" and "That" in the policy manual, but didn't find any reference to board policy, though it did say, "See *AWT* volumes." The supervisor checked the *Academic Writ Tome* (*AWT*) for "This" and "That" and found this unhelpful direction: "See *Policy Manual*."

The supervisor pondered the complaints of the students and had an inspiration: Hang on, darn it. Mann did *not* wear a blue necktie.

He mentioned that fact to one of the complainers, who said with a straight face, "Oh, yeah, real distracting to all of us. It's either brown—"

"Or he doesn't have one on at all," another complainer added.

The supervisor met with Professor Mann and discussed this deficiency. Mann then read the *Academic Writ Tome* and saw that it did not have any rule requiring the wearing of blue neckties.

Evaluation time came in February, and Professor Mann received "Satisfactory, but Needs Improvement." The evaluation stated, "Professor does not understand the need for proper professional attire and should wear a blue necktie as recommended by knowledgeable academics."

During that year, Professor Mann did not put on a blue necktie, though he wore a teal-and-gold clip-on, a yellow bowtie, and on special days a black mask like Zorro's.

By the next February, the rating had changed to "Unsatisfactory," and Professor Mann was *ordered* to wear a blue necktie.

Professor Mann then wrote to the president, all 64 vice presidents, 232 of the 983 associate vice presidents asking them to confirm that the *Academic Writ Tome* did not say you *had* to wear a blue necktie. Two responses tried to give Professor Mann the impression that the *AWT* required what his supervisor said. The other vice presidents and associate vice presidents did not respond since they were involved in a study to get greater efficiency from the 20 full-time instructors and 16,000 adjunct faculty at the college.

Professor Mann applied for a grievance hearing to pin down this blue necktie rule and his obligation to obey it. The supervisor said it could not be grieved, but gave it to an Ad Hoc Complaint committee composed of Amelia Earhart, Ambrose Bierce, and D.B. Cooper. Neither his grievance nor the committee itself was ever heard of again.

Next, Professor Mann received a certified letter notifying him that the college was recommending to the board that he be terminated because he was guilty of gross insubordination in not obeying a valid command related to the performance of his job in the Widgetry Department.

Professor Mann grieved the termination because the validity of the rule still had not been examined. The president and the battalion of vice presidents ignored the request, and Mann was terminated.

MORAL: When a bureaucracy wants to lynch someone, any neckwear will do for a noose.

A MATRIX CHRISTMAS TO EVERYONE

Dr. Franklin T. Foxwhistle of the Bureau of Bureaucracies frowned at the bearded gentleman and gestured for him to take a seat. He flipped through a file for several minutes in silence. "You know why you're here, Claus?"

The old man made a nervous joke, which he swallowed in awkward silence.

Foxwhistle merely stared at him through thick glasses that made his eyes the size of pie-graphs projected on a screen. "The B.O.B. has noticed that you have been delivering all of these presents by yourself. Is that true?"

"I had some helpers. I can't take all the credit."

"Helpers, helpers." Foxwhistle flipped through the folder. "I don't see any W-4 forms on these personnel."

"*Er*, they're not salaried." Santa encountered the big eyes again. "They help out because, well, they care."

Foxwhistle scribbled on his pad and muttered, "Unsalaried assistants. I don't suppose you pay any liability insurance for them?" He glanced up a second and sighed at Santa's blank look. "I thought not. Do you supervise them?"

"They're responsible and professional. It hasn't—"

"Unsupervised assistants." Foxwhistle drummed on the table.

"Do your assistants ever have any injuries on the job?"

"Yes, sir, now and then, usually nothing serious."

"Usually?" Foxwhistle gave him a dubious look. "You have coverage for Workman's Comp?"

"I don't know Mr. Workman, sir."

"Claus, who do you report to, some sort of indefinite Higher Power, I suppose?"

Claus fidgeted and cleared his throat. "Well, that and to all the boys and girls. I *do* have to satisfy them."

"You don't have any annual supervisory evaluation?"

Santa's mouth had dried up, and he only managed a bleat in response.

Foxwhistle made two more entries on the file and frowned at the old man. "Claus, bureaucratically your operation is a disaster. To remedy the problem, we are creating a president of holiday eleemosynary activities, with six vice presidents: one for each continent, of course. Then we'll have assistant vice presidents for males and females respectively in each zone. Under these necessary officials, we shall have associate assistant vice presidents, with responsibilities for presents-mechanical (non-battery or non-electronic), presents-electronic and battery-driven, presents-biological (flowering plants, mink, and so forth)."

"Won't these responsibilities overlap?"

"You don't know about matrix management, do you?"

Santa sighed. "Very well, I'll tell the reindeer."

"Oh, that's another thing: We're replacing Donner, Blitzen, and the rest with program managers."

Defeated, Santa left the office of the Bureau of Bureaucracies humming, "We wish you a Matrix Christmas, We wish you—"

No Bad Administrators: Train Edu-Crats the Schoolhouse Way

BY BARBARA SCHOOLHOUSE

You hear a lot of rubbish from faculty about the hopelessness of dealing with administrators. Having now taught for almost four decades and having dealt with all breeds of administrators, I have earned the right to express my views about bureaucratic behavior due to my experience over the decades at Barkshire College in the U.K.

During nearly four decades, I have heard faculty despairing about their destructive and uncontrollable supervisors. Collective bargaining, of course, is the quickest and best solution, but many timid faculty wish to know what to do until bargaining comes about.

Consider this: Unless a supervisor is out-right savage or mentally unbalanced, he or she can be made a useful member of your educational institution. My code has always been, "There aren't any 'bad' administrators; there are only lazy and timid faculty."

What behaviours do faculty complain about in administrators? They whine about the following: The supervisors stick together. They trash classrooms. They trample on rights. They spend the institution's money on fads and frills. They engage in favouritism. They lose sight of the real purpose of the institution.

Isn't it natural that the administrators should transgress in these ways?

Let's consider the nature of the beast: Administrators are pack animals. They feel comfortable having a lot of their kind around. Consequently, a typical system for state colleges or universities, will have one administrator for every four full-time instructors. For camouflage, the administrators only like officially to recognise a small number, as they try to redefine a pack of directors, coordinators, and the like using various mongrel titles.

What inattentive faculty have permitted to develop is a change in the pack behaviour. Formerly, the pack consisted of the classroom professionals, who selected one of their kind to be department chair, dean, or president, or, under another scenario, the pack evolved after a highly competent classroom professional established a school with himself or herself as president or principal and then hired other professionals as needed. The *alpha* professional, though, was the leader.

Under the current programme, however, the *alpha* professional is so separated from the normal pack that he or she only identifies with other neglected administrators. This perverted pack then loses sight of the larger purpose and misbehaves. It is appalling the number of administrators whose eyes show scant intelligence, whose understanding of the meaning of basic educational principles is lacking, and whose main preoccupation is either sitting in a meeting or giving reports to others.

What is the solution?

First, the faculty need to look at their own attitudes and behaviour. If they are too unimaginative to cope with administrators, they are possibly too short-sighted to handle students either. They might consider other occupations: sorting potatoes or being quiz-show hosts on the telly.

Second, faculty should use a metaphorical choke-chain with their supervisors. The most effective choke-chain, as you may well surmise, involves collective bargaining. Sans contract, though, the choke-chain should be jerked whenever the administrator goes against the best interests of the authentic pack. You can get their attention by using memoranda jointly signed by the faculty, reports to faculty groups about specific infractions, letters of complaint further up the chain of command, or letters outside the institution to state officials and the media. It is not necessary to jerk the chain hard or to cut off the air supply. I always say, "Each loving jerk will cure the supervisor of becoming an unlovable jerk."

When administrators respond positively, conscientious faculty members will let them know it. Praise them each time and do so straight-forwardly, without irony, since irony only confuses and discourages them. Use their name, and I've found it most effective if you preface your praise with the word *what*: "*What* a *good* dean, Dr. Jones! *What* an *excellent* way to monitor class sizes! *Good* administrator, *what* a *good* administrator you are, Dr. Jones!"

Insist that they teach at least one class per semester to remain refreshed and to maintain their identity with the authentic pack. And don't forget the praise: "*What* a *wonderful* instructor you are, Dr. Jones!"

Despite the folk wisdom that "the only good administrator is a dead administrator," I maintain that it is rare that an administrator really needs to be put down. They are not all attack dogs or obese lap-dogs. If faculty are firm, exciting, full of fun, outgoing, and angry when appropriate, the administrator will try to please the classroom professionals.

Whenever it is time for *talkies*, whether in meetings or classes, you will find that an administrator, properly trained, can be a teacher's best friend.

A PASSION FOR SEARCHING FOR ACADEMIC EXCELLENCE OR SOMETHING

Once upon a time, the vagaries of a college's management drove me from my familiar shelves in the library with their titles by Mary Renault, V.S. Naipaul, and James Thurber to the strange volumes to be found on shelves devoted to business administration. Although these tomes lacked the wit of essays by, say, Gore Vidal, these books did enable me to understand the way *good* managers think, evaluate, evaluate success, and treat their employees.

Over the years, this English-lit major plowed through tomes by (ex-)presidents of such firms as ITT and Chrysler, through a few *Reader's Digest*-level how-to-manage-better books, along with the coffee-table best-sellers, *A Passion for Excellence*, *In Search of Excellence*, *Restructuring the Corporation*, and Tom Peters' *Thriving for Chaos*. On campus, you would see administrators carrying *Chaos*, since it was the book *du jour*.

A business instructor, of course, has read all of the works of such management experts as Peter Drucker and could recommend a dozen other works to review. However, non-business readers may not wish to lose their claim to dilettantism by plowing through M.B.A.-land and, as I desire, may only wish to know the major recommendations of these books.

For readers who are mildly curious about the content of these books, here is a summary of the major points:

1. A firm (or college or public agency) should demand quality and refuse to accept anything less. They speak of G.I.G.O.—or "garbage in, garbage out" or of "the bad drives out the good." (Therefore, we infer that, if faculty turn their classes into play periods, we drive off serious students and only keep, and attract, students who wish to play.)
2. A firm should find its essence and emphasize that primary purpose: that is, a shirt manufacturer should not saddle itself with cookie factories and tire-recapping franchises. If the firm's expertise is in food, it should focus on food. (Therefore, a college is supposed to *teach*; everything else is secondary or tertiary.)
3. A firm should get rid of excessive layers of management. Managers should also wander around and be close to the action of producing the product and satisfying the customers, but, if the managers simply fill nebulous slots in middle management, they should be given productive jobs or handed pink slips. (Higher education sometimes uses fake designations and job classifications, but, after any camouflage is removed, we have one administrator for every four full-time faculty members; therefore—)
4. To produce a better product, a firm should consult the men and women actually producing the product. The firm should go to the workers themselves and solicit the expertise, and the potential energy that is there.

5. A firm should treat its employees decently and should establish an environment of trust.
6. Firms should be responsive to customer complaints and suggestions.
7. Employees and managers should measure, measure, measure quality.

Many of these points carry over into higher education and into other public agencies, although not necessarily to the extent that any trend-following administrators may prefer. However, as public employees pursue excellence and thrive on "chaos," we should note the spots where the business-and-education analogy breaks down.

For example, although it is true that faculty and staff have a product to deliver, our product differs from such solid consumer items as automobiles, computers, or hamburgers. At times, our partially infotainment product is akin to movies, plays, concerts, or television shows in that it will entertain and occupy the mind. The entertainment may be "cotton candy," "bubblegum," or, as William Shatner said years ago of his cop show, *T. J. Hooker*, "chip and dip" of the mind. Customers may flick the channels or turn off shows that bore them; they may very well be bored by anything that demands more than car chases and prime-time cat-fights on the soaps.

By contrast, our product, quality education, seeks to evoke a *change* in our customers: They should have acquired a new skill (e.g., welding, musicianship, etc.) or an appropriate, and higher, degree of knowledge (e.g., of philosophy, humanities, microbiology, etc.).

We deal in changed responses, in learned behavior, and the acquisition of knowledge (which may be a combination of skills, facts, and awareness). Whereas customers going into a hamburger joint are always right because they know exactly how they want their burgers and fries, our customers should not always have it their way. They may often be exploring new territory. As they encounter new ways of thinking, they will meet the normal frustrations of dealing with a new environment; they may well have to contend with their biggest obstacles: themselves and their past patterns of "learning" or thinking.

At this point, our customers are not necessarily right, and our appropriate metaphor should not be the assembly-line turning out a reliable laptop, i-phone, or Blackberry. Although coaxing and enticing are the preferred approaches for us to use, to paraphrase Gore Vidal, the student may have to be dragged, kicking and screaming, into the world of knowledge. That is because, as Herbert Spencer says, "Education has for its objective the formation of character."

In this respect, we recreate the essential conflict in *Karate Kid* or *An Officer and a Gentleman*, which are stories of change, dedication, and acceptance of new standards. Each student experiences his or her equivalent of a *Bildungsroman* (coming of age story).

By sharp contrast to the pupils from Japanese and European schools and the better-run schools in America (perhaps even Marva Collins' school in Chicago), our students often come to us with the worst imaginable habits and with defective educational standards. They may have neglected attendance through high school, even dropping out to pursue the freedom from regimen found in G.E.D. programs. Not students at all, but more enrollees, they may view classes as times to socialize and be entertained. They may approve of classes that remind them of MTV, with swirls of disjointed images, background music, and (to pay homage to our exalted purpose) an exercise in name-dropping masquerading as knowledge ("Who has heard of Edward Jenner? No, Bubba, Edward Jenner did not want to have a sex change. Oh, come on, let's hear it for Immanuel Kant!").

In addition, the students may have worked all night at some job and, absolutely exhausted, use class time to sleep. As victims of alcoholism, abuse, or poverty, they may truly live in *chaos*, and, although doing little in class, they should receive some praise for simply being able to function in chaos. Such chaos does not automatically entitle the student to a passing grade since the student still needs to pass.

Trendy management books notwithstanding, people do not thrive in chaos. Chaos is William Butler Yeats' rough beast rising to slouch through the madness of revolutionary Ireland. Chaos is the horror, the cannibalism, the murder of the terrified passengers on the raft of Gericault's *Medusa.* Chaos is the killing fields of Cambodia, post-Arabian springs in Iraq, Libya, Syria, Somalia, or the Gaza Strip. Contrary to Peters' title, chaos is *not* fluctuating energy prices or stiff competition, or, in our case, students refusing to sign up for classes exactly as we have scheduled them.

No, people, colleges, and firms thrive, not on chaos, but on flux, mutability, on change, all operating within the framework of order. In actual chaos, "the best lack all conviction," while the "worst are full of passionate intensity." In the private sector, a typical firm will meet a blank and pitiless state by going bankrupt if it (like Enron or the mega-banks) ignores the proper mixture of striving for quality, of adjusting to the market, and of avoiding the waste of administrative featherbedding, golden parachutes, and ecological irresponsibility. In the public sector, however, an agency may drag its slow thighs through the metaphorical mud, slowing increasingly as the weight collects on its feet.

At one time, it was managerially stylish to develop extensive administrative procedures manuals, but the pendulum swung the other way, and experts such as Peters were recommending getting rid of these volumes. Peters suggests a "one-sentence" procedures system based on a system of trust, thus presenting us with a chicken-or-the-egg problem.

Extensive rules for agencies are often written when state auditors complain that resources are being wasted or stolen, that no one knows where inventory items are, that employees are mistreated, etc.

In another area, employees may have been given widely different treatment under similar circumstances, or are told drastically different interpretations of policies by supervisors. So, to ensure that public monies are being spent wisely, the agency may devise procedures.

These procedures may even outline a typical three- or four-step grievance system to provide a safety valve. Hence, because there is distrust in the ability of a bureaucracy to spend wisely or supervise uniformly, the agency or firm developed uniform procedures; because uniform supervisors were not trusted, a safety net was created.

Let's focus on the people-procedures, while keeping in mind that, to state officials, wise management of funds is more important than merely being courteous and kind to people.

Peters says that firms and employees, by golly, will just have to put up with a period of uncertainty in order to establish the trust that can be found in a "one-sentence" management. Especially in the public sector where quarterly statements do not measure progress, Peters' oxymoronic advice ignores these valid requirements of public agencies: They have to make certain that they adjudicate their problems fairly and that they keep sufficient records to demonstrate fair treatment when the fairness of decisions is questioned. At the worst, his advice of "operate by the seat of your pants" may produce chaos, or, at more benign times, merely shiny double-knits. When distorted, the one-sentence system may result in the organization relying excessively on the "orders" of its supervisors; each "order" that is not obeyed may be perceived as insubordination, though the so-called order itself was ill-advised or even illegal to begin with.

As colleges, in theory, thrive on flux and work for an environment of trust, they certainly should trim any massive volumes of administrative procedures manuals (APMs). At times, the APMs may become downright silly in their specificity, perhaps even telling a faculty member how to write a letter to a textbook publisher to request a desk copy of a textbook.

A college APM system may even evolve into chaos in unnecessary ways. First, the APMs supposedly are the procedures or principles by which colleges operate. However, many colleges may make changes in the APMs without even notifying their employees that a new rule/procedure is in effect. New APMs may appear without notations that "APM #-xyz (dated—-) supersedes the earlier APM #-xyz." Some APMs may be clearly obsolete.

At Fairy Land College, the procedures/rules would be adopted according to an ideal system that involves maximum participation of the employees. (Or a truly utopian system would feature what *I* want.)

Under a system endorsed by the coffee-table books on pursuing excellent management, a college would at least send notices to faculty or other employees: "Enclosed see the proposed revisions for APM-xyz. Please read and make any recommendations for changes to——."

A college should leave enough procedures in place for employees and the "customers," the student, to know what to expect. Fairly stated and publicized procedures help a college to reduce tensions and stay out of court. Fair rules and procedures also promote, as Abraham Lincoln wrote in another context, a "sense of attachment" between faculty and management and between all of us and other customers. The absence of this "sense of attachment" creates an environment in which only Yeatsian beasts thrive.

HOBGOBLINS AND AMERICAN BOSSES

A foolish consistency is the hobgoblin of little minds, adored by little statesmen and philosophers and divines. With consistency a great soul has simply nothing to do.

— Ralph Waldo Emerson

I normally hang out in the wading pool of philosophy and try not to plunge into the currents and riptides where you find Emerson, Heidegger, Kant, and other deep thinkers. However, Emerson's quote floated in the wind over to my wading pool one summer long ago, and I have read and re-read it over the years. It's often incorrectly quoted without the word "foolish," which augurs that we can bounce all over the place.

In politics, some people think they must be consistent, come high water or wading pools, even when they end up being foolish. For example, it is axiomatic that modern Republicans believe that unions are corrupt. They protect the lazy and the incompetent.

Having taken that position, they want to be consistent and, therefore, ignore any counter-argument about any benefit of unions. You may have noticed that Frau Anne

Coulter in her columns bemoans the presence of work rules from a collective bargaining contract. They prevent the supervisor from kicking butt and compelling his or her employees to get down to work.

In this mindset, there is no attempt to see what good the unions perform.

Quick digression: Unions *are* corrupt, but so are governments, corporations, churches, families, bridge-clubs, sports booster clubs, publications, professional athletes, etc. If we skip stones across this lake of human endeavors, they will touch upon a Jim Jones at Jamestown, the 1919 Black Sox players, a plethora of pederast priests and adulterous and predatory preachers, Pope Alexander VI, Kenneth Lay, Tom Delay, the administrations of U.S. Grant and Warren G. Harding, and so on.

Since Frau Coulter is enamored of being the darling of the far right, she ignores this key fact: Many Republicans, Democrats, Liberals, Tea Partiers, independents, etc. have worked under lousy bosses and supervisors. If you talk to people at the right time and coax them to describe their worst bosses ever, you will be sprayed by a geyser of frustrations.

Let's look at some lousy bosses in pop culture. Naturally, the Michael Scott character in *The Office* is an example of what not to do. In *9 to 5*, scriptwriters Patricia Resnick and Colin Higgins created the character Franklin Hart Jr. (Dabney Coleman). Hart was a boss who was a sexist, deceiving, hypocritical jerk. Scott Adams' comic strip *Dilbert* chronicles the stupidity and even criminality of managers and top execs.

Pop culture also provides us with examples of poor employees: Dagwood Bumstead, Wally in *Dilbert*, and Beetle Bailey, plus the lay-abouts Andy Capp and Snuffy Smith.

In real life, these lousy bosses are all around us and at happy hour may cause us to pop quarters in the juke box to listen to Johnny Paycheck singing David Allen Coe's lyrics for

"Take This Job and Shove It." We can grumble about our fool of a foreman or supervisor who thinks he is cool with his "brand new flat top." We grouse about this "regular dog-the-line boss."

Of course, sometimes supervisors need to nag at those on an assembly line, but even that can be taken to an extreme. Decades ago, we read with disgust of autoworkers deliberately dropping new cars off of forklifts. Such vandalism, such sabotage! Damned unions!

Some time later, John DeLorean wrote about the rest of the story. Management had insisted that the line keep running, no matter what. The line didn't stop even if the workers were being forced to put in defective parts. A major component (alternator or fuel injector) was defective, but that part was still being installed, and consumers would wind up buying lemons that would not run properly. A dealer, of course, would fix the car under warranty, but why should a customer have to tolerate that? To show their contempt, some workers began dropping the cars.

Driven by William Edwards Deming's principles, Japanese car makers began winning the loyalty of American motorists by adhering to Deming's rules, including these two:

"Cease dependence on inspection to achieve quality. Eliminate the need for massive inspection by building quality into the product in the first place."

"End the practice of awarding business on the basis of price tag. Instead, minimize total cost."

To his credit, Henry Ford refined the modern assembly line, instituted a higher wage, and reduced the work hours, but, to Ford's discredit, in the late 1920s, the company began to speed up its assembly line beyond the point where workers could keep up a reasonable pace. Ford hired spies; they dogged their workers, who weren't permitted to smile, tell one-liners, or whatever on the line.

The workers developed the "Ford stare," faces void of emotion even on their days off when they were with their children in a grocery store.

We find bad bosses elsewhere, in offices, on sales floors, in hospitals, and on campuses.

A new top exec comes in and tries to discard every procedure and practice of the former leadership. No one other than the new boss could have had any good ideas.

A new boss attends meetings, more meetings, and even additional meetings, but she isn't focused on doing any actual work. Meetings substitute for productivity; each meeting strokes some exec's ego.

A new boss looks the part, but he spends his time decorating his office or surfing the net.

A lower-level boss can be so afraid of making a mistake that she procrastinates on making even simple "yes" or "no" decisions. She delays so long that she ends up making a different mistake.

A boss is supposed to see that his employees are doing what needs to be done. A subordinate may ask for a job description, but the boss never gets around to creating or even asking the employee to provide him with a draft that can be adapted.

A boss wants to micromanage everything. In effect, she ends up interfering with everyone's work and having satisfactory work re-done until it meets her usually elusive standard.

A boss should be aware of a goof-off in the department, but he hopes it will work itself out or go away. He lets Wally be Wally instead of kicking butt as Mr. Dithers and Sgt. Snorkle would do.

Another boss finds defects in one employee, but she ignores that several other employees are worse.

Headquarters wants regular reports about how the

business or office is doing. Local management decides that it will report only what makes itself look good. If someone argues "but these figures aren't right," he is told to sign the form anyway...or else.

Employees go long stretches without knowing the status of their work. If members of their department are supposed to have, say, occupational liability insurance, the boss may lock up the paperwork and be evasive if the matter is brought up in meetings.

In education, the boss may tell a teacher this aphorism from the 1960s: "If one student has failed, the teacher has failed." The bad boss may say, "If you fail the student, you'll just have her in your class next year."

If a teacher has a major disruptive student or two in class, the boss may tell him to tolerate it because "we don't want the parents to sue."

Luckily, we have many more good bosses, but we should never forget that bad bosses are out there. If the top execs impose a standard of negativity on an organization, even pro-management politicos may be surprised by this frequent consequence:

Poor management is the best union organizer in the whole world. Employees, especially in the South, are often reluctant to join or vote for a union. Philosophically, they may oppose the concept of unionism, but, when the work environment becomes too chaotic and threatening, they turn to a union to act as mechanism to let them work in peace.

The organizer is almost never able to recruit Wally, Dagwood, Andy Capp, and Snuffy. Goof-offs rely on lousy managers for their protection.

THE PARABLE OF THE CHICKENS

One of my favorite people was my maternal uncle Joe Stephenson. He ranked high in my universe because he was handsome (reminding me of the actor Robert Sterling as George Kerby in the old *Topper* TV series) and was good natured; moreover, minus the premature gray hair, he was an echo of my belovéd grandfather Pappy. Unlike me, Joe was a people person, who enjoyed chit-chatting with people and exchanging anecdotes; that skill helped him in small businesses that ranged from cafés and barber shops to small-scale coal mining and gentleman farming.

My grandfather, who could be reserved and distant, opened up with his grandchildren and would take two to four grandchildren out into the country to visit his farm property and friends' farms and perhaps to discuss livestock or land deals with the farmers of Walker and Winston Counties. While the adults talked, I was more interested in watching the mules and climbing into the lofts of barns and avoiding stepping barefoot into chicken droppings.

After Pappy's death, Joe also touched base with his nephews to see if any wanted to go out into the country. I always did, even though I was now too old to fight Black Bart and Geronimo amid the barns and outbuildings.

Whereas Pappy drove the company pickup from Kilgore

and Sons Livestock, Joe would generally have, say, a Pontiac for Lynnette and the children but would drive a junker when he went fishing or traveled down unpaved roads to check out property.

On one occasion, Joe said he had purchased a pig and had it in the back seat to take it out to the farm.

A friend wanted to go into the country with him, and, during the course of the ride, the friend lit up a cigarette.

As the ash grew longer, the polite but uncomfortable friend looked about the car for an ashtray. "What do you need?" Joe asked eventually.

"Somewhere to put my ashes." Despite there being a pig in the backseat, the passenger explained, "I don't want to mess up your car."

Apparently, the pig had been equally courteous and thoughtful, at least on that trip.

Once when Joe and I were riding out for him to check on his chicken business (he had one or two long rectangular buildings, each containing, say, 500 chickens), I asked him what were some of the special problems that a chicken farmer faced.

He said they had to be watched because they were bad to clump together and form mounds or pyramids that would suffocate a bunch of them.

"They are also bad to peck each other, and, if they see a speck of blood on one chicken, they'll peck it to death. In fact, we keep bottles of white liquid shoe polish on hand to hide the blood spots. We also cut the red circles out from the feed sacks and staple them to the wall so they will peck these instead of each other."

I laughed, figuring he was pulling my leg, but, after a bit, I realized he was dead serious about it. Years later, I learned about factory farming of chickens: They stay in cages; they evolve into genetic freaks; they even have their beaks burned off so they won't harm each other. Joe's era was more humane.

Joe's little facts about the behavior of chickens stuck with me, and twenty years later, when I was helping fellow employees in grievance-style situations, I would remember those chickens and realize that we humans were equally prone to peck at each other, especially at wounded colleagues. We would deny that, of course, for we like to think we are God's noblest creatures. True, we can't leap tall buildings in a single bound; instead, we sit on our roosts in our cubicles, clucking to ourselves that we really need to get down to business and peck some doofus sorely in need of it.

For that reason, in nastier grievance situations, I advise individuals, as much as possible, to stay away from those who might be destructive. I repeat the Parable of the Chicken to emphasize the point.

Quick digression: When a bureaucratic fight turns its nastiest, colleagues will then fly the coop when an individual enters a room. They clam up just as some of us may do when we know a colleague has Stage 2 or 3 cancer. We don't know what to say, and perhaps we are afraid of catching the ailment, even though intellectually we know it's not contagious. Would that be the behavior of chickens if, say, a hawk or owl has grabbed one of their number for supper?

I got to thinking along these lines because my mosaic mind connects chickens with the McCarthy era hearings and Florida's own version of it with the Charlie Johns committee.

After World War II, many American politicians conveniently forgot that Stalin and the Soviet Union had been our allies against the Hitler and the Nazis. Winston Churchill had joked, "If Hitler invaded hell, I would make at least a favorable reference to the devil in the House of Commons." In the post-war years, any Machiavellian alliances with the Reds were suspect and worthy of investigations.

If we were grading the eggs in the baskets of accused U.S. communists or ex-reds, we would find these stacks:

> **Grade A**: Hard-core members (or the Destructive hard-shell reds) were awaiting a phone call to counter the fascists in the U.S., to aid Moscow, or to sabotage a train or a plant.
>
> **Grade B**: These Idealists thought of themselves as good eggs and believed that Marx and Engels had a good notion. These move up to Grade A if, like Alger Hiss, they start giving away secrets.
>
> **Grade C**: The Discouraged had given up on the Republicans and Democrats and were looking for another solution to the country's problems. Those major party screwballs had messed up the world with the Great War and then the Great Depression. It was time to try something else.
>
> **Grade D**: The Curious had attended some meetings to see what it was all about and drifted away when they got a job or became bored.
>
> **Grade E**: These pitiable souls simply knew someone in Grade C or D.

When the investigations went on, some zealots were trying to smear Grades D and E with the same intensity that those in Grade A might deserve.

In Florida nearly sixty years ago, the state did not have a lieutenant governor to take over if the governor died, as Daniel T. McCarty did in 1953. So the Senate President, Charlie Johns, assumed the governorship for two years. He wasn't elected to his own term, losing to the more progressive and modern Leroy Collins. Johns returned to the state Senate, where he chaired the Florida Legislative Investigation Committee, also known as the "Johns

Committee." This committee not only investigated communists and homosexuals, but also Jewish academics and civil rights advocates. The Johns Committee was following in the footsteps of the Federal Bureau of Investigation, Joe McCarthy's Senate investigators, and the House Un-American Activities Committee. Now we associate these techniques more with the Stasi of East Germany and the KGB of the Soviets. Johns terrorized the students and faculty of the chicken houses of Florida's university system.

I was fortunate enough to come across a copy of Julian E. Farris' novel *The Sin Warriors*, which changed people's names to protect the innocent and guilty during Florida's Red Scare. The Johns investigators could drag in some student or faculty member and try to get him to admit being a homosexual and a communist. Those who strongly protested they were neither were given the third degree until they at least named some names. (If you want to know more about the Farris book, go to http://www.julianearlfarris.com.)

Old habits die hard, and foul politicians still want to peck at people in an opposing political party. Florida's U.S. Rep. Allen West was exhibit A. In April 2012, when he was asked how many card-carrying Marxists and socialists were in Congress, he estimated 78 to 81—those Democrats who comprise the Congressional Progressive Caucus. He was tearing a page out of the playbook of Joe McCarthy.

We don't have to sound alarums at every stupid statement from politicians. Many office-holders seem to adopt the motto, "Think not, but bloviate," as they speak about "legitimate rape" and God's intentions.

However, we do need to exert eternal vigilance to ensure that such silliness doesn't get out of control. We may take comfort in the typical trajectory of such witch hunts.

McCarthy, of course, was pinned to the wall in 1954 when during the Army-McCarthy hearings attorney Joseph

Welch asked, "Have you no sense of decency, sir? At long last, have you left no sense of decency?" The American public picked up on the foolishness of the investigations when the head of the John Birch Society argued that General Dwight Eisenhower, now President Eisenhower, was a communist. Russell Kirk, a conservative intellectual, retorted, "Ike is no communist; he's a golfer."

Other so-called communists identified by the John Birch head included Secretary of State John Foster Dulles, CIA chief Allen Dulles, and Ike's brother Milton. Any short-wave radio fan back then knew that Radio Moscow was not an admirer of either Dulles or Milton Eisenhower.

Excesses also did in the Charlie Johns Committee when it published "the purple book," a meticulous report about homosexuality and questionable sexuality in Florida. It became a "dirty book" and horrified respectable and prudish legislators. The "pornographic" book was even trucked to New York and other cities where it sold out with folks chortling, "It can't be pornography. It's put out by the State of Florida for God's sakes!"

Similarly, when Ken Starr was independent counsel investigating Vince Foster's suicide, the pecking in the hen house expanded to include Whitewater and even Bill Clinton's misbehavior with Monica and his lying under oath about it. The righties in the U.S. House apparently wanted pay-back for the attacks in the 1970s on Saint Richard the Reluctant Confessor, but the sober right, the mischievous middle, and the lascivious left felt the Starr report was a bit, well, smutty and disturbingly obsessive. Besides, we males lie about sex and fidelity all the time; we have no sense of morals and decency. Duh? It took a three-judge panel and millions of taxpayers' funds to come up with this conclusion? Any three women at a happy hour could have told them this.

There is a solution for the perennial craziness of

American politics. Print up a page of American flags, each about two inches wide, and staple these to the walls of Congress and state legislatures. Intersperse these with miniature images of the Liberty bell and a Minuteman soldier. Give the lawmakers plenty of room so they can peck at the odious objects. Allow ample ventilation so they won't pile into scrums and suffocate themselves.

Thank you, Joe Stephenson, for this insight.

IS A CANDIDATE FROM BUSINESS THE BEST CHOICE?

How many times have you heard a candidate say, "I'm the best choice for [this office] because I'm the only one in the race who has ever made a payroll"? The implication is that the candidate knows what it's like to watch expenses and make sure there's a profit.

That, of course, led to my thinking of a fellow named Buford Such, for Such was his name. When he drove up to Lattes R Us in a new Hummer, someone whistled at the expense, but Buford shrugged it off. "I figure I'm entitled to it. It's my business and my money. I started it, I took the risks, and now that I've prospered I'm entitled to reward myself."

When Buford Such added a 54-foot yacht at a price that work-a-proles couldn't comprehend, he said, "It's my business and my money. I take the chances; I reap the rewards."

It goes like that from acquisition to acquisition until one day he begins contemplating other trinkets, like a mayorship. "Buford Such for mayor" sounds good. "Mayor Buford Such" sounds even better. He campaigns by telling voters we should run government like a business and that he'll be excellent because he knows balance sheets and keeping up with revenue and expenditures. He's regularly met a payroll.

Eventually, he ends up with 52 percent of the votes and sets about to prove how clever he is in managing the taxpayers' money.

He does well for several months, closing this office and consolidating those two. Then one day the motor pool tells him he needs to replace the city car set aside for his official use. He decides on a Cadillac because it is a prestige vehicle and the mayor is entitled. "I manage the money," he says, "like it was my own." Then he gets a bright idea: "Besides, what would potential businessmen think if I pulled up in a Ford Give-Me-a-Break Escort?"

A couple of friends come to him with a plan that will benefit him and the city. He nobly says he can take care of himself thank you very much, but he does find the $500,000 the friends will need for their job-creation project. He coaxes the city council members to okay the deal. Later, he never asks if the new jobs materialized, and, if he seems inclined to ask, his chums shake their heads and complain that the terrible economy is really playing havoc with all the businesses of their fair city. That's the fault of the cowboy or the Kenyan in the White House.

Things build until by and by the TV news media open every program with "Critics think Mayor treats taxpayers' money as if it's his own."

The simple solution might seem to be to fill public offices with, say, public education officials or agents from the Widgets Division. They haven't run any businesses, but they have managed budgets. Individuals may claim that they have earned ten straight years of clean audits for their agency. Here's where the parable of the talents may come in.

A very rich man, according to the rabbi from Nazareth, had to go away, and he called upon three of his workers to manage his money. He gave five talents (say, $1 million in today's money) to one employee; two talents ($400,000) to a second one; and one talent ($200,000) to a third.

When he returned, Mr. Five Talents returned ten talents ($2 million); Mr. Two, four talents ($800,000). The boss congratulated both of them for being "good and faithful servants." Then Mr. One returned the one talent, proudly saying that he had buried it to keep the money safe from thieves and con artists.

I believe it was the Book of Bubba that reported, verily verily, forsooth, and prithee thee, that the boss wigged out and said he was a churl who was dumber than a truckload of dried cow patties.

In reality, public servants don't strive to make a profit or even to save money. Each year, they automatically receive about the same amount of money. They can generally go along without close observation, willy-nilly spending much of the taxpayers' funds. However, someone may change from being a good and faithful servant into a person who wants to "build an empire." She may be the director of widgetry with a secretary, but she finagles the agency into creating a position called "assistant director of widgetry," also with a secretary. The office is so busy that some entry-level positions are added. Each sounds reasonable. At the end of the fiscal year, if the widgetry budget finds itself with a surplus of, say, $250,000, they call a meeting to figure out how to spend that money. "We can't return it because they'll just reduce what we receive next year by $250K."

Sometimes a Buford Such-type can even create unfaithful public servants. A Captain Bligh cracks a metaphorical whip and tongue-lashes his subordinates in front of other employees. He rules by terror and paralyzes subordinates who might be Mr. Five or Two Talents. His motto is "It's my way or the highway."

In a healthy organization, a matter landing in the in-basket would be dealt within a day or two, but Mr. One Talent worries about what Bligh will say or do. The issue still hasn't been addressed after two weeks, then a month, finally a quarter. The basket gets full, and another has to be added to handle the overflow.

We should not assume that experience in business, or education, or the legal system, or whatever gives an individual a leg up on everyone else when we are evaluating potential officeholders. We have to consider individuals' energy, enthusiasm, and fairness for us to avoid voting for a party hack, a Mr. One Talent, or a Captain Bligh.

JUST BEWARE, 'ENRY 'IGGINS, JUST BEWARE

You need to be careful if you are using recent findings about straight or gay speech in your fiction-writing. Your version of Professor Henry Higgins might get into trouble if you rely on the research of Erik Tracy from Ohio State University.

Since this criticism comes from the erstwhile editor of *The International Journal of Elvisology and the Elvisian Era*, I realize I may be a cast-iron pot complaining about a Teflon-coated kettle.

Nonetheless, that cognitive psychologist has said: "Other researchers have done various acoustic analyses to understand why gay and heterosexual men produce vowels differently. Whatever this difference is, it seems that listeners are using it to make this sexual orientation decision."

U.S. News and World Report said the study used seven gay and seven straight guys pronouncing such one-syllable words as "mass" or "soap." The studies had listeners concentrate on first the first letter (not successful) but then on two letters (successful 75 percent of the time).

On the MSNBC website, Nidhi Subbaraman said the volunteer college students ranked each speaker's sexual orientation on a scale from 1 (straight) to 7 (gay). "The gay speakers received a score of 4.42," Subbaraman said, "compared to the heterosexual speakers, who received an average score of 3.45."

A psychologist in Alberta, Canada, complained the study assumes that there is "such a thing as 'gay speech,' and that the test subjects were responding to traces of the flamboyant dialogue that has become the generalization and stereotype for how gay men talk."

That observation reminds me of what Ed Sullivan said about his impersonators: Most of them really weren't imitating Ed. Instead, he said they were mimicking Will Jordan's dead-on impersonation of him. Similarly, we let the stereotypes from *Boys in the Band* and various sit-coms implant the gay sound in our minds. We tend to forget the formal trained speech of Raymond Burr's Perry Mason or George Takei's Sulu, not to mention such giants as Sir John Gielgud or Sir Ian McKellen.

Other than the Canadian psychologist's valid complaint, there are at least four other problems with the study:

1. It has a relatively small sampling to come up with any major conclusions. (Old jungle saying: Beware of any studies and surveys that have fewer than 250 participants.)

2. The college participants in the study very likely were from linguistics, psych, and science programs. Speakers and guessers should have been more diverse; they should have been bakers, butchers, candle-stick makers; they should have been of varied ages and social backgrounds.

3. With only two options (gay or straight), that's not much of a challenge. Moreover, there was only a .97 difference between the two categories. Instead, the participants should have been asked to guess about a mix of factors: (a) age of speaker, (b) social status, (c) probable

occupation, (d) home state (or country), and then (e) the sexual orientation of the speaker.

4. Such clumsy studies may encourage people to draw inaccurate conclusions from weak data.

It's fascinating to study how people talk and how their words and sounds differ from region to region, whether the speakers are gay, straight, male, female, Californian or Floridian. A few decades ago, *The Birmingham News* had a full-page article in its Sunday paper on the linguistic differences from Huntsville down to Mobile and Dothan. For example, some areas preferred to call a certain pan a "skillet," while one area might call it a "spider." (The spider was a skillet with three legs attached to the bottom, so that it could be stabilized if used on a camp fire or a fireplace.)

The Sears & Roebuck catalog came along in 1888 and standardized Americans' usage so that most people ended up calling it a "frying pan."

When I mentioned the *News*' word-usage article to Frank Green of the Bard Society (oldest writing group in Northeast Florida), he mentioned Cleanth Brooks' *The Relation of the Alabama-Georgia Dialect to the Provincial Dialects of Great Britain* (Kennikat Press, 1935, 1972).

Brooks noted that John Aubrey had reported in his *Brief Lives* that Sir Walter Raleigh spoke in a "broad Devon" accent throughout his life. (Devon is on the southwest protrusion of England on the way to Cornwall and Plymouth.) Brooks notes: "If Raleigh, a well-educated man, a great nobleman and a court favorite, retained so much of the provincial coloring of his native county, even at court, what must have been true of the small farmer, the indentured servant, and the shop-keeper in the provincial town, so many of whom made up the body of the seventeenth century immigrants to America?"

I first noticed the sounds and dialects when I was around five or six. One of my Southern-born cousins came down from New Jersey where her father had been stationed at Picatinny Arsenal. When she pronounced the word "school," she (and others infected by "Yankee" speech) said the word with almost two syllables (*schoo-ule*, with a hint of the word "screw" in the pronunciation). I was accustomed to hearing only one syllable like "pool" or "cool." Readers have pointed out that you also hear a shortened form: "scoo," as in "I'm late for scoo.")

The sounds of our universe included the voices on the radio. Instead of having this discussion become a paean to classic radio, let's just focus on Fred Allen's characters in Allen's Alley: the Yiddish Mrs. Malaprop Pansy Nussbaum (played by Minerva Pious), the laconic New England farmer Titus Moody (Parker Fennelly), and my favorite, the blowhard Senator Beauregard Claghorn (Kenny Delmar). Mel Blanc essentially did the same voice for Foghorn Leghorn in Warner Bros. cartoons. Blanc denied stealing from Delmar; he claimed there had been a performer doing a similar act in vaudeville in the 1920s.

During my time in junior high, there were no interstates in my stomping grounds, so we mostly traveled on two-lane roads from Pensacola up to Walker County north of Birmingham. As we stopped for gas, lunch, or pit stops in Atmore, Greenville, or Demopolis, I noticed first of all that the water tasted different. The words that residents used were also different from what we heard perhaps only 50 to 150 miles apart.

In those days, not only did a locale have its own sound, but you would find that different ages picked up each other's speech patterns. I learned this in the 1980s while eating a hamburger at the counter of People's Drugs in my home town. Behind me, near the circular community table, I heard my uncle, Joe Stephenson, bantering with his friends...except Joe had died at age 60 of diabetes. When I turned around, I saw that the speaker was of his age and was possibly a classmate at Walker High. A little later, I was on campus in Jacksonville using the photocopier when I met an employee from another campus who had been a friend of my family. As we introduced ourselves, I heard the voice and cadence of my aunt, Jane Stephenson Root (younger sister of Joe). Ah, said I to myself, a different sound and cadence for a specific location and a specific generation.

That generational difference was made clearest to me when I heard Mawmaw and Pawpaw Price on their farm in Cullman County. Mawmaw (a Kilpatrick) used the archaic "hit" for "it" and could easily say, "Hit don't make no nevermind." (You will find "hit" in Chaucer's "Canterbury Tales.") Their daughter and two sons didn't say "hit's time," but they still sounded country.

When judging manuscripts for the now defunct Florida First Coast Writers' Festival, I'd occasionally put on a critique sheet "all the characters in this story/novel sound alike." Individuals would complain, "But they do talk alike!" No, there is a difference even with some similarities.

It was also frustrating decades ago when some actors tried to do Southern accents. Some might do a nasal Appalachian twang for a South Carolina banker, when (as Senator Ernest Hollings would show) the sound should suggest that the speaker's tongue had been shot full of Novocain. A Tidewater dialect exists in different varieties from Virginia down the coast. At Pensacola's Blount Junior High in the ninth grade, no doubt influenced by Scots, Miz White taught algebra and peppered her lectures with "aboot," "a boot in the water," "go oot of the hoose."

When our Navy family transferred to Norfolk, I was horrified to know that for two years I was going to be swimming against the current of this Tidewater linguistic riptide. What shy, introverted fifteen-year-old wants to return to his home territory infected by "oot and aboot"?

Canadians will say "oot and aboot," again influenced by their Scottish settlers, but both Canadians and Tidewater residents will soften it at times with a soft "a": "haose" or "boaot" (as the late Peter Jennings did).

By and by, my family acquired a reel-to-reel tape-recorder, and we killed time testing one two three and how nowing the brown cow. In effect, we were policing our dialect and moving more toward the Midwest standard. Remnants of our old speech remained for years. Even so, two decades later, She Who Knows All broke into laughter when she heard me pronouncing "mail" as "mel" and "arrow" as "error." In truth, I have also never done well differentiating the sounds of "pin," "pan," and "pen."

The question also comes up, "Can you tell when a speaker is black or white?" At one time, I would have answered in the affirmative.

But Cleanth Brooks stated that "the speech of the negro and of the white is essentially the same, the characterically negro forms turning out to be survivals of earlier native English forms."

We could play around with a Southern dialect tree, with one limb representing Uncle Remus and another Senator Claghorn.

In dealing with freshman papers, anyone would recognize that a young African American in the 1970s was making certain errors (it go, he have, am unconcern), while the white student from a similar economic background would make others (ain't, have wrote, I knowed). Occasionally an instructor would spot a paper with the errors of an African American, but the student would turn out to be white.

So it is in speaking: If we are butchers, bakers, plumbers, or sales persons, we tend to talk like our customers, to bond with them; it may be close to the way we talk at home. But if we are professionals who realize the importance of the Power Dialect, we have tried to weed out speech patterns that label us as uneducated blacks or rednecks. We may want to move from our modest entry-level jobs into executive positions. We know that the Power Dialect can still be Southern, Midwestern, Mid-Atlantic, or whatever, as long as it is understood.

I have more things to do than survey everyone in the U.S., but I suspect these percentages are close to what we would find:

Five percent of people don't realize how they talk. Some of these are tone-deaf (or vowel-deaf), perhaps like General Grant, who could only recognize that one song was the national anthem and another one wasn't. Oliver Sacks in *Musicophilia: Tales of Music and the Brain* discusses those who simply don't get music, whether they are listening to Bach, Benny Goodman, Bob Wills, or the Big Bopper.

About 10 to 15 percent of us just talk and don't think about proper pronunciation.

Some people (15 to 20 percent) talk like their friends, neighbors, and acquaintances. When my aunt Victoria worked in Washington, her speech was more northern urban, but, when she retired to my hometown, it reclaimed its magnolia quality.

Another 15 to 20 percent deliberately lose much or more of their accents. Perhaps they are aspiring actors who have learned stage English; they may want jobs speaking on TV, radio, and videos. Tom Wicker of *The New York Times* said his Southern accent gave him an advantage when he first tackled the big leagues in New York. "Some people thought I was ignorant or stupid, and it gave me an edge up on them," he said.

When I began hanging around newsrooms as a flunky sports reporter, I learned that the voice doesn't have to match our image of the speaker on the radio. When one radio announcer came in with a news release to publicize his son's Little League event, I saw that he was a pencil-neck geek with horn-rims and an Adam's apple the size of a softball instead of what I had visualized: a handsome hero-of-the-air with a gimlet eye and a cleft chin. Today, that radio announcer might be black, white, or Asian.

Except for skilled impressionists, such as Rich Little or Kevin Spacey, most of us are stuck with our voice boxes and range of voices. Even so, some critics complained that Peggy Lee was copying Billie Holliday. Perry Como started out imitating Bing Crosby (in Der Bingle's middle years); Sammy Davis Jr. sounded like Sinatra in his early recordings (until Frank told him his own voice was fine). Billy Eckstein and Al Hibbler had similar voices.

Mamie Eisenhower pointed out that Ike sounded like Clark Gable. You can confirm this by saying "Frankly, my dear, I don't give a damn" and then applying the same voice to Ike, as comedian Will Jordan did: "Good evening, this is Eisenhower, the president of the United States of [pause as he turns a page in his speech] America."

During Watergate, I was listening to the different Southern voices of Senators Howard Baker of Tennessee, Sam Ervin (a bit too Senator Claghornish for my tastes), and Herman Talmadge of Georgia. Like Allen's Alley, the Senate Watergate Committee gave us the Asian-Hawaiian-American sound of Daniel Inouye, Hispanic-American sound of Joseph Montoya of New Mexico; Edward Gurney of Florida, and Lowell Weicker Jr. of Connecticut.

Any halfway decent mimic could do an agonizing imitation of Sam Ervin, but Talmadge's voice interested me the most. It had the flat quality of eastern and central

Georgia, which was the home turf of Oliver Hardy ("bud" for "bird"; "gull" for "girl." In fact, when I played my LP of speeches by Will Rogers (out of Claremore, Oklahoma, with Southern and Cherokee influences), I detected that Talmadge of Georgia and Rogers of Oklahoma sounded very much alike.

Those who would find gayness in others' speech might consider the observation that went around from the 1950s onward: "All Englishmen sound like they're homosexuals." So, if you had been to a Hugh Grant film festival, would that infect you enough to give you a gay score in the Ohio State study?

The observation about all Englishmen is incorrect anyway. Not all Brit males are gay. There is a straight one working as an accountant in Winchester, a mechanic in Coventry, and a billiard ball salesman in Shrewsbury.

Oh, don't go PC on me.

As the rooster Foghorn J. Leghorn would remind us, "Ah say, that's a joke, son! I keep pitchin' 'em and yoah keep standin' theah with yo mouth open catchin' flies with yo' go-gitter."

THE NAMING OF THINGS, GENERALLY SPEAKING

You may have followed the perennial brouhaha in some Southern state (Mississippi most recently) where some of the Sons of the Confederacy wanted to honor General Nathan Bedford Forrest with a specialty license tag. Gov. Haley Barbour, not wanting to be a GOP kamikaze pilot in future elections, said the legislature would never approve such a proposal.

People need to be careful about whom they put on a tag, a courthouse, or a school; sometimes they give due honor to a citizen, but on occasion they make a mistake. In 1927, Jacksonville, Florida, for example, did all right when it named one new high school after General Andy Jackson. He never visited here but was in Pensacola as governor of the Florida territory for a while. Since Cowford, our town's original name, lacked a certain cachet, they renamed it after the Tennessean.

In 1928, Lee High was named after the Confederate States of America general; he did visit the area and established Yellow Bluff Fort to guard the St. Johns River during the War of Southern Exasperation. Lee tried to pattern his life after George Washington's and, after the war, worked as an educator to unify the country and head off the guerilla warfare that Jefferson Davis and a few other stubborn Southerners toyed with in their weaker moments. If Southerners in general had been convinced they should engage in perpetual guerilla warfare, our country would have gone down a bloody road that we might still be on, so we should all thank Lee, Longstreet, Forrest, and other CSA generals.

In 1959, during the school integration fight, some defiant citizens in Jacksonville got a second high school named after a Confederate general, this time Nathan Bedford Forrest. They did this despite (or because of) his connection with the Ku Klux Klan. They couldn't nullify the Brown v. Board of Education ruling of the U.S. Supreme Court, but, by God, they could spit in the eyes of the court and all the agitators out there.

If you are a Civil War buff, you can speak of the many admirable qualities of General Forrest: He was aggressive, energetic, brave, and innovative. Yankee generals such as Grant and Sherman feared his ability to attack supply lines and gallop to other unexpected sites and attack again. War Colleges today still study his tactics and military philosophies.

On the negative side, Nathan Bedford Forrest traded in slaves and made fortunes doing so. He got saddled with the blame for the massacre of African American Union troops at Fort Pillow. An argument can be made that he didn't order, or approve of, his troops' actions. After World War II, that's what some Japanese generals said about some of the atrocities during their occupations, but Allied military tribunals weren't buying it and executed some Japanese generals anyway for failing to have their troops under control.

On the positive side, Forrest had nearly fifty of his own slaves driving wagons, handling supplies, etc., and he promised to free them if the South won. He also told them that, if the North won, they would be freed regardless. He kept his contingent together to the end of the war.

On the minus side, after the war, he joined with other planters to form the Ku Klux Klan. Supposedly, the Klan was established to rein in the out-of-control freed slaves, who were said to be murdering and raping citizens. That's part of the Southern Gospel about the Glories of the Lost Cause. It's worth reading books by Valdosta State historian David Williams (e.g., *Bitterly Divided: The South's Inner Civil War* and *The People's History of the Civil War: Struggles for the Meaning of Freedom*). Williams noted that the planters mainly used the Klan to keep their former slaves on the plantation, almost in the same status as before emancipation. A typical Klan trick was for night-riders to go to the dwelling of a black leader or to the hotel room of a white advocate, lynch or shoot them, and then claim to have been fifteen miles away playing poker with friends when the crime occurred (other night-riders were "witnesses" to their poker games).

On the plus side, he eventually disbanded his Klan organization.

Also on the plus side, he was not interested in the stubborn recalcitrance of "we'll fight on and on and on," "hell, no, we ain't forgetting," or "the South will rise again." In his farewell address as a CSA general, he urged his former soldiers and others to suck it up, be good citizens, and obey the laws of the U.S. In 1873, when it looked as if the U.S. might be going to war with Spain because of the *Virginius* Affair, he volunteered to put on the Union uniform and help out. The incident blew over, but General Sherman sent him a letter saying he would have been proud to have him as a colleague.

One eventually wants to know why the Sons of the Confederacy didn't put forward the names of some actual Civil War generals from Mississippi. But have you ever heard of William Barksdale, Carnot Posey, Wirt Adams, Earl Van Dorn, and Benjamin G. Humphreys? Most people haven't, even casual Civil War buffs. By contrast, Florida had a dozen CSA generals to fall back on for naming purposes, but they wouldn't have made a socio-political statement in 1959.

As George Wallace had learned in the losing 1958 campaign against John Patterson, a Southern politician back then did not want to be "out-segged" (a tamer term than the "n"-word variant actually used), so Jacksonville's power structure would instinctively look the other way when many acts of violence occurred. A year later, in August 1960, most police curiously had other assignments when a peaceful downtown sit-in occurred at a lunch counter. That was when over 200 white racists descended on the demonstrators with ax handles and baseball bats. (Check this out at http://rodneyhurst.com/ for an in-depth look.)

The white mindset back in the 1950s and 1960s juggled these beliefs: "They've got to be kept in their place...We are very close to a war between blacks and whites...Our colored people are good people, but a bunch of outsiders are coming in here and stirring things up...They're Communist agitators." The whites might not admit it, but they had feared black people, even before the Nat Turner Rebellion in Virginia in 1831.

You would think that a Southern city might have given the benefit of a doubt to the motives of Jacksonville school teacher Rutledge Pearson, student Rodney Hurst, and dozens of others who demonstrated here in the 1960s, but a glance at the Federal Writers Project book, *Washington, City and Federal* (1937), shows the other side of the "local" coin: "In 1830, there were 6,152 free Negroes in the District of Columbia compared with 6,152 slaves [sic]; in 1840, 8,361 compared with 4,694 slaves; and in 1860, 11,131 compared with only 3,185."

As these African Americans prospered in Washington, how did the whites react? "These free Negroes were an ever present 'Bad example' to the slaves of the District and of the surrounding slave States, and the more they prospered, the 'worse example' they became."

That type of thinking caused most Southern cities and towns to assume the worst and perhaps inadvertently to ally themselves with the Klan or the White Citizens' Councils.

In recent years, teachers, students, and African Americans have been looking at the controversy concerning the name of Nathan Bedford Forrest High School. In 2008, the school board voted 5-2 for the status quo. The mindset of those resisting change was this: "Forrest has been receiving F's on statewide evaluations, so let's worry about that before we spend any more time on the name...The name has been in place for almost half a century...A lot of students just know they attended Forrest. They aren't that aware of who he was, or they don't care, so let's move on."

Some advocates for a new name suggested the school should be named after Navy pilot Lt. Scott Speicher (the first combat casualty in the first Gulf War and a Forrest High graduate). Others argued it should be named after Eartha M. M. White (an African American native of Jacksonville and a philanthropist). Both were excellent candidates and deserved to have, say, TV movies based on their stories, although, with Speicher, it would focus on friends and families hoping to get him released as a POW. The anti-climax would be eventual discovery of his bones during the second Iraq war.

Ms. White had one handicap: Jacksonville already has a White High School, one named after Ed White, who was burned up in a NASA space training accident with Gus Grissom and Roger Chaffee. Her name is useful because it shows that people were thinking of naming schools after local historic figures. The potential name pool could include scientists, inventors, social workers, and educators.

Inventors? The city had one school named after an inventor, Dr. John Gorrie, who created the first device that was a refrigerator/air conditioner. (The school is now a condominium for retirees.)

How about naming the school after Lee De Forest, who is remembered as one of the fathers of the electronic age, thanks to his invention of the Albion (a vacuum tube)? His father, a minister, had been president of the African American college Talladega College in Alabama. Okay, perhaps not the best choice. You'd have to add "De" to the school's sign and remove an "r."

Hang on, what's this in the biography of Nathan Bedford Forrest?

Hmm, he had a great-grandson, a NBF the Third. He served in World War II in the Army Air Force. He was a brigadier general who was the first American general to become a combat casualty in Europe. His B-17 Flying Fortress was hit in June 1943, when he was on a bombing raid on Nazi submarine yards at Kiel. He died because he stayed at the controls while his crew safely bailed out. Before he could escape, his plane exploded. His body was washed up on Sept. 23, 1943. He was posthumously given a Distinguished Flying Cross. He was buried in Europe and later was reburied at Arlington National Cemetery.

Could this be the solution, "Nathan Bedford Forrest III High School"? No major change, and it honors a valiant soldier who died for his men and his country. And no Ku Klux Klan or slavery baggage.

Think about it.

POST SCRIPT: The school board eventually changed the name to Westside High School, having decided NOT to name this (or presumably any) school after a person.

THE OBSCENITY OF 'TAJ MAHAL SCHOOLS'

President Dwight Eisenhower warned Americans against a "military industrial complex" that could bankrupt the nation and lead to danger and mischief if unchecked. It was hard to pooh-pooh what he said since he was a five-star general who led the Allies to victory in Europe. On the other hand, time will wipe clean a nation's consciousness so that we can wind up with the turn-of-the-century Asian wars.

Probably in the 1940s, some wag created the term, "edifice complex," which is a cousin to the later "military industrial" variety. It can be updated to "educational-construction industry complex." This complex ensures that public (college and university) buildings will go up at the drop of a hat.

If we look far enough back into the past, we find that legislatures were approving funds for building construction, only to have some counties and cities spending the money on salaries, utilities, and other expenses. The legislatures then divided appropriations into Operational funds and Capital funds. The latter HAD to be used for buildings. That worked fine when a state was establishing a system of state colleges back in the 1950s and 1960s or replacing wooden school structures in the 1940s.

But it came to pass that, when the various systems had essentially been completed, the "educational-construction" complex wanted the funds to continue. States then came up with funding mechanisms often called public education capital outlay (PECO) bonds. Even when critics said a system had enough new buildings, the PECO funds paid for even more structures. Bureaucrats would say, "What are we going to do? We HAVE to use the funds, duh!"

That sort of mentality led California to spend $578 million for one new high school in Los Angeles, and some educrats are just so gosh-darn proud they are about to bust their buttons. For example, Joe Agron, editor-in-chief of *American School & University*, a school construction journal, said, "There's no more of the old, windowless cinderblock schools of the '70s where kids felt, 'Oh, back to jail.' Districts want a showpiece for the community, a really impressive environment for learning."

The American School & University website contains a lot of useful information about school construction in general, but it is a shame that the organization felt it had to ignore the excesses of the proposal and even to act as a defense attorney for such a guilty client.

L.A. also spent $377 million on the Edward R. Roybal Learning Center, which opened in 2008, and $232 million on the Visual and Performing Arts High School that opened its doors in 2009.

All of this is occurring during the Great Recession. Los Angeles was firing 3,000 teachers. California was facing a $640 million deficit. The Race to the Top grants were being distributed in Washington, and Maryland was raking in a $250 million, which L.A. would say is chicken feed.

We may see some parallels to Ronald Reagan's Strategic Defense Initiative (SDI), which would gobble up billions and be nicknamed "Star Wars Defense," since the U.S. then (and now) did not have the technology to shoot down an enemy missile any more than it could fire a bullet to shoot down another bullet. By and by, the "military-industrial" complex faked some tests that cost taxpayers $27 billion (chicken feed to them). The project earns an additional nickname: "Star Wars as It Might be Run by Boss Tweed and Al Capone."

Critics of lavish school projects have called them "Taj Mahal schools," but its defenders have tried to brazen their way through the argument. Sure, they say, our students are worth the very best. We need to show that we hold excellence in high regard. And so on.

That's total baloney, of course. Some buildings and structures in the world are unique and impressive because of their rarity. These architectural jewels include the actual Taj Mahal, of course, but also the Great Pyramids of Giza and St. Peter's Cathedral and the Pantheon in Rome. They are not as mundane as public schools, courthouses, and Woopsy-Doodle Burger franchises.

Let's use an automobile analogy. We wouldn't want our schools to be constructed like the Zastava Koral, better known to us as the lowly Yugo. No one would want a school that continually refused to start or that broke down repeatedly. Elsewhere in the world, we regularly read about school buildings and hotels collapsing without the aid of an earthquake, largely due to shoddy construction and non-existent code inspections.

By the same token, we wouldn't want our schools to be the equivalent of the Lamborghini Aventador, since only millionaires could afford it. Not only would such schools bankrupt a state or a school district, it is doubtful that they would give an adequate bang for the buck.

Consumer Reports is an excellent forum for rating the efficiency and efficacy of everything from autos to PC's. They have a "best buy" designation for products that are affordable and superior in quality. Recent best-buy models include the Chevrolet Silverado and Traverse, Mazda5, Nissan Altima, Subaru Forester, and Volkswagen GTI, not a Taj Mahal vehicle among them.

Another reason to object to Taj Mahal schools is the nature of young people. Bill Cosby pointed out that "all children are brain damaged," and, dating back to Plato nearly 2,400 years ago, you could find reams of zingers about the flaws of teenagers:

> The children now love luxury; they have bad manners, contempt for authority; they show disrespect for elders and love chatter in place of exercise. Children are now tyrants, not the servants of their households. They no longer rise when elders enter the room. They contradict their parents, chatter before company, gobble up dainties at the table, cross their legs, and tyrannize their teachers.

So, Socrates, let me ask you: Would you want to turn a teenager loose in a Lamborghini or perhaps hope that the kid would do less damage in a used Ford Escort, uncool though it might be?

Since it is the nature of the brain-damaged beast to gripe and complain, it is foolish to think that the youths might not consider their Taj Mahal High as anything except a jail. If they are required to attend, it's a jail; if they can't leave a classroom, it's a jail; if they can't chew gum or have cell phones, it's a jail; if they can't grope each other, it's a jail; and, if they have to watch the cool kids grope each other, it's a jail.

Taj Mahal advocates have a common thread in their argument: We must make the environment better so that the youths will learn better. To them, WE always must take actions; the students, passive and hopefully docile, will be forced to learn.

In reality, learning and excellence can occur in a one-room school house, in a building from the 1920s with wooden floors and window fans, and even in a cinderblock structure of recent vintage.

The old adage is that, when the student is ready, the teacher will be there. That also suggests that, when the student is ready and wanting to learn, the building isn't of utmost importance.

CURTAIN LINE AND RIDING OFF INTO THE SUNSET

You may remember Brewster Barlow almost falling out of his saddle when his horse What's Its Name reared up at the end of *Shoot-Out with a Wild-Eyed Moderate.* He was trying to shout something, but his bottle fell out of his saddlebags. His bottle of sassparilla, the studio said.

You certainly recall the Lone Ranger's more elegant exit.

With our 21st Century Wild-Eyed Moderate, you may imagine the author adjusting his top-hat and monocle. He hits the horn, and we hear:

"Honk, honk away! Good people, remember: Get the lead out!"

(Come back on a future Saturday, boys and girls, when our hero rides again in *Gunfight with a Wild-Eyed Moderate.*)

About the Author

Howard Denson is a newspaper-Navy brat who has mainly moved from one part of the South to another. A native of Jasper, Alabama, he has been living in Jacksonville, Florida, since the administration of Saint Richard the Reluctant Confessor.

At what is now Florida State College at Jacksonville, he taught composition, literature, and creative writing, plus humanities courses in the ancient world and Middle Ages, the Renaissance to the modern world, art appreciation, American art and culture.

He was closely involved in a town-and-gown writers' conference, the Florida First Coast Writers' Festival, and attended similar conferences at Samford University, Birmingham-Southern College, the University of Florida, and especially at St. Petersburg's excellent Florida Suncoast Writers' Conference.

He has been an editor and/or contributor to *The State Street Review*, *The Penchant*, *The International Journal of Elvisology and the Elvisian Era*, *The Write Stuff*, *The FCCFF Update*, and *Kassandra's Kitchen*. For the Writers' Festival, he helped run and judge contests in novels, short fiction, poetry, and plays.

He and his smarter bride of thirty-eight years Michele Boyette currently have seven four-legged children: the meowers, Eddie, CeeCee, Billy, Wally, Frieda, and Amber; and the barkers, Mr. Darcy, and Daphne.

To keep up with similar discussions, go to his website at http://howarddenson.webs.com.

THANKS TO

Brad Hall for his sharp eye in proofing and for his valuable editorial suggestions.

OTHER BOOKS BY HOWARD DENSON

Check on Amazon.com and Kindle for these books in the near future:

MOWBRAY AND THE SHARKS, a novel set in 1936-37. Martin Mowbray has a good life with his ward/foster-son/stepson Tommy Watson...until two New York City hoods confuse him with Tommy-Gun Watson, a psychopathic bank robber coming to NYC to make a name for himself.

GUNFIGHT WITH A WILD-EYED MODERATE, another collection that applies humor to serious subjects by a writer whose intellectual and spiritual guide was Charlie McCarthy. Also features Brewster Barlow talking about his memories of his scraping out a living working for Gene Autry, Tommy (Little Beaver) Cook, Smiley Burnette, and Edgar Bergen.

A QUANDARY OF FIBBLES, fantasy, fiction, satire. Traces the frustrated love of Princess Esmeralda for her clumsy knight, Sir Jonathan d'Klutz, through transmigrations of their souls finally into a pot-bellied stove and a junkman.

FIBBLE-FABBLES, fantasy, fiction, satire. Traces Emperor Leonidas the Lion and his animal subjects in the Land of Fibbles through fables that reveal who is wise or foolish. Other tales focus on Star-Freight Captain Bailey George, the Porkertons, and Dolly Passionata and a couple of angels.

THE WRONG STUFF: FINDINGS OF A FORENSIC GRAMMARIAN, nonfiction. The forensic grammarian searches out example of flawed writing in newspapers, magazines, and respected websites and deduces the chain of events that led to raids by Grammar Nazis.

www.ingramcontent.com/pod-product-compliance
Lightning Source LLC
LaVergne TN
LVHW020537100826
845148LV00010B/1501
9780615692739